BLACK LEGACY PRESS™
WWW.BLACKLEGACYPRESS.ORG

SLAVE NARRATIVES

VOLUME II
ARKANSAS NARRATIVES
PART 5

By
United States.
Work Projects Administration

Copyright © 2024 by BLACKLEGACYPRESS.ORG

All rights reserved. No part of this publication may be reproduced or transmitted in any form or by any means electronic or mechanical, including information storage and retrieval systems without permission in writing from the publisher, except for student research using the appropriate citations.

ISBN: 978-1-63652-220-3

SLAVE NARRATIVES

A Folk History of Slavery in the United States.
From Interviews with Former Slaves

**UNITED STATES.
WORK PROJECTS ADMINISTRATION**

TYPEWRITTEN RECORDS PREPARED BY
THE FEDERAL WRITERS' PROJECT
1936-1938
ASSEMBLED BY
THE LIBRARY OF CONGRESS PROJECT
WORK PROJECTS ADMINISTRATION
FOR THE DISTRICT OF COLUMBIA
SPONSORED BY THE LIBRARY OF
CONGRESS

WASHINGTON 1941

VOLUME II
ARKANSAS NARRATIVES
PART 5

Prepared by
The Federal Writers' Project of
The Works Progress Administration
For the State of Arkansas

CONTENTS

Charlie McClendon 1
Lizzie McCloud 5
Lizzie McCloud 9
Avalena McConico 11
Ike McCoy 15
Richard H. McDaniel 19
Waters McIntosh 21
Cresa Mack 31
Warren McKinney 33
Warren McKinney 37
Victoria McMullen 41
Nannie P. Madden 49
Perry Madden 51
Lewis Mann 59
Angeline Martin 61
Josie Martin 63
Bess Mathis 65
Caroline Matthews 67
Malindy Maxwell 71
Nellie Maxwell 79
Ann May 81
Joe Mayes 83

Jesse Meeks	87
Jesse Meeks	89
Jeff Metcalf	91
Hardy Miller	93
Henry Kirk Miller	99
H.k Miller	107
Matilda Miller	113
Nathan Miller	117
Sam Miller	119
W.D. Miller	121
Mose Minser	123
Gip Minton	125
A.J. Mitchell	129
Gracie Mitchell	133
Hettie Mitchell	139
Mary Mitchell	143
Moses Mitchell	145
Ben Moon	151
Emma Moore	153
Patsy Moore	157
Ada Moorehead	159
Mrs. Mary Jane (Mattie) Mooreman	163
Evelina Morgan	171
James Morgan	177

Olivia Morgan	183
Tom Morgan	187
Charity Morris	189
Emma Morris	193
Claiborne Moss	197
Frozie Moss	211
Mose Moss	213
S.O. Mullins	215
Alex Murdock	219
Bessie Myers	221
Mary Myhand	223
Griffin Myrax	225
Tom Wylie Neal	227
Sally Nealy	231
Sally Neeley	235
Wylie Nealy	239
Emaline Neland	245
Henry Nelson	249
Henry Nelson	253
Iran Nelson	255
James Henry Nelson	257
John Nelson	261
Lettie Nelson	263
Mattie Nelson	265

Dan Newborn	267
Sallie Newsom	269
Pete Newton	273
Charlie Norris	277
Emma Oats	279
Helen Odom	285
Jane Oliver	287
Ivory Osborne	291
Jane Osbrook	293
Annie Page	297
Annie Page	299
Annie Page	301
Fannie Parker	303
J.M. Parker	305
Judy Parker	313
R.F. Parker	319
Annie Parks	321
Austin Pen Parnell	327
Frank A. Patterson	343
John Patterson	353
Sarah Jane Patterson	357
Solomon P. Pattillo	365
Carry Allen Patton	371
Harriett McFarlin Payne	375

John Payne	379
Larkin Payne	381
Cella Perkins	383
Maggie Perkins	387
Marguerite Perkins	391
Rachel Perkins	393
Dinah Perry	397
Dinah Perry	401
Alfred Peters	403
Mary Estes Peters	405
John Peterson	415
Louise Pettis	419
Henry C. Pettus	423
Dolly Phillips	429
Tony Piggy	431
Ella Pittman	433
Ella Pittman	435
Sarah Pittman	437
Mary Poe	441
W.L. Pollacks	443
"Doc" John Pope	445
William Porter	449
Bob Potter	453
Louise Prayer	457

Interviewer: Mrs. Bernice Bowden
Person interviewed: Charlie McClendon
708 E. Fourth Avenue, Pine Bluff, Arkansas
Age: 77

CHARLIE MCCLENDON

"I don't know exactly how old I am. I was six or seven when the war ended. I member dis—my mother said I was born on Christmas day. Old master was goin' to war and he told her to take good care of that boy—he was goin' to make a fine little man.

"Did I live up to it? I reckon I was bout as smart a man as you could jump up. The work didn't get too hard for me. I farmed and I sawmilled a lot. Most of my time was farmin'.

"I been in Jefferson County all my life. I went to school three or four sessions.

"About the war, I member dis—I member they carried us to Camden and I saw the guards. I'd say, 'Give me a pistol.' They'd say, 'Come back tomorrow and we'll give you one.' They had me runnin' back there every day and I never did get one. They was Yankee soldiers.

"Our folks' master was William E. Johnson. Oh Lord, they was just as good to us as could be to be under slavery.

"After they got free my people stayed there a year or two and then our master broke up and went back to South Carolina and the folks went in different directions.

Oh Lord, my parents sho was well treated. Yes ma'm. If he had a overseer, he wouldn't low him to whip the folks. He'd say, 'Just leave em till I come home.' Then he'd give em a light breshin'.

"My father run off and stay in the woods one or two months. Old master say, 'Now, Jordan, why you run off? Now I'm goin' to give you a light breshin' and don't you run off again.' But he'd run off again after awhile.

"He had one man named Miles Johnson just stayed in the woods so he put him on the block and sold him.

"I seed the Ku Klux. We colored folks had to make it here to Pine Bluff to the county band. If the Rebels kotch you, you was dead.

"Oh Lord yes, I voted. I voted the Publican ticket, they called it. You know they had this Australia ballot. You was sposed to go in the caboose and vote. They like to scared me to death one time. I had a description of the man I wanted to vote for in my pocket and I was lookin' at it so I'd be sure to vote for the right man and they caught me. They said, 'What you doin' there? We're goin' to turn you over to the sheriff after election!' They had me scared to death. I hid out for a long time till I seed they wasn't goin' to do nothin'.

"My wife's brother was one of the judges of the election. Some of the other colored folks was constables and magistrates—some of em are now—down in the country.

"I knew a lot about things but I knew I was in the United States and had to bow to the law. There was the compromise they give the colored folks—half of the offices and then they got em out afterwards. John M. Clayton was runnin' for the senate and say he goin' to see the colored people had equal rights, but they killed him as he was gwine through the country speakin'.

"The white people have treated me very well but they don't pay us enough for our work—just enough to live on and hardly that. I can say with a clear conscience that if it hadn't been for this relief, I don't know what I'd do—I'm not able to work. I'm proud that God Almighty put the spirit in the man (Roosevelt) to help us."

United States. Work Projects Administration

Interviewer: Mrs. Bernice Bowden
Person interviewed: Lizzie McCloud
1203 Short 13th Street, Pine Bluff, Arkansas
Age: 120?

LIZZIE MCCLOUD

"I was one of 'em bless your heart. Yes ma'm, Yes ma'm, I wouldn't tell you a lie 'bout that. If I can't tell you the truth I'm not goin' tell you nothin'!

"Oh yes, I was a young lady in slavery times—bred and born in Tennessee. Miss Lizzie and Marse John Williams—I belonged to them—sho did! I was scared to death of the white folks. Miss Lizzie—she mean as the devil. She wouldn't step her foot on the ground, she so rich. No ma'm wouldn't put her foot on the ground. Have her carriage drive up to the door and have that silk carpet put down for her to walk on. Yes Lord. Wouldn't half feed us and they went and named me after her.

"I know all about the stars fallin'. I was out in the field and just come in to get our dinner. Got so dark and the stars begin to play aroun'. Mistress say, 'Lizzie, it's the judgment.' She was just a hollerin'. Yes ma'm I was a young woman. I been here a long time, yes ma'm, I been here a long time. Worked and whipped, too. I run off many a time. Run off to see my mammy three or four miles from where I was.

"I never was sold but they took we young women and brought us down in the country to another plantation where they raised corn, wheat, and hay. Overseer whipped us too. Marse John had a brother named Marse Andrew and he was a good man. He'd say to the overseer, 'Now don't whip these girls so much, they can't work.' Oh, he was a good man. Oh, white folks was the devil in slavery tines. I was scared to death of 'em. They'd have these long cow hide whips. Honey, I was treated bad. I seen a time in this world.

"Oh Lord, yes, that was long 'fore the war. I was right down on my master's place when it started. They said it was to free the niggers. Oh Lord, we was right under it in Davidson County where I come from. Oh Lord, yes, I knowed all about when the war started. I'se a young woman, a young woman. We was treated just like dogs and hogs. We seed a hard time—I know what I'm talkin' about.

"Oh God, I seed the Yankees. I saw it all. We was so scared we run under the house and the Yankees called 'Come out Dinah' (didn't call none of us anything but Dinah). They said 'Dinah, we're fightin' to free you and get you out from under bondage.' I sure understood that but I didn't have no better sense than to go back to mistress.

"Oh Lord, yes, I seed the Ku Klux. They didn't bother me cause I didn't stay where they could; I was way under the house.

"Yankees burned up everything Marse John had. I looked up the pike and seed the Yankees a coming'. They say 'We's a fightin'' for you, Dinah!' Yankees walked in, chile, just walked right in on us. I tell you I've seed a time. You talkin' 'bout war—you better wish no more war come. I know when the war started. The Secessors on this side and the Yankees on that side. Yes, Miss, I seen enough. My brother went and jined the Secessors and they killed him time he got in the war.

"No, Missy, I never went to no school. White folks never learned me nothin'. I believes in tellin' white folks the truth.

"White folks didn't 'low us to marry so I never married till I come to Arkansas and that was one year after surrender.

"First place I landed on was John Clayton's place. Mr. John Clayton was a Yankee and he was good to us. We worked in the field and stayed there two years. I been all up and down the river and oh Lord, I had a good time after I was free. I been treated right since I was free. My color is good to me and the white folks, too. I ain't goin' to tell only the truth. Uncle Sam goin' send me 'cross the water if I don't tell the truth. Better not fool with dat man!"

United States. Work Projects Administration

Interviewer: Mrs. Bernice Bowden
Person interviewed: Lizzie McCloud
1203 E. Short 13th Street, Pine Bluff, Arkansas
Age: 103
[TR: Appears to be same as previous informant despite age discrepancy.]

LIZZIE MCCLOUD

"Well, where you been? I been wonderin' 'bout you. Yes Lawd. You sure is lookin' fine.

"Yes, honey, I was bred and bawn in Davidson County, Tennessee. Come here one year after surrender.

"My daughter there was a baby jus' sittin' alone, now, sittin' alone when I come here to this Arkansas. I know what I'm talkin' about.

"Lizzie Williams, my old missis, was rich as cream. Yes Lawd! I know all about it 'cause I worked for 'em.

"I was a young missis when the War started. I was workin' for my owners then. I knowed when they was free—when they said they was free.

"The Yankees wouldn't call any of the colored women anything but Dinah. I didn't know who they was till they told us. Said, 'Dinah, we's comin' to free you.'

"The white folks didn't try to scare us 'bout the Yankees 'cause they was too scared theirselves. Them Yankees wasn't playin'; they was fitin'. Yes, Jesus!

"Had to work hard—and whipped too. Wasn't played with. Mars Andrew come in the field a heap a times and say, 'Don't whip them women so hard, they can't work.' I thought a heap of Mars Andrew.

"I used to see the Yankees ridin' hosses and them breastplates a shining'. Yes Lawd. I'd run and they'd say, 'Dinah, we ain't gwine hurt you.' Lawd, them Yankees didn't care for nothin'. Oh, they was fine.

"My husband was a soldier—a Yankee. Yes ma'am. They sends me thirty dollars every month, before the fourth. Postman brings it right to me here at the house. They treats me nice.

"When I come here, I landed on John Clayton's place. He was a Yankee and he was a good white man too.

"I'm the onliest one left now in my family."

Interviewer: Mrs. Irene Robertson
Person Interviewed: Avalena McConico
on the [---- ----] west of Brinkley, Arkansas
Age: 40[?]

[TR: Much of this interview smeared and difficult to decipher; illegible words indicated by [----], questionable words followed by [?].]

AVALENA MCCONICO

"Grandma was a slave woman. Her name was Emma Harper. She was born in Chesterville, Mississippi. Her young master was Jim and Miss Corrie Burton. The old man was John Burton. I aimed[?] to see them once. I seen both Miss Corrie and Mr. Jim. My grandparents was never sold. They left out after freedom. They stayed there a long time but they left.

"The first of the War was like dis: Our related folks was having a dance. The Yankees come in and was dancing. Some "fry boys" [---- ----] them. The next day they were all in the field and heard something. They went to the house and told the white folks there was [----] a fire. They heard it. [----] he [----] about. Master told them it was war. Miss Burton was crying. They heard about [----] in [----] at Harrisburg where they could hear the shooting.

"They put the slaves to digging. They dug two weeks. They buried their meat and money and a whole heap of things. They never found it. A little white,[?] Mollita[?], was out where they were digging. She went in the house.

She said, Mama, is the devil coming? They said he was." Master had them come to him. He questioned them. They told him they got so tired [----] of them said he [----] he [---- ----] the [----] Yankees come he'd tell them where all this was, but he was just talking. But when the Yankees did come they was so scared they never got close to a Yankee. They was scared to death. They never found the meat and money. They [----] and cut the turkeys' heads off and the turkey fell off the rail fence, the head drop on one side and the body on the other. They milked a cow and cut both hind quarters off and leave the rest of the cow there and the cow not dead yet.

"Mr. South[?] Strange at Chesterville, Mississippi had a pony named Zane. The Yankees hemmed him and four more men in at Malone Creek and killed the four men. Zane rared up on hind legs and went up a steep cliff and ran three miles. Mr. Strange's coat was cut off from him. It was a gray coat. Mr. Strange was a white man.

"Uncle Frank Jones was forty years old when they gathered him up out of the woods and put him in the battle lines. All the runaway black folks in the woods was hunted out and put in the Yankee lines. Uncle Frank lived in a cave up till about then. His master made him mean. He got better as he got old. His master would sell him and tell him to run away and come back to his cave. He'd feed him. He never worked and he went up for his provisions. He was sold over and over and over. His master learnt him in books and to how to cuss. He learnt him how to trick the dogs and tap trees like a coon. At the end of the trail the dogs would turn on the huntsman. Uncle Frank was active when he was old. He was hired out to race other boys sometimes. He never wore glasses. He could see well when he was old. He told me he was raised out from England, Arkansas.

"When freedom was told 'em Uncle Frank said all them in the camps hollered and danced, and marched and sung. They was so glad the War was done and so glad they been freed.

"Grandma was sold in South Carolina to Mississippi and sold again to Dr. Shelton. Now that was my father's father and mother. She said they rode and walked all the way. They came on ox wagons. She said on the way they passed some children. They was playing. A little white boy was up in a persimmon tree settin' on a limb eating persimmons. He was so pretty and clean. Grandma says, 'You think you is some pumpkin, don't you, honey child.' He says, 'Some pumpkin and some 'simmon too.' Grandma was a house girl. She got to keep her baby and brought him. He was my father. Uncle was born later. Then they was freed. Grandma lived to be ninety-five years old. Mrs. Dolphy Wooly and Mrs. Shelton was her young mistresses. They kept her till she died. They kept her well.

"Grandma told us about freedom. She was hired out to the Browns to make sausage and dry out lard. Five girls was in the field burning brush. They was white girls— Mrs. Brown's girls. They come to the house and said some Blue Coats come by and said, 'You free.' They told them back, 'That's no news, we was born free.' Grandma said that night she melted pewter and made dots on her best dress. It was shiny. She wore it home next day 'cause she was free, and she never left from about her own white folks till she died and left them.

"Times seem very good on black folks till hard cold winter and spring come, then times is mighty, mighty bad. It is so hard to keep warm fires and enough to eat. Times have been good. Black folks in the young generation need more heart training and less book learning. Times is so fast the young set is too greedy. They is wasteful too. Some is hard workers and tries to live right.

"I wash and irons and keep a woman's little chile so she can work. I owns my home."

Interviewer: Mrs. Irene Robertson
Person Interviewed: Ike McCoy, Biscoe, Arkansas
Age: 65
[TR: Illegible words indicated by [----], questionable words followed by [?].]

IKE MCCOY

"My parents named Harriett and Isaac McCoy. Far as I knew they was natives of North Kaline (Carolina). He was a farmer. He raised corn and cabbage, a little corn and wheat. He had tasks at night in winter I heard him say. She muster just done anything. She knit for us here in the last few years. She died several years ago. Now my oldest sister was born in slavery. I was next but I came way after slavery.

"In war time McCoys hid their horses in the woods. The Yankees found them and took all the best ones and left their [----] (nags). Old boss man McCoy hid in the closet and locked himself up. The Yankees found him, broke in on him and took him out and they nearly killed him beating him so bad. He told all of 'em on the place he was going off. They wore him out. He didn't live long after that.

"Things got lax. I heard her say one man sold all his slaves. The War broke out. They run away and went back to him. She'd see 'em pass going back home. They been sold and wouldn't stay. Folks got to running off to war. They thought it look like a frolic. I heard some of them say they wish they hadn't gone off to war 'fore it was done. Niggers didn't know that[?] war no freedom was 'ceptin' the Yankees come tell them something and then they couldn't understand how it all be. Black folks was mighty ignant then. They is now for that matter. They look to white folks for right kind of doings[?].

"Ma said every now and then see somebody going back to that man tried to get rid of them. They traveled by night and beg along from black folks. In daytime they would stay in the woods so the pettyrollers wouldn't run up on them. The pettyrollers would whoop 'em if they catch 'em.

"Ma told about one day the Yankees come and made the white women came help the nigger women cook up a big dinner. Ma was scared so bad she couldn't see nothing she wanted. She said there was no talking. They was too scared to say a word. They sot the table and never a one of them told 'em it was ready.

"She said biscuits so scarce after the War they took 'em 'round in their pockets to nibble on they taste so good.

"I was eighteen years old when pa and ma took the notion to come out here. All of us come but one sister had married, and pa and one brother had a little difference. Pa had children ma didn't have. They went together way after slavery. We got transportation to Memphis by train and took a steamboat to Pillowmount. That close to Forrest City. Later on I come to Biscoe. They finally come too.

"I been pretty independent all my life till I getting so feeble. I work a sight now. I'm making boards to kiver my house out at the lot now. I goiner get somebody to kiver it soon as I get my boards made.

"We don't get no PWA aid 'ceptin' for two orphant babies we got. They are my wife's sister's little boys.

"Well sir-ree, folks could do if the young ones would. Young folks don't have no consideration for the old wore-out parents. They dance and drink it bodaciously out on Saturday ebening and about till Sunday night. I may be wrong but I sees it thater way. Whan we get old we get helpless. I'm getting feebler every year. I see that. Times goiner be hard ag'in this winter and next spring. Money is scarce now for summer time and craps laid by. I feels that my own self now. Every winter times get tough."

Interviewer: Miss Irene Robertson
Person interviewed: Richard H. McDaniel, Brinkley, Arkansas
Age: 73

RICHARD H. MCDANIEL

"I was born in Newton County, Mississippi the first year of the surrender. I don't think my mother was sold and I know my father was never sold. Jim McDaniel raised my father and one sister after his mother died. One sister was married when she died. I heard him say when he got mad he would quit work. He said old master wouldn't let the mistress whoop him and she wouldn't let him whoop my father. My father was a black man but my mother was light. Her father was a white man and her mother part Indian and white mixed, so what am I? My mother was owned by people named Wash. Dick Wash was her young master. My parents' names was Willis and Elsie McDaniel. When it was freedom I heard them say Moster McDaniel told them they was free. He was broke. If they could do better go on, he didn't blame them, he couldn't promise them much now. They moved off on another man's place to share crop. They had to work as hard and didn't have no more than they had in slavery. That is what they told me. They could move around and visit around without asking. They said it didn't lighten the work none but it lightened the rations right smart. Moster McDaniel nor my father neither one went to war.

"From the way I always heard it, the Ku Klux was the

law like night watchman. When I was a boy there was a lot of stealing and bushwhacking. Folks meet you out and kill you, rob you, whoop you. A few of the black men wouldn't work and wanted to steal. That Ku Klux was the law watching around. Folks was scared of em. I did see them. I would run hide.

"I farmed up till 1929. Then I been doing jobs. I worked on relief till they turned me off, said I was too old to work but they won't give me the pension. I been trying to figure out what I am to do. Lady, could you tell me? Work at jobs when I can get them.

"I allus been voting till late years. If they let some folks vote in the first lection, they would be putting in somebody got no business in the gover'ment. All the fault I see in white folks running the gover'ment is we colored folks ain't got work we can do all the time to live on. I thought all the white folks had jobs what wanted jobs. The conditions is hard for old men like me. I pay $3 for a house every month. It is a cold house.

"This present generation is living a fast life. What all don't they do?"

Interviewer: Samuel S. Taylor
Person interviewed: Waters McIntosh
1900 Howard Street, Little Rock, Arkansas
Age: 76

WATERS MCINTOSH

"I was born July 4, 1862 at 2:08 in the morning at Lynchburg, Sumter County, South Carolina.

Parents

"My mother was named Lucy Sanders. My father was named Sumter Durant. Our owner was Dr. J.M. Sanders, the son of Mr. Bartlett Sanders. Sumter Durant was a white man. My mother was fourteen years old when I was born I was her second child. Durant was in the Confederate army and was killed during the War in the same year I was born, and before my birth.

Sold

"When I was a year old, my mother was sold for $1500 in gold, and I was sold for $500 in gold to William Carter who lived about five miles south of Cartersville. The payment was made in fine gold. I was sold because my folk realized that freedom was coming and they wanted to obtain the cash value of their slaves.

Name

"My name is spelled 'Waters' but it is pronounced 'Waiters.' When I was born, I was thought to be a very likely child and it was proposed that I should be a waiter. Therefore I was called Waters (but it was pronounced Waiters). They did not spell it w-a-i-t-e-r-s, but they pronounced it that way.

How Freedom Came

"My mother said that they had been waiting a long time to hear what had become of the War, perhaps one or two weeks. One day when they were in the field moulding corn, going round the corn hoeing it and putting a little hill around it, the conk sounded at about eleven o'clock, and they knew that the long expected time had come. They dropped their hoes and went to the big house. They went around to the back where the master always met the servants and he said to them, 'You are all free, free as I am. You can go or come as you please. I want you to stay. If you will stay, I will give you half the crop.' That was the beginning of the share cropping system.

"My mother came at once to the quarters, and when she found me she pulled the end out of a corn sack, stuck holes on the sides, put a cord through the top, pulled out the end, put it on me, put on the only dress she had, and made it back to the old home (her first master's folk).

What the Slaves Expected

"When the slaves were freed, they got what they expected. They were glad to get it and get away with it, and that was what mother and them did

Slave Time Preaching

"One time when an old white man come along who wanted to preach, the white people gave him a chance to preach to the niggers. The substance of his sermon was this:

"'Now when you servants are working for your masters, you must be honest. When you go to the mill, don't carry along an extra sack and put some of the meal or the flour in for yourself. And when you women are cooking in the big house, don't make a big pocket under your dress and put a sack of coffee and a sack of sugar and other things you want in it."

"They took him out and hanged him for corrupting the morals of the slaves.

Conditions After the War

"Immediately after the War, there was a great scarcity of food. Neither Negroes nor white folk had anything to eat. The few white people who did have something wouldn't let it be known. My grandmother who was sixty-five years old and one of the old and respected inhabitants of that time went out to find something for us to eat. A white woman named Mrs. Burton gave her a sack of meal and told her not to tell anybody where she got it.

"My grandmother brought the meal home and cooked it in a large skillet in a big cake. When it got done, she cut it into slices in the way you would cut up a pie and divided it among us. That all we had to eat.

House

"The white people in those days built their houses back from the front. In South Carolina, there were lots of farms that had four to twelve thousand acres. From what mother told me, Master Bill's place set back from the road. Then there was a great square place they called the yard. A fence divided the house and the yard adjoining it from that part of the grounds which held the barn. The yard in front and back of the house held a grove.

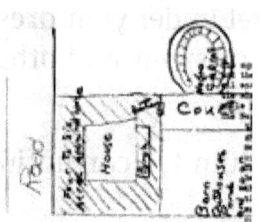

The square around the house and the Negro quarters were all enclosed so that the little slaves could not get out while parents were at work. The Negroes assembled on the porch when the gong called them in the morning. The boss gave orders from the porch. There was an open space between the quarters and the court (where the little slaves played). There was a gate between the court and the big house.

"On the rear of the house, there was a porch from which the boss gave orders usually about four o'clock in the morning and at which they would disband in the evening between nine and ten—no certain time but more or less not earlier than nine and not often later than ten. Back of the house and beyond it was a fence extending clear across the yard. In one corner of this fence was a gate leading into the court. Leading out of the court was an opening surrounded by a semi-circular fence which enclosed the Negro quarters.

"The cabins were usually built on the ground—no floors. The roofs were covered with clapboards.

"When I was a boy we used to sing, 'Rather be a nigger than a poor white man.' Even in slavery they used to sing that. It was the poor white man who was freed by the War, not the Negroes.

Furniture

"There wasn't any furniture. Beds were built with one post out and the other three sides fastened to the sides of the house.

Marrying Time

"I remember one night the people were gone to marry. That was when all the people in the community married immediately after slavery.

Ghosts

"We had an open fireplace. That was at Bartlett Sanders' place. He had close on to three thousand acres. Every grown person had gone to the marrying, and I was at home in the bed I just described.

"My grandfather's mother[HW: ?] had a chair and that was hers only. She was named Senia and was about eighty years old. We burned nothing but pine knots in the hearth. You would put one or two of those on the fire and they would burn for hours. We were all in bed and had been for an hour or two. There were some others sleeping in the same room. There came a peculiar knocking on grandmother's[HW: great grandmother?] chair. It's hard to describe it. It was something like the distant beating of a drum. Grandmother was dead, of course. The boys got up and ran out and brought in some of the hands. When they came in, a little thing about three and a half feet high with legs about six or eight inches long ran out of the room.

Ku Klux Klan

"Whenever there was a man of influence, they terrorized him. They were at their height about the time of Grant's election. Many a time my mother and I have watched them pass our door. They wore gowns and some kind of helmet. They would be going to catch same leading Negro and whip him. There was scarcely a night they couldn't take a leading Negro out and whip him if they would catch him alone. On that account, the Negro men did not stay at home in Sumter County, South Carolina at night. They left home and stayed together. The Ku Klux very seldom interfered with a woman or a child.

"They often scared colored people by drinking large quantities of water. They had something that held a lot of water, and when they would raise the bucket to their mouths to drink, they would slip the water into it.

White Caps

"The white caps operated further to the northwest of where I lived. I never came in contact with them. They were not the same thing as the Ku Klux.

Voting

"In South Carolina under the Reconstruction, we voted right along. In 1868 there were soldiers at all of the election places to see that you did vote.

Career Since the War

"In 1881 I married. The year after that, in '83,[HW: ?] I merchandised a little. Then I got converted. I got it in my head that it was wrong to take big profits from business, so I sold out. Then I was asked to assist the keeper of the jail.

"In 1888 I went to school for the first time. I was then twenty-six years old. By the end of the first term, I knew all that the teacher could teach, so he sent me to Claflin University. I left there in the third year normal.

"When I returned home, I taught school, at first in a private school and later in a public school for $15 a month.

"A man named Boyle told me that he had some ground to sell. I saved up $45, the price he asked for it. When I offered it to him, he said that he had decided not to sell it. I went to town and spent my $45. A few days later, he met me and offered me the place again. I told him I had spent my money. He then offered it to me on time. There was plenty of timber on the place, so I got some contracts with a man named Roland and delivered wood to him. When I went to collect the money, he said he would not pay me in money.

"A man named Pennington offered me 20¢ a day for labor. I asked if he would pay in money.

"He replied, 'If you're looking for money, don't come.'

"I went home and said to my wife, 'I am going to leave here.'

"I came to Forrest City, Arkansas January 28, 1888. I farmed in Forrest City, making one crop, and then I entered the ministry, and then I preached at Spring Park for two years.

"Then I entered Philander Smith College where I stayed from 1891-1897. I preached from the time I left Philander until 1913.

"Then I studied law and completed the American Correspondence course in Law when I was fifty years old. I am still practicing.

Wife and Family

"In 1897, when I graduated from Philander, my wife and six children were sitting on the front seat.

"I have eleven sons and daughters, of whom six are living. I had seven brothers and sisters.

"My wife and I have been married fifty-six years. I had to steal her away from her parents, and she has never regretted coming to me nor I taking her."

Interviewer's Comment

"Brother Mack" as he is familiarly and affectionately known to his friends is a man keen and vigorous, mentally and physically. He attends Sunday school, church both in the morning and evening, and all departments of the Epworth League. He takes the Epworth Herald, the Southwestern Christian Advocate, the Literary Digest, some poultry and farm magazines, the Arkansas Gazette, and the St. Louis Democrat, and several other journals. He is on omnivorous reader and a clear thinker. He raises chickens and goats and plants a garden as avocations. He has on invincible reputation for honesty as well as for thrift and thought.

Nothing is pleasanter than to view the relationship between him and his wife. They have been married fifty-six years and seem to have achieved a perfect understanding. She is an excellent cook and is devoted to her home. She attends church regularly. Seems to be four or five years younger than her husband. Like him, however, she seems to enjoy excellent health.

United States. Work Projects Administration

Interviewer: Mrs. Bernice Bowden
Person interviewed: Cresa Mack
1417 Short Indiana St., Pine Bluff, Ark.
Age: 85

CRESA MACK

"I can tell you something about slavery days. I was born at South Bend, Arkansas on the old Joe Clay place. I 'member they used to work 'em scandalous. They used me at the house and I used to wait on old mistress' brother. He was a old man named Cal Fletcher.

"I 'member when they said the Yankees was comin' the boss man put us in wagons and runned us to Texas. They put the women and chillun in the wagons but the men had to walk. I know I was something over twelve years old.

"Old mistress, Miss Sarah Clay, took her chillun and went to Memphis.

"My white folks treated us very well. I never seed 'em whip my mother but once, but I seen some whipped till they's speechless. Yes ma'm I have.

"I can 'member a lot 'bout the war. The Lord have mercy, I'se old. I 'member they used to sing

  'Run nigger run,
  The paddyrollers'll ketch you,
  Run nigger run.'

"Corse if they ketch you out without a pass they'd beat you nearly to death and tell you to go home to your master.

"One time I was totin' water for the woman what did the washin'. I was goin' along the road and seed somethin' up in a tree that look like a dog. I said 'Look at that dog.' The overseer was comin' from the house and said 'That ain't no dog, that's a panther. You better not stop' and he shot it out. Then I've seen bears out in the cane brakes. I thought they was big black bulls. I was young then—yes mam, I was young.

"When the Yankees come through they sot the house afire and the gin and burned up 'bout a hundred bales a cotton. They never bothered the niggers' quarters. That was the time the overseer carried us to Texas to get rid of the Yankees.

"After the surrender the Yankees told the overseer to bring us all up in the front yard so he could read us the ceremony and he said we was as free as any white man that walked the ground. I didn't know what 'twas about much cause I was too busy playin'.

"I didn't know what school was 'fore freedom, but I went about a month after peace was declared. Then papa died and mama took me out and put me in the field.

"I was grown, 'bout twenty-four or five, when I married. Now my chillun and grand chillun takes care of me."

Interviewer: Miss Irene Robertson
Person interviewed: Warren McKinney, Hazen, Arkansas
Age: 85

WARREN MCKINNEY

I was born in Edgefield County, South Carolina. I am eighty-five years old. I was born a slave of George Strauter. I remembers hearing them say "Thank God Ize free as a jay bird." My ma was a slave in the field. I was eleven years old when freedom was declared. When I was little, Mr. Strauter whipped my ma. It hurt me bad as it did her. I hated him. She was crying. I chunked him with rocks. He run after me, but he didn't catch me. There was twenty-five or thirty hands that worked in the field. They raised wheat, corn, oats, barley, and cotton. All the children that couldn't work stayed at one house. Aunt Mat kept the babies and small children that couldn't go to the field. He had a gin and a shop. The shop was at the fork of the roads. When de war come on my papa went to build forts. He quit ma and took another woman. When de war closed ma took her four children, bundled em up and went to Augusta. The government give out rations there. My ma washed and ironed. People died in piles. I don't know till yet what was de matter. They said it was the change of living. I seen five or six wooden, painted coffins piled up on wagons pass by our house. Loads passed every day lack you see cotton pass here. Some said it was cholorea and some took consumption. Lots of de colored people nearly starved. Not much to get to do and not much house room. Several families had to live in one house. Lots of the colored folks went up north and froze to death. They couldn't stand the cold. They wrote back about them dieing. No they never sent them back. I heard some sent for money to come back. I heerd plenty bout the Ku Klux. They scared the folks to death. People left Augusta in droves. About a thousand would all meet and walk going to hunt work and new homes. Some of them died. I had a sister and brother lost that way. I had another sister come to Louisiana that way. She wrote back.

I don't think the colored folks looked for a share of land. They never got nothing cause the white folks didn't have nothing but barren hills left. About all the mules was wore out hauling provisions in the army. Some folks say they ought to done more for de colored folks when dey left, but dey say dey was broke. Freeing all de slaves left em broke.

That reconstruction was a mighty hard pull. Me and ma couldn't live. A man paid our ways to Carlisle, Arkansas and we come. We started working for Mr. Emenson. He had a big store, teams, and land. We liked it fine, and I been here fifty-six years now. There was so much wild game living was not so hard. If a fellow could get a little bread and a place to stay he was all right. After I come to dis state I voted some. I have farmed and worked at odd jobs. I farmed mostly. Ma went back to her old master. He persuaded her to come back home. Me and her went back and run a farm four or five years before she died. Then I come back here. I first had 300 acres at Carlisle. I sold it and bought 80 acres at Green Grove. I married in South Carolina. We had a fine weddin, home weddin. Each of our families furnished the weddin supper. We had 24 waiters. That is all the wife I ever had. We lived together 57 years. It is hard for me to keep up with my mind since she died. She been dead five years nearly now. I used to sing but I forgot all the songs. We had song books. I joined the church when I was twelve years old.

I think the times are worse than they use to be. The people is living mighty fast I tell you. I don't get no help from the government. They won't give me the pension. I can't work and I can't pay taxes on my place. They just don't give me nothing but a little out of the store. I can't get no pension.

United States. Work Projects Administration

Little Rock District
FOLKLORE SUBJECTS
Name of Interviewer: Irene Robertson
Subject: Ex-Slave—History
Story—Information

This Information given by: Warren McKinney
Place of Residence: Hazen, Green Grove Settlement, Arkansas
Occupation: Farming
Age: 84

[TR: Information moved from bottom of first page.]

WARREN MCKINNEY

Warren McKinney was born in Edgefield County, South Carolina. He was born a slave. His master was George Strauter. He had a big plantation and worked twenty-five or thirty work hands. There were twenty-five or thirty children too small to work in the field. They raised cotton, corn, oats, and wheat. His mother washed and ironed and cooked. He was small but well remembers once when his mother had been sick and had just gotten out. George Strauter whipped her with a switch on her legs. Warren did not approve of it. Rocks were plentiful and he began throwing at him. He said Mr. George took out after him but didn't catch or whip him.

George Strauter tried to teach them all how to be good farmers and be saving. Warren knew war was going on but he didn't see any of it. His father came home several times. He was off building forts. He said he remembered a big "hurly-burly" and he heard 'em saying, "Thank God I'ze free as a jay bird." He didn't know why they were fighting so he didn't know then why they were saying that.

George Strauter had a shop at the fork of the roads. He had his own gin. They sold cotton and bought provisions at Augusta, Georgia. They made some of their meal and flour and raised all their meat and made enough lard to do the year around.

He heard them talking about the "Yankees" burning up Augusta, but he saw where they had burned Hamburg, South Carolina or North Augusta they call it.

After they were free he remembers his mother bundling up her things and her family and them all going in an ox cart to Augusta to live. Warren's mother washed, cooked and ironed for a living. Her husband went off and lived with another woman after freedom. Warren was about eleven years old then. The Government furnished food for them too. One thing that distressed Warren was the way people died for more than a year. He saw five or six coffins piled up on a wagon being taken out to be buried. He thought it was changing houses and changing ways of living. They didn't have shoes and warm clothes and weren't fed from white folks smoke house. Lots of the slaves had Consumption and died right now. Stout men and women didn't live two years after they were freed. Lots of them said they didn't like that freedom and wanted to go back but the masters were broke and couldn't keep many of them if they went back.

When Warren was about fifteen years old, there was a white man or two, but colored leaders mostly got about a thousand colored people to start for the West walking. Warren had sisters and brothers who started on this trip.

Warren had some fussy brothers, his mother was afraid would get in jail. They kept her uneasy. They shipped their "stuff" by boat and train. He never saw them any more but he heard from them in Louisiana. Louisiana had a bad name in those days.

When Warren was about fourteen and fifteen, his mother had them on a farm, farming near Hamburg.

When he was sixteen or seventeen, his mother and the other children came on the train to about where Carlisle now is but it wasn't called by that name. There were very few houses of any kind. Mr. Emerson had a big store and lots of land. He worked black and white. Mr. Emerson let them have seven or eight mules and wagons and they farmed near there. He remembers pretty soon there was a depot where the depot now stands, a bank, a post office, and two or three more stores, all small buildings. He liked coming to Arkansas because he got to ride on the train a long ways. It was easy to live here. There were lots of game and fish.

Warren never shot anything in his life. He was no hunter. Nats were awful. Warren made smoke to run the nats from the cows. Four or five deer would come to the smoke. Cows were afraid of them and would leave the smoke. When he would go the deer would leap four or five feet in the air at the sight of him.

When Warren lived in Augusta, Georgia, they had schools a month at a time but Warren never did get to go to any, so he can't read or write. But he learned to save his money. He joined a church when he was twelve years old in South Carolina and belongs to the Baptist church at Green Grove now.

The old master in South Carolina persuaded his mother to come back. They all went back four or five years before his mother died. While Warren was there he married a woman on a joining farm.

Interviewer: Samuel S. Taylor
Person interviewed: Victoria McMullen
1416 E. Valmar, Little Rock, Arkansas
Age: 54
Occupation: Seamstress

VICTORIA MCMULLEN

"My mother was born March 16, 1865, and knew nothing of slavery.

"Both my grandmothers and both grandfathers were slaves. My father was born in the same year as my mother and like my mother knew nothing of slavery although both of them might have been born slaves.

"I knew my mother's mother and father and my father's mother, but I didn't know my father's father.

"He was from Texas and he always stayed there. He never did come out to Louisiana where I was born. My mother was born in Louisiana, but my father was born in Texas. I don't know what county or city my father was born in. I just heard my grandmother on his side say he was born in Texas.

"During the War (he was born in '65 when the War ceased), Grandmother Katy—that was her name, Katy, Katy Elmore—she was in Louisiana at first—she was run out in Texas, I suppose, to be hidden from the Yankees. My father was born there and my grandfather stayed there. He died in Texas and then Grandma Katy come back to Louisiana with my father and settled in Ouachita Parish.

"Grandma Katy was sold from South Carolina into Louisiana to Bob McClendon, and she kept the name of Elmore who was her first owner in South Carolina. It was Bob McClendon who run her out in Texas to hide her from the Yankees. My grandfather in Texas kept the name of Jamison. That was the name of his master in Texas. But grandma kept the name of Elmore from South Carolina because he was good to her. He was better than Bob McClendon. The eastern states sold their slaves to the southern states and got all the money, then they freed the slaves and that left the South without anything.

"Grandma Katy had Creek Indian blood in her. She was of medium size and height, copper colored, high cheek bones, small squinchy eyes, black curly hair. Her hair was really pretty but she didn't curl it. It was just naturally curly. She was a practical nurse as they call it, but she did more of what some people call a midwife. They call it something else now. They got a proper word for it.

"They got it in these government agencies. That is what she was even in slavery times. She worked for colored people and white people both. That was after she was freed until she went blind. She went blind three years before she died. She died at the age of exactly one hundred years. She treated women and babies. They said she was a real good doctor in her day. That is been fifty-four years ago. [I will be fifty-four years old tomorrow—September 18, 1938.] In slavery times my grandma was almost as free as she was in freedom because of her work.

"She said that Bob McClendon was cruel to her. Sometimes he'd get angry and take the shovel and throw hot ashes on the slaves. And then he'd see them with blisters on them and he would take a handsaw or a flat plank and bust the blisters. Louisiana was a warm country and they wouldn't have much clothes on. When the slaves were freed, he went completely broke. He had scarcely a place to live.

"I seen him once. Be look like on old possum. He had a long beard down to his waist and he had long side burns too. Just a little of his face showed. He was tall and stooping and he wore his hair long and uncut down on his neck. You know about what he looked like. He had on blue jeans pants and brogan shoes and a common shirt—a work shirt. He wore very common clothes. When they freed the Negroes, it broke him up completely. He had been called a 'big-to-do' in his life but he wasn't nothing then. He owned Grandma Katy.

"Grandma Katy had a sister named Maria and a brother named Peter. He owned all three of them. I have seen all of them. Grandma Katy was the oldest. She and Uncle Peter stayed close together. He didn't have no wife and she didn't have no husband. But Aunt Maria had a husband. She lived off from them after freedom. It was about twelve miles away. My great-aunt and great-uncle—they were Maria and Peter—that was what they were. Uncle Peter died first before I left Louisiana, but Aunt Maria and Grandma Katy died after I came to Arkansas. Grandma Katy lived four years after I came here.

"After they was free and my father had gotten large enough to work and didn't have no horse, my grandma was going 'round waiting on women—that is all she did—all the rest of the people had gotten large and left home. Papa made a crop with a hoe. He made three bales of cotton and about twelve loads of corn with that hoe. He used to tell me, 'You don't know nothin' 'bout work. You oughter see how I had to work.' After that he bought him a horse. Money was scarce then and it took something to buy the place and the horse both. They were turned loose from slavery without anything. Hardly had a surname—just Katy, Maria, and Peter.

"I knew more about the slave-time history of my mother's folks than I did about my father's but I'll tell you that some other time. My grandmother on my mother's side was born in Richmond, Virginia. She was owned by a doctor but I can't call his name. She gets her name from her husband's owners. They came from Virginia. They didn't take the name of their owners in Louisiana. They took the name of the owners in Virginia. She was a twin—her twin was a boy named June and her name was Hetty. Her master kept her brother to be a driver for him. She was sent from Virginia to Louisiana to people that were related to her Virginia people. She called her Louisiana mistress 'White Ma;' she never did call her 'missis.' The white folks and the colored folks too called her Indian because she was mixed with Choctaw. That's the Indian that has brown spots on the jaw. They're brownskin. It was an Indian from the Oklahoma reservation that said my mother belonged to the Choctaws.

"She rode from Virginia to Louisiana on a boat at the age of twelve years. She was separated from her mother and brothers and sisters and never did see them again. She was kept in the house for a nurse. She was not a midwife. She nursed the white babies. That was what she was sent to Louisiana for—to nurse the babies. The Louisiana man that owned her was named George Dorkins. But I think this white woman came from Virginia. She married this Louisiana man, then sent back to her father's house and got grandma; she got her for a nurse. She worked only a year and a half in the field before peace was declared. After she got grown and married, my grandfather—she had to stay with him and cook and keep house for him. That was during slavery time but after George Dorkins died. Dorkins went and got hisself a barrel of whiskey—one of these great big old barrels—and set it up in his house, and put a faucet in it and didn't do nothin' but drink whiskey. He said he was goin' to drink hisself to death. And he did.

"He was young enough to go to war and he said he would drink hisself to death before he would go, and he did. My grandma used to steal newspapers out of his house and take them down to the quarters and leave them there where there were one or two slaves that could read and tell how the War was goin' on. I never did learn how the slaves learned to read. But she was in the house and she could steal the papers and send them down. Later she could slip off and they would tell her the news, and then she could slip the papers back.

"Her master drank so much he couldn't walk without falling and she would have to help him out. Her mistress was really good. She never allowed the overseer to whip her. She was only whipped once in slave time while my father's mother was whipped more times than you could count.

"Her master often said, 'I'll drink myself to death before I'll go to war and be shot down like a damn target.'

She said in living with them in the house, she learned to cuss from him. She said she was a cussin' soul until she became a Christian. She wasn't 'fraid of them because she was kin to them in some way. There was another woman there who was some kin to them and she looked enough like my grandma for them to be kin to each other. We talked it over several times and said we believed we were related; but none of us know for sure.

"When the slaves wanted something said they would have my grandma say it because they knew she wouldn't be whipped for it. 'White Ma' wouldn't let nobody whip her if she knew it. She cussed the overseer out that time for whipping her.

"When grandma was fourteen or fifteen years old they locked her up in the seed house once or twice for not going to church. You see they let the white folks go to the church in the morning and the colored folks in the evening, and my grandma didn't always want to go. She would be locked up in the seed bin and she would cuss the preacher out so he could hear her. She would say, 'Master, let us out.' And he would say, 'You want to go to church?' And she would say, 'No, I don't want to hear that same old sermon: "Stay out of your missis' and master's hen house. Don't steal your missis' and master's chickens. Stay out of your missis' and master's smokehouse. Don't steal your missis' and master's hams." I don't steal nothing. Don't need to tell me not to.'

"She was tellin' the truth too. She didn't steal because she didn't have to. She had plenty without stealin'! She got plenty to eat in the house. But the other slaves didn't git nothin' but fat meat and corn bread and molasses. And they got tired of that same old thing. They wanted something else sometimes. They'd go to the hen house and get chickens. They would go to the smokehouse and get hams and lard. And they would get flour and anything else they wanted and they would eat something they wanted. There wasn't no way to keep them from it.

"The reason she got whipped that time, the overseer wanted her to help get a tree off the fence that had been blown down by a storm. She told him that wasn't her work and she wasn't goin' to do it. Old miss was away at that time. He hit her a few licks and she told old miss when she came back. Old 'White Ma' told the overseer, 'Don't never put your hands on her no more no matter what she does. That's more than I do. I don't hit her and you got no business to do it.'

"Her husband, my grandfather, was a blacksmith, and he never did work in the field. He made wagons, plows, plowstocks, buzzard wings—they call them turning plows now. They used to make and put them on the stocks. He made anything-handles, baskets. He could fill wagon wheels. He could sharpen tools. Anything that come under the line of blacksmith, that is what he did. He used to fix wagons all the time I knowed him. In harvest time in the fall he would drive from Bienville where they were slaves to Monroe in Ouachita Parish. He kept all the plows and was sharpening and fixing anything that got broke. He said he never did get no whipping.

"His name was Tom Eldridge. They called him 'Uncle Tom'. They was the mother and father of twelve children. Six lived and six died. One boy and five girls lived. And one girl and five boys died—half and half. He died at the age of seventy-five, June 6, 1908. She died January 1920.

"I came out here in January 1907. I lived in Pine Bluff. From Louisiana I came to Pine Bluff in 1906. In 1907 I went to Kerr in Lonoke County and lived there eight years and then I came to Little Rock. I farmed at Kerr and just worked 'round town those few months in Pine Bluff. Excusing the time I was in Pine Bluff and Little Rock I farmed. I farmed in Ouachita Parish, Louisiana."

Interviewer: Miss Irene Robertson
Person interviewed: Nannie P. Madden,
West Memphis, Arkansas
Age: 69

NANNIE P. MADDEN

"I am Martha Johnson's sister. I was born at Lake Village, Arkansas. I am 69 years old. I was born on Mr. Ike Wethingtons place. Pa was renting. Mother died in 1876 on this farm. We called it Red Leaf plantation. Father died at Martha Johnson's here in West Memphis when he was 88 years old.

"Mother was not counted a slave. Her master's Southern wife (white wife) disliked her very much but kept her till her death. Mother had three white children by her master. After freedom she married a black man and had four children by him. We are in the last set.

"We was born after slavery and all we know is from hearing our people talk. Father talked all time about slavery. He was a soldier. I couldn't tell you straight. I can give you some books on slavery:

>Booker T. Washington's Own Story of His Life and Work,
>64 page supplement, by Albon L. Holsey

>Authentic Edition--in office of Library of Congress,
>Washington, D.C., 1915, copywrighted by J.L.

Nichols Co.

The Master Mind of a Child of Slavery--
Booker T. Washington,
by Frederick E. Drinker, Washington, D.C.

I have read them both. Yes, they are my own books.

"I farmed and cooked all my life."

Interviewer: Samuel S. Taylor
Person interviewed: Perry Madden, Thirteenth Street, south side, one block east of Boyle Park Road, Route 6, Care L.G. Cotton, Little Rock, Arkansas
Age: About 79

PERRY MADDEN

Birth and Age

"I have been here quite a few years. This life is short. A man ought to prepare for eternity. I had an uncle who used to say that a person who went to torment stayed as long as there was a grain of sand on the sea.

"I was a little boy when slavery broke. I used to go out with my brother. He watched gaps. I did not have to do anything; I just went out with him to keep him company. I was scared of the old master. I used to call him the 'Big Bear.' He was a great big old man.

"I was about six years old when the War ended, I guess. I don't know how old I am. The insurance men put me down as seventy-three. I know I was here in slavery time, and I was just about six years old when the War ended.

Schooling

"I got my first learning in Alabama. I didn't learn anything at all in slavery times. I went to school. I would go to the house in slavery tine, and there wouldn't be nobody home, and I would go to the bed and get under it because I was scared. When I would wake up it would be way in the night and dark, and I would be in bed.

"I got my schooling way after the surrender. We would make crops. The third time we moved, dad started me to school. I had colored teachers. I was in Talladega County. I made the fifth grade before I stopped. My father died and then I had to stop and take care of my mother.

An "Aunt Caroline" Story

"I know that some people can tell things that are goin' to happen. Old man Julks lived at Pumpkin Bend. He had a colt that disappeared. He went to 'Aunt Caroline'—that's Caroline Dye. She told him just where the colt was and who had it and how he had to get it back. She described the colt and told him that was what he come to find out about before he had a chance to ask her anything. She told him that white people had it and told him where they lived and told him he would have to have a white man go and git it for him. He was working for a good man and he told him about it. He advertised for the colt and the next day, the man that stole it came and told him that a colt had been found over on his place and for him to come over and arrange to git it. But he said, 'No, I've placed that matter in the hands of my boss.' He told his boss about it, but the fellow brought the horse and give it to the boss without any argument.

Family and Masters

"My old master's slaves were called free niggers. He and his wife never mistreated their slaves. When any of

Madden's slaves were out and the pateroles got after them, if they could make it home, that ended it. Nobody beat Madden's niggers.

"My father's name was Allen Madden and my mother's name was Amy Madden. I knew my grandfather and grandmother on my mother's side. My grandfather and grandmother never were 'round me though that I can remember.

"When the old man died, the Negroes were divided out. This boy got so many and that one got so many. The old man, Mabe Madden, had two sons, John and Little Mabe. My mother and father went to John. They were in Talladega because John stayed there.

"My father's mother and father fell to Little Mabe Madden. They never did come to Alabama but I have heard my father talk about them so much. My father's father was named Harry. His last name must have been Madden.

"My grandfather on my mother's side was named Charlie Hall. He married into the Madden family. He belonged to the Halls before he married. Old man Charlie, his master, had a plantation that wasn't far from the Madden's plantation. In those days, if you met a girl and fell in love with her, you could git a pass and go to see her if you wanted to. You didn't have to be on the same plantation at all. And you could marry her and go to see her, and have children by her even though you belonged to different masters. The Maddens never did buy Hall. Grandma never would change her name to Hall. He stayed at my house after we married, stayed with me sometimes, and stayed with his other son sometimes.

"My mother was born a Madden. She was born right at Madden's place. When grandma married Hall, like it is now, she would have been called Hall. But she was born a Madden and stayed Madden and never did change to her husband's name. So my mother was born a Madden although her father's name was Hall.

"I don't know what sort of man Mabe was, and I only know what my parents said about John. They said he was a good man and I have to say what they said. He didn't let nobody impose on his niggers. Pateroles did git after them and bring them in with the hounds, but when they got in, that settled it. Madden never would allow white people to beat on his niggers.

"They tried to git my daddy out so that they could whip him, but they couldn't catch him. They shot him—the pateroles did—but he whipped them. My daddy was a coon. I mean he was a good man.

Early Life

"My brother was big enough to mind gaps. That was in slavery times. They had good fences around the field. They didn't have gates like they do now. They had gaps. The fence would zigzag, and the rails could be lifted down at one section, and that would leave a gap. If you left a gap, the stock would go into the field. When there was a gap, my brother would stay in it and keep the stock from passing. When the folks would come to dinner, he would go in and eat dinner with them just as big as anybody. When they would leave, the gap would stay down till night. It stayed down from morning till noon and from one o'clock till the men come in at night. The gap was a place in the rails like I told you where they could take down the rails to pass. It took time to lay the rails down and more time to place then back up again. They wouldn't do it. They would leave them down till they come back during the work hours and a boy that was too small to do anything else was put to mind them. My brother used to do that and I would keep him company. When I heard old master coming there, I'd be gone, yes siree. I would see him when he left the house and when he got to the gap, I would be home or at my grandfather's.

Occupational Experiences

"I have followed farming all my life. That is the sweetest life a man can lead. I have been farming all my life principally. My occupation is farming. That is it was until I lost my health. I ain't done nothin' for about four years now. I would follow public work in the fall of the year and make a crop every year. Never failed till I got disabled. I used to make all I used and all I needed to feed my stock. I even raised my own wheat before I left home in Alabama. That is a wheat country. They don't raise it out here.[HW: ?]

"I came here—lemme see, about how many years ago did I come here. I guess I have been in Arkansas about twenty-eight years since the first time I come here. I have gone in and out as I got a chance to work somewheres. I have been living in this house about three years.

"I preached for about twenty or more years. I don't know that I call myself a preacher. I am a pretty good talker sometimes. I have never pastored a church; somehow or 'nother the word come to me to go and I go and talk. I ain't no pulpit chinch. I could have taken two or three men's churches out from under them, but I didn't.

Freedom and Soldiers

"I can't remember just how my father got freed. Old folks then didn't let you stan' and listen when they talked. If you did it once, you didn't do it again. They would talk while they were together, but the children would have business outdoors. Yes siree, I never heard them say much about how they got freedom.

"I was there when the Yankees come through. That was in slave time. They marched right through old man Madden's grove. They were playing the fifes and beating the drums. And they were playing the fiddle. Yes sir, they were playing the fiddle too. It must have been a fiddle; it sounded just like one. The soldiers were all just a singin'. They didn't bother nobody at our house. If they bothered anything, nothing was told me about it. I heard my uncle say they took a horse from my old manager. I didn't see it. They took the best horse in the lot my uncle said. Pardon me, they didn't take him. A peckerwood took him and let the Yankees get him. I have heard that they bothered plenty of other places. Took the best mules, and left old broken down ones and things like that. Broke things up. I have heard that about other places, but I didn't see any of it.

Right after the War

"Right after the War, my father went to farming— renting land. I mean he sharecropped and done around. Thing is come way up from then when the Negroes first started. They didn't have no stock nor nothin' then. They made a crop just for the third of it. When they quit the third, they started givin' them two-fifths. That's more than a third, ain't it? Then they moved up from that, and give them half, and they are there yet. If you furnish, they give you two-thirds and take one-third. Or they give you so much per acre or give him produce in rent.

Marriage

"I was married in 1883. My wife's name was Mary Elston. Her mother died when she was an infant. Her grandmother was an Elston at first. Then she changed her name to Cunningham. But she always went in the name of Elston, and was an Elston when she married me. My wife I mean. I married on a Thursday in the Christmas week. This December I will be married fifty-five years. This is the only wife I have ever had. We had three children and all of them are dead. All our birthed children are dead. One of them was just three months old when he died. My baby girl had three children and she lived to see all of them married.

Opinions

"Our own folks is about the worst enemies we have. They will come and sweet talk you and then work against you. I had a fellow in here not long ago who came here for a dollar, and I never did hear from him again after he got it. He couldn't get another favor from me. No man can fool me more than one time. I have been beat out of lots of money and I have got hurt trying to help people.

"The young folks now is just gone astray. I tell you the

truth, I wouldn't give you forty cents a dozen for these young folks. They are sassy and disrespectful. Don't respect themselves and nobody else. When they get off from home, they'll respect somebody else better 'n they will their own mothers.

"If they would do away with this stock law, they would do better everywhere. If you would say fence up your place and raise what you want, I could get along. But you have to keep somebody to watch your stock. If you don't, you'll have to pay something out. It's a bad old thing this stock law. It's detrimental to the welfare of man."

Interviewer: Mrs. Bernice Bowden
Person interviewed: Lewis Mann
1501 Bell Street, Pine Bluff, Arkansas
Age: 81

LEWIS MANN

"As nigh as I can come at it, I was bout five or six time of the war. I remember when the war ceasted. I was a good-sized chap.

"Durin' the war my mother's master sent us to Texas; western Texas is whar they stopped me. We stayed there two years and then they brought us back after surrender.

"I remember when the war ceasted and remember the soldiers refugeein' through the country. I'm somewhar round eighty-one. I'm tellin' you the truf. I ain't just now come here.

"I was born right here in Arkansas. My mother's master was old B.D. Williams of Tennessee and we worked for his son Mac H. Williams here in Arkansas. They was good to my mother. Always had nurses for the colored childrun while the old folks was in the field.

"After the war I used to work in the house for my white folks—for Dr. Bob Williams way up there in the country on the river. I stayed with his brother Mac Williams might near twenty-five or thirty years. Worked around the house servin' and doin' arrands different places.

"I went to school a little bit a good piece after the war and learned to read and write.

"I've heard too much of the Ku Klux. I remember when they was Ku Kluxin' all round through here.

"Lord! I don't know how many times I ever voted. I used to vote every time they had an election. I voted before I could read. The white man showed me how to vote and asked me who I wanted to vote for. Oh Lord, I was might near grown when I learned to read.

"I been married just one time in my life and my wife's been dead thirteen years.

"I tell you, Miss, I don't know hardly what to think of things now. Everything so changeable I can't bring nothin' to remembrance to hold it.

"I didn't do nothin' when I was young but just knock around with the white folks. Oh Lord, when I was young I delighted in parties. Don't nothin' like that worry me now. Don't go to no parades or nothin'. Don't have that on my brain like I did when I was young. I goes to church all the place I does go.

"I ain't never had no accident. Don't get in the way to have no accident cause I know the age I is if I injure these bones there ain't anything more to me.

"My mother had eight childrun and just my sister and me left. I can't do a whole day's work to save my life. I own this place and my sister-in-law gives me a little somethin' to eat. I used to be on the bureau but they took me off that."

Interviewer: Mrs. Bernice Bowden
Person interviewed: Angeline Martin, Kansas City, Missouri
Visiting at 1105 Louisiana St., Pine Bluff, Arkansas
Age 80

ANGELINE MARTIN

"Well, I was livin' then. I was born in Georgia. Honey, I don't know what year. I was born before the war. I was about ten when freedom come. I don't remember when it started but I remember when it ended. I think I'm in the 80's—that's the way I count it.

"My master was dead and my mistress was a widow—Miss Sarah Childs. She had a guardeen.

"When the war come, old mistress and her daughter refugeed to Mississippi. The guardeen wouldn't let me go, said I was too young.

"My parents stayed on the plantation. My white folks' house was vacant and the Yankees come and used it for headquarters. They never had put shoes on me and when the Yankees shot the chickens I'd run and get em. They didn't burn up nothin', just kill the hogs and chickens and give us plenty.

"I didn't know what the war was about. You know chillun in them days didn't have as much sense as they got now.

"After freedom, my folks stayed on the place and

worked on the shares. I want to school right after the war. I went every year till we left there. We come to this country in seventy something. We come here and stopped at the Cummins place. I worked in the field till I come to town bout fifty years ago. Since then I cooked some and done laundry work.

"I married when I was seventeen. Had six children. I been livin' in Kansas City twenty-three years. Followed my boy up there. I like it up there a lot better than I do here. Oh lord, yes, there are a lot of colored people in Kansas City."

Interviewer: Miss Irene Robertson
Person interviewed: Josie Martin
R.F.D., Madison, Arkansas
Age: 86

JOSIE MARTIN

"I was born up near Cotton Plant but took down near Helena to live. My parents named Sallie and Bob Martin. They had seven children. I heard mother say she was sold on a block in Mississippi when she was twelve years old. My father was a Creek Indian; he was dark. Mother was a Choctaw Indian; she was bright. Mother died when I was but a girl and left a family on my hands. I sent my baby brother and sister to school and I cooked on a boarding train. The railroad hands working on the tracks roomed and et on the train. They are all dead now and I'm 'lone in the world.

"My greatest pleasure was independence—make my money, go and spend it as I see fit. I wasn't popular with men. I never danced. I did sell herbs for diarrhea and piles and 'what ails you.' I don't sell no more. Folks too close to drug stores now. I had long straight hair nearly to my knees. It come out after a spell of typhoid fever. It never come in to do no good." (Baldheaded like a man and she shaves. She is a hermaphrodite, reason for never marrying.) "I made and saved up at one time twenty-three thousand dollars cooking and field work. I let it slip out from me in dribs.

"I used to run from the Yankees. I've seen them go in droves along the road. They found old colored couple, went out, took their hog and made them barbecue it. They drove up a stob, nailed a piece to a tree stacked their guns. They rested around till everything was ready. They et at one o'clock at night and after the feast drove on. They wasn't so good to Negroes. They was good to their own feelings. They et up all that old couple had to eat in their house and the pig they raised. I reckon their owners give them more to eat. They lived off alone and the soldiers stopped there and worked the old man and woman nearly to death.

"Our master told us about freedom. His name was Master Martin. He come here from Mississippi. I don't recollect his family.

"I get help from the Welfare. I had paralysis. I never got over my stroke. I ain't no 'count to work."

Interviewer: Miss Irene Robertson
Person interviewed: Bess Mathis, Hazen, Arkansas
Age: 82

BESS MATHIS

"I was born in De Sota County, Mississippi. My parents' owners was Mars Hancock. Mama was a cook and field hand. Papa milked and worked in the field. Mama had jes' one child, that me. I had six childern. I got five livin'. They knowed they free. It went round from mouth to mouth. Mama said Mars Hancock was good er slave holder as ever lived she recken. I heard her come over that er good many times. But they wanted to be free. I jes' heard em talk bout the Ku Klux. They said the Ku Klux made lot of em roamin' round go get a place to live and start workin'. They tell how they would ride at night and how scarry lookin' they was. I heard em say if Mars Hancock didn't want to give em meat they got tree a coon or possum. Cut the tree down or climb it and then come home and cook it. They had no guns. They had dogs or could get one. Game helps out lots.

"The women chewed for their children after they weaned em. They don't none of em do that way now. Women wouldn't cut the baby's finger nails. They bite em off. They said if you cut its nails off he would steal. They bite its toe nails off, too. And if they wanted the children to have long pretty hair, they would trim the ends off on the new of the moon. That would cause the hair to grow long. White folks and darkies both done them things.

"I been doin' whatever come to hand—farmin', cookin', washin', ironin'.

"I never expects to vote neither. I sure ain't voted.

"Conditions pretty bad sometimes. I don't know what cause it. You got beyond me now. I don't know what going become of the young folks, and they ain't studyin' it. They ain't kind. Got no raisin' I call it. I tried to raise em to work and behave. They work some. My son is takin' care of me now."

Interviewer: Mrs. Bernice Bowden
Person interviewed: Caroline Matthews
812 Spruce Street, Pine Bluff, Arkansas
Age: 79

CAROLINE MATTHEWS

"Yes'm, I was born in slavery times in Mississippi. Now, the only thing I remember was some soldiers come along on some mules. I remember my mother and father was sittin' on the gallery and they say, 'Look a there, them's soldiers.'

"And I remember when my parents run off. I was with 'em and I cried for 'em to tote me.

"My mother's first owner was named Armstrong. She said she was about eleven years old when he bought her. I heard her say they just changed around a lot.

"Freedom was comin' and her last owners had carried her to a state where it hadn't come yet. That's right—it was Texas.

"Her first owners was good. She said they wouldn't 'low the overseer to 'buke the women at all.

"But her last owners was cruel. She said one day old missis was out in the yard and backed up and fell into a pan of hot water and when her husband come she told him and he tried to 'buke my mother. You know if somebody tryin' to get the best of you and you can help yourself, you gwine do it. So mama throwed up her arm and old master hit it with a stick and cut it bad. So my parents run off. That was in Texas.

"She said we was a year comin' back and I know they stopped at the Dillard place and made a crop. And they lost one child on the way—that was Kittie.

"I heard mama say they got back here to Arkansas and got to the bureau and they freed 'em. I know the War wasn't over yet 'cause I know I heard mama say, 'Just listen to them guns at Vicksburg.'

"When I was little, I was so sickly. I took down with the whoopin' cough and I was sick so long. But mama say to the old woman what stayed with me, 'This gal gwine be here to see many a winter 'cause she so stout in the jaws I can't give her no medicine.'

"When I commenced to remember anything, I heered 'em talkin' 'bout Grant and Colfax. Used to wear buttons with Grant and Colfax.

"But I was livin' in Abraham Lincoln's time. Chillun them days didn't know nothin'. Why, woman, I was twelve years old 'fore I knowed babies didn't come out a holler log. I used to go 'round lookin' in logs for a baby.

"I had seven sisters and three brothers and they all dead but me. Had three younger than me. They was what they called freeborn chillun.

"After freedom my parents worked for Major Ross. I know when mama fixed us up to go to Sunday-school we'd go by Major Ross for him to see us. I know we'd go so early, sometimes he'd still be in his drawers.

"I know one thing—when I was about sixteen years old things was good here. Ever'body had a good living."

United States. Work Projects Administration

Interviewer: Miss Irene Robertson
Person interviewed: Malindy Maxwell, Madison, Arkansas
Age: Up in 80's

MALINDY MAXWELL

"I was born close to Como and Sardis, Mississippi. My master and mistress was Sam Shans and Miss Cornelia Shans. I was born a slave. They owned mama and Master Rube Sanders owned pa. Neither owner wouldn't sell but they agreed to let ma and pa marry. They had a white preacher and they married out in the yard and had a big table full of weddin' supper, and the white folks et in the house. They had a big supper too. Ma said they had a big crowd. The preacher read the ceremony. Miss Cornelia give her a white dress and white shoes and Miss Cloe Wilburn give her a veil. Miss Cloe was some connection of Rube Sanders.

"They had seven children. I'm the oldest—three of us living.

"After 'mancipation pa went to see about marrying ma over agen and they told him that marriage would stand long as ever he lived.

"Mama was sold at twelve years old in Atlanta, Georgia. Ma and pa was always field hands. Grandma got to be one of John Sanders' leading hands to work mong the women folks. They said John Sanders was meanest man ever lived or died. According to pa's saying, Mars Ruben was a good sorter man. Pa said John Sanders was too mean a man to have a wife. He was mean to Miss Sarah. They said he beat her, his wife, like he beat a nigger woman.

"Miss Sarah say, 'Come get your rations early Saturday morning, clean up your house, wash and iron, and we'll go to preaching tomorrow—Sunday. I want you to all come out clean Monday morning.' They go ask Mars John Sanders if they could go to preaching. I recken from what they said they walked. Mars John, when they git their best clothes on, make them turn round and go to the field and work all day long. He was just that mean. Work all day long Sunday.

"Miss Sarah was a Primitive Baptist and that is what I am till this day. Some folks call us Hardshell Baptist. The colored folks set in the back of the church. The women all set on one side and the men on the other. If they had a middle row, there was a railing dividing mens' seats from the womens' seats on the very same benches.

"Miss Cloe, Miss Cornelia, and Miss Sarah cook up a whole lot of good things to eat and go to camp meeting. Sometimes they would stay a week and longer. They would take time bout letting the colored folks go long. We had big times. My grandpa took a gingercake cutter with him and sold gingercakes when they come out of the church. He could keep that money his own. I don't know how he sold them. My sister has the cutter now I expect. My girl has seen it. It was a foot long, this wide (5 inches), and fluted all around the edges, and had a handle like a biscuit cutter. They was about an inch thick. He made good ones and he sold all he could ever make. Grandpa took carpet sacks to carry his gingercakes in to sell them. I remember that mighty well. (The shape of the cutter was like this: 🔊) He purt nigh always got to go to all the camp meetings. Folks got happy and shouted in them days. It would be when somebody got religion. At some big meetings they didn't shout.

"When I was born they had a white mid-wife, Miss Martin. My mistress was in the cabin when I was born. I was born foot foremost and had a veil on my face and down on my body a piece. They call it a 'caul.' Sometimes I see forms and they vanish. I can see some out of one eye now. But I've always seen things when my sight was good. It is like when you are dreaming at night but I see them at times that plain in day.

"I don't know how old I am but I was a good size girl when 'mancipation come on. Miss Cornelia had my age in her Bible. They done took me from the cabin and I was staying at the house. I slept on a trundle bed under Miss Cornelia's bed. Her bed was a teaster—way high up, had a big stool to step on to go up in there and she had it curtained off. I had a good cotton bed and I slept good up under there. Her bed was corded with sea grass rope. It didn't have no slats like beds do now.

"Colored folks slept on cotton beds and white folks—some of em at least—picked geese and made feather beds and down pillows. They carded and washed sheep's wool and put in their quilts. Some of them, they'd be light and warm. Colored folks' bed had one leg. Then it was holes hewed in the wall on the other three sides and wooden slats across it. Now that wasn't no bad bed. Some of them was big enough for three to sleep on good. When the children was small four could sleep easy cross ways, and they slept that way.

"They had shelves and tables and chairs. They made chests and put things in there and set on top of it too. White folks had fine chests to keep their bed clothes in. Some of them was made of oak, and pine, and cypress. They would cook walnut hulls and bark and paint them dark with the tea.

"I recollect a right smart of the Civil War. We was close nough to hear the roar and ramble and the big cannons shake the things in the house. I don't know where they was fighting—a long ways off I guess.

"I saw the soldiers scouting. They come most any time. They go in and take every drop of milk out of the churn. They took anything they could find and went away with it. I seen the cavalry come through. I thought they looked so pretty. Their canteens was shining in the sun. Miss Cornelia told me to hide, the soldiers might take me on with them. I didn't want to go. I was very well pleased there at Miss Cornelia's.

"I seen the cavalry come through that raised the 'white sheet.' I know now it must have been a white flag but they called it a white sheet to quit fighting. It was raised a short time after they passed and they said they was the ones raised it. I don't know where it was. I reckon it was a big white flag they rared up. It was so they would stop fighting.

"Mars Sam Shan didn't go to no war; he hid out. He said it was a useless war, he wasn't going to get shot up for no use a tall, and he never went a step. He hid out. I don't know where. I know Charles would take the baskets off. Charles tended to the stock and the carriage. He drove the wagon and carriage. He fetched water and wood. He was a black boy. Mars Sam Shan said he wasn't goiner loose his life for nothing.

"Miss Cornelia would cook corn light bread and muffins and anything else they had to cook. Rations got down mighty scarce before it was done wid. They put the big round basket nearly big as a split cotton basket out on the back portico. Charles come and disappear with it.

"Chess and Charles was colored overseers. He didn't have white overseers. Miss Cornelia and Miss Cloe would walk the floor and cry and I would walk between. I would cry feeling sorry for them, but I didn't know why they cried so much. I know now it was squally times. War is horrible.

"Mars Sam Shan come home, went down to the cabins—they was scattered over the fields—and told them the War was over, they was free but that they could stay. Then come some runners, white men. They was Yankee men. I know that now. They say you must get pay or go off. We stayed that year. Another man went to pa and said he would give him half of what he made. He got us all up and we went to Pleasant Hill. We done tolerable well.

"Then he tried to buy a house and five acres and got beat out of it. The minor heirs come and took it. I never learnt in books till I went to school. Seem like things was in a confusion after I got big nough for that. I'd sweep and rake and cook and wash the dishes, card, spin, hoe, scour the floors and tables. I would knit at night heap of times. We'd sing some at night.

"Colored folks couldn't read so they couldn't sing at church lessen they learnt the songs by hearing them at home. Colored folks would meet and sing and pray and preach at the cabins.

"My first teacher was a white man, Mr. Babe Willroy. I went to him several short sessions and on rainy days and cold days I couldn't work in the field. I worked in the field all my life. Cook out in the winter, back to the field in the spring till fall again.

"Well, I jes' had this one girl. I carried her along with me. She would play round and then she was a heap of help. She is mighty good to me now.

"I never seen a Ku Klux in my life. Now, I couldn't tell you about them.

"My parents' names was Lou Sanders and Anthony Sanders. Ma's mother was a Rockmore and her husband was a Cherokee Indian. I recollect them well. He was a free man and was fixing to buy her freedom. Her young mistress married Mr. Joe Bues and she heired her. Mr. Joe Bues drunk her up and they come and got her and took her off. They run her to Memphis before his wife could write to her pa. He was Mars Rockmore.

"Grandma was put on a block and sold fore grandpa could cumerlate nough cash to buy her for his wife. Grandma never seen her ma no more. Grandpa followed her and Mr. Sam Shans bought her and took her to Mississippi with a lot more he bought.

"My pa's ma b'long to John Sanders and grandpa b'long to Rube Sanders. They was brothers. Rube Sanders bought grandpa from Enoch Bobo down in Mississippi. The Bobo's had a heap of slaves and land. Now, he was the one that sold gingercakes. He was a blacksmith too. Both my grandpas was blacksmiths but my Indian grandpa could make wagons, trays, bowls, shoes, and things out of wood too. Him being a free man made his living that way. But he never could cumolate enough to buy grandma.

"My other grandma was blacker than I am and grandpa too. When grandpa died he was carried back to the Bobo graveyard and buried on Enoch Bobo's place. It was his request all his slaves be brought back and buried on his land. I went to the burying. I recollect that but ma and pa had to ask could we go. We all got to go—all who wanted to go. It was a big crowd. It was John Sanders let us go mean as he was.

"Miss Cornelia had the cistern cleaned out and they packed up their pretty china dishes and silver in a big flat sorter box. Charles took them down a ladder to the bottom of the dark cistern and put dirt over it all and then scattered some old rubbish round, took the ladder out. The Yankees never much as peared to see that old open cistern. I don't know if they buried money or not. They packed up a lot of nice things. It wasn't touched till after the War was over.

"I been farming and cooking all my life. I worked for Major Black, Mr. Ben Tolbert, Mr. Williams at Pleasant Hill, Mississippi. I married and long time after come to Arkansas. They said you could raise stock here—no fence law.

"I get $8 and commodities because I am blind. I live with my daughter here."

Interviewer: Miss Irene Robertson
Person interviewed: Nellie Maxwell, Biscoe, Arkansas
Age: 63

NELLIE MAXWELL

"Mama was Harriett Baldwin. She was born in Virginia. Her owners was Mistress Mollie Fisher and Master Coon Fisher. It was so cold one winter that they burned up their furniture keeping a fire. Said seemed like they would freeze in spite of what all they could do.

"Grandpa was sold away from grandma and three children. He didn't want to be sold nary bit. When they would be talking about selling him he go hide under the house. They go on off. He'd come out. When he was sold he went under there. He come out and went on off when they found him and told him he was sold to this man. Grandma said he was obedient. They never hit him. He was her best husband. They never sold grandma and she couldn't 'count for him being let go. Grandma had another husband after freedom and two more children. They left there in a crowd and all come to Arkansas. Grandma was a cook for the field hands. She had charge of ringing a big dinner-bell hung up in a tree. She was black as charcoal. Mama and grandma said Master Coon and old Mistress Mollie was good to them. That the reason grandpa would go under the house. He didn't want to be sold. He never was seen no more by them.

"Grandma said sometimes the meals was carried to the fields and they fed the children out of troughs. They took all the children to the spring set them in a row. They had a tubful of water and they washed them dried them and put on their clean clothes. They used homemade lye soap and greased them with tallow and mutton suet. That made them shine. They kept them greased so their knees and knuckles would ruff up and bleed.

"Grandma and mama stopped at Fourche Dam. They was so glad to be free and go about. Then it scared them to hear talk of being sold. It divided them and some owners was mean.

"In my time if I done wrong most any grown person whoop me. Then mama find it out, she give me another one. I got a double whooping.

"Times is powerful bad to raise up a family. Drinking and gambling, and it takes too much to feed a family now. Times is so much harder that way then when I was growing."

Interviewer: Miss Sallie C. Miller
Person interviewed: Ann May, Clarksville, Arkansas
Age: 82

ANN MAY

"I was born at Cabin Creek (Lamar now, but I still call it Cabin Creek. I can't call it anything else). I was sold with my mother when I was a little girl and lived with our white folks until after the war and was freed. We lived on a farm. My father belong to another family, a neighbor of ours. We all lived with the white folks. My mother took care of all of them. They was always as good as they could be to us and after the war we stayed on with the white folks who owned my father and worked on the farm for him. His master gave us half of everything we made until we could get started our selves, then our white folks told my father to homestead a place near him, and he did. We lived there until after father died. We paid taxes and lived just like the white folks. We did what the white folks told us to do and never lost a thing by doing it. After I married my husband worked at the mill for your father and made a living for me and I worked for the white folks. Now I am too old to cook but I have a few washin's for the white folks and am getting my old age pension that helps me a lot.

"I don't know what I think about the young generation. I aim at my stopping place.

"The songs we sang were

'Come ye that love the Lord and let your Joys be known'
'When You and I Were Young, Maggie'
'Juanita'
'Just Before the Battle, Mother'
'Darling Nellie Gray'
'Carry Me Back to Old Virginia'
'Old Black Joe'

Of course we sang 'Dixie.' We had to sing that, it was the leading song."

Interviewer: Miss Irene Robertson
Person interviewed: Joe Mayes, Madison, Arkansas
Age: ?

JOE MAYES

"I was born a slave two years. I never will forget man come and told mother she was free. She cooked. She never worked in the field till after freedom. In a few days another man come and made them leave. They couldn't hold them in Kentucky. The owners give her provisions, meat, lasses, etc. They give her her clothes. She had four children and I was her youngest. The two oldest was girls. Father was dead. I don't remember him. Mother finally made arrangements to go to Will Bennett's place.

"Another thing I remember: Frank Hayes sold mother to Isaac Tremble after she was free. She didn't know she was free. Neither did Isaac Tremble. I don't know whether Frank Mayes was honest or not. The part I remember was that us boys stood on the block and never was parted from her. We had to leave our sisters. One was sold to Miss Margaret Moxley, the other to Miss Almyra Winder. (He said "Miss" but they may have been widows. He didn't seem to know—ed.) Father belong to a Master Mills. All our family got together after we found out we had been freed.

"The Ku Klux: I went to the well little after dark. It was a good piece from our house. I looked up and saw a man with a robe and cap on. It scared me nearly to death. I nearly fell out. I had heard about the 'booger man' and learned better then. But there he was. I had heard a lot about Ku Klux.

"There was a big gourd hanging up by the well. We kept it there. There was a bucket full up. He said, 'Give me water.' I handed over the gourd full. He done something with it. He kept me handing him water. He said, 'Hold my crown and draw me up another bucket full.' I was so scared I lit out hard as I could run. It was dark enough to hide me when I got a piece out of his way.

"The owners was pretty good to mother to be slavery. She had clothes and enough to eat all the time. I used to go back to see all our white folks in Kentucky. They are about all dead now I expect. Mother was glad to be free but for a long time her life was harder.

"After we got up larger she got along better. I worked on a steamboat twelve or thirteen years. I was a roustabout and freight picker. I was on passenger boats mostly but they carried freight. I went to school some. I always had colored teachers. I farmed at Hughes and Madison ever since excepting one year in Mississippi.

"I live alone. I get $8 and commodities from the Sociable Welfare.

"The young folks would do better, work better, if they could get work all time. It is hard at times to get work right now. The times is all right. Better everything but work. I know colored folks is bad managers. That has been bad on us always.

"I worked on boats from Evansville, St. Louis, Memphis to New Orleans mostly. It was hard work but a fine living. I was stout then."

United States. Work Projects Administration

Interviewer: Mrs. Bernice Bowden
Person interviewed: Jesse Meeks
707 Elm Street, Pine Bluff, Arkansas
Age: 76
Occupation: Minister

JESSE MEEKS

"I am seventy-six. 'Course I was young in slavery times, but I can remember some things. I remember how they used to feed us. Put milk and bread or poke salad and corn-meal dumplin's in a trough and give you a wooden spoon and all the children eat together.

"We stayed with our old master fourteen years. They were good folks and treated us right. My old master's name was Sam Meeks—in Longview, Drew County, Arkansas, down here below Monticello.

"I got a letter here about a month ago from the daughter of my young mistress. I wrote to my young mistress and she was dead, so her daughter got the letter. She answered it and sent me a dollar and asked me was I on the Old Age Pension list.

"As far as I know, I am the onliest one of the old darkies living that belonged to Sam Meeks.

"I remember when the Ku Klux run in on my old master. That was after the War. He was at the breakfast table with his wife. You know in them days they didn't have locks and keys. Had a hole bored through a board and put a peg in it, and I know the Ku Klux come up and stuck a gun through the auger hole and shot at old master but missed him. He run to the door and shot at the Ku Klux. I know us children found one of 'em down at the spring bathin' his leg where old master had shot him.

"Oh! they were good folks and treated us right."

FOLKLORE SUBJECTS
Name of Interviewer: Mrs. Bernice Bowden
Subject: Superstitions
Story:—Information

This information given by: Jesse Meeks
Place of residence: 707 Elm Street, Pine Bluff, Arkansas
Occupation: Minister
Age: 76

[TR: Information moved from bottom of first page.]

JESSE MEEKS

"I remember there was on old man called Billy Mann lived down here at Noble lake. He said he could 'give you a hand.' If you and your wife wasn't gettin' along very well and you wanted to get somebody else, he said he could 'give you a hand' and that would enable you to get anybody you wanted. That's what he said.

"And I've heard 'em say they could make a ring around you and you couldn't get out.

"I don't believe in that though 'cause I'm in the ministerial work and it don't pay me to believe in things like that. That is the work of the devil."

United States. Work Projects Administration

Interviewer: Miss Irene Robertson
Person interviewed: Jeff Metcalf
R.F.D., Brinkley, Arkansas
Age: 73

JEFF METCALF

"My mother's name was Julia Metcalf and my father's name was Jim Metcalf. They belong to an old bachelor named Bill Metcalf. I think I was born in Lee County, Mississippi. They did not leave when the war was over. They stayed on the Bill Metcalf place till they died. I reckon I do remember him.

"I can't tell you 'bout the war nor slavery. I don't know a thing 'bout it. I heard but I couldn't tell you it been so long ago. They didn't expect nothing but freedom. They got along in the Reconstruction days about like they had been getting along. Seemed like they didn't know much about the war. They heard they was free. I don't remember the Ku Klux Klan. I heard old folks talk 'bout it.

"I don't know if my father ever voted but I guess he did. I have voted but I don't vote now. In part I 'proves of the women votin'. I think the men outer vote and support his family fur as he can.

"I come here in 1914 from Mississippi. I got busted farmin'. I knowed a heap o' people said they was doing so well I come too. I come on the train.

"I ain't got no home, no land. I got a hog. No garden.

Two times in the year now is hard—winter and simmer. In some ways times is better. In some ways they is worser. When a trade used to be made to let you have provisions, you know you would not starve. Now if you can't get work you 'bout starve and can't get no credit. Crops been good last few years and prices fair fur it. But money won't buy nothin' now. Everything is so high. Meat is so high. Working man have to eat meat. If he don't he get weak.

"The young folks do work. They can't save much farmin'. If they could do public work between times it be better. I had a hard time in July and August. I got six children, they grown and gone. My wife is 72 years old. She ain't no 'count for work no more. The Government give me an' her $10 a month between us two. Her name is Hannah Metcalf.

"I wish I did know somethin' to tell you, lady, 'bout the Civil War and the slavery times. I done forgot 'bout all I heard 'em talkin'. When you see Hannah she might know somethin'."

Interviewer: Mrs. Bernice Bowden
Person interviewed: Hardy Miller
702-1/2 W. Second Avenue, Pine Bluff, Arkansas
Age: 85
Occupation: Yardman

HARDY MILLER

"Mistress, I'll tell you what my mother said. She said she birthed me on Christmas morning in 1852 in Sumpter County, Georgia. It was on her old master's place. Bright Herring was his name. Old mistress' name was Miss Lizzie. My father belonged to a different owner.

"Mac McClendon and John Mourning was two nigger traders and they brought my mother and sister Nancy and sister Liza and my sister Anna and Hardy Miller—that's me—out here on the train from Americus, Georgia to Memphis and put us on a steamboat and brought us here to Pine Bluff and sold me to Dr. Pope. He was a poor white man and he wanted a pair of niggers. He bought me and Laura Beckwith. In them days a doctor examined you and if your heart was sound and your lungs was sound and you didn't have no broken bones—have to pay one hundred dollars for every year you was old. That was in 1862 and I was ten years old so they sold me for one thousand dollars and one thousand dollars for Laura cause she was sound too. Carried us down to Monticello and when I got free my mammy come after me.

"Fore I left Georgia, my daddy belonged to a man

named Bill Ramsey. You see niggers used the name of their masters.

"I can remember when I was a boy Bill Ramsey set my father free and give him a free pass and anybody hire him have to pay just like they pay a nigger now. My daddy hired my mammy from her master. My mammy was her master's daughter by a colored woman.

"My daddy had a hoss named Salem and had a cart and he would take me and my mammy and my sister Liza and go to Americus and buy rations for the next week.

"I member when the war started in 1861 my mammy hired me out to Mrs. Brewer and she used to git after me and say, 'You better do that good or I'll whip you. My husband gone to war now on account of you niggers and it's a pity you niggers ever been cause he may get killed and I'll never see him again.'

"I member seein' General Bragg's men and General Steele and General Marmaduke. Had a fight down at Mark's Mill. We just lived six miles from there. Seen the Yankees comin' by along the big public road. The Yankees whipped and fought em so strong they didn't have time to bury the dead. We could see the buzzards and carrion crows. I used to hear old mistress say, 'There goes the buzzards, done et all the meat off.' I used to go to mill and we could see the bones. Used to got out and look at their teeth. No ma'm, I wasn't scared, the white boys was with me.

"Dr. Pope was good to me, better to me than he was to Master Walter and Master Billy and my young Miss, Aurelia, cause me and Laura was scared of em and we tried to do everything they wanted.

"When the war ended in 1865 we was out in the field gettin' pumpkins. Old master come out and said, 'Hardy, you and Laura is free now. You can stay or you can go and live with somebody else.' We stayed till 1868 and then our mammies come after us. I was seventeen.

"After freedom my mammy sent me to school. Teacher's name was W.H. Young. Name was William Young but he went under the head of W.H. Young.

"I went to school four years and then I got too old. I learned a whole lot. Learned to read and spell and figger. I done pretty good. I learned how to add and multiply and how to cancel and how to work square root.

"What I've been doin' all my life is farmin' down at Fairfield on the Murphy place.

"Vote? Good lord! I done more votin'. Voted for all the Presidents. Yankees wouldn't let us vote Democrat, had to vote Republican. They'd be there agitatin'. Stand right there and tell me the ones to vote for. I done quit votin'. I voted for Coolidge—we called him College—that's the last votin' I did. One of my friends, Levi Hunter, he was a colored magistrate down at Fairfield.

"Ku Klux? What you talkin' about? Ku Klux come to our house. My sister Ellen's husband went to war on the Yankee side durin' the war—on the Republican side and fought the Democrats.

"After the war the Ku Klux came and got the colored folks what fought and killed em. I saw em kill a nigger right off his mule. Fell off on his sack of corn and the old mule kep' on goin'.

"Ku Klux used to wear big old long robe with bunches of cotton sewed all over it. I member one time we was havin' church and a Ku Klux was hid up in the scaffold. The preacher was readin' the Bible and tellin' the folks there was a man sent from God and say an angel be here directly. Just then the Ku Klux fell down and the niggers all thought 'twas the angel and they got up and flew.

"Ku Klux used to come to the church well and ask for a drink and say, 'I ain't had a bit of water since I fought the battle of Shiloh.'

"Might as well tell the truth—had just as good a time when I was a slave as when I was free. Had all the hog meat and milk and everything else to eat.

"I member one time when old master wasn't at home the Yankees come and say to old mistress, 'Madam, we is foragin'.' Old mistress say, 'My husband ain't home; I can't let you.' Yankees say, 'Well, we're goin' to anyway.' They say, 'Where you keep your milk and butter?' Old mistress standin' up there, her face as red as blood and say, 'I haven't any milk or butter to spare.' But the Yankees would hunt till they found it.

"After a battle when the dead soldiers was layin' around and didn't have on no uniform cause some of the other soldiers took em, I've heard the old folk what knowed say you could tell the Yankees from the Rebels cause the Yankees had blue veins on their bellies and the Rebels didn't.

"Now you want me to tell you bout this young nigger generation? I never thought I'd live to see this young generation come out and do as well as they is doin'. I'm goin' tell you the truth. When I was young, boys and girls used to wear long white shirt come down to their ankles, cause it would shrink, with a hole cut out for their head. I think they is doin' a whole lot better. Got better clothes. Almost look as well as the white folks. I just say the niggers dressin' better than the white folks used to.

"Then I see some niggers got automobiles. Just been free bout seventy-two years and some of em actin' just like white folks now.

"Well, good-bye—if I don't see you again I'll meet you in Heaven."

Interviewer: Beulah Sherwood Hagg
Person interviewed: [HW: Henry Kirk] H.K. Miller
1513 State Street, Little Rock, Arkansas
Age: 86

HENRY KIRK MILLER

"No ma'am, it will not bother me one bit if you want to have a long visit with me.... Yes, I was a little busy, but it can wait. I was getting my dishes ready for a party tomorrow night.

"Yes ma'am, I was born during slavery. I was born at a little place called Fort Valley in Georgia, July 25, 1851. Fort Valley is about 30 miles from Macon. I came to Little Rock in 1873. My old mistress was a widow. As well as I can remember she did not have any slaves but my father and mother and the six children. No ma'am, her name was not Miller, it was Wade.... Where did I get my name, then? It came from my grandfather on my father's side.... Well, now, Miss, I can't tell you where he got that name. From some white master, I reckon.

"We got free in Georgia June 15, 1865. I'll never forget that date. What I mean is, that was the day the big freedom came. But we didn't know it and just worked on. My father was a shoemaker for old mistress. Only one in town, far as I recollect. He made a lot of money for mistress. Mother was houseworker for her. As fast as us children got big enough to hire out, she leased us to anybody who would pay for our hire. I was put out with another widow woman who lived about 20 miles. She worked me on her cotton plantation. Old mistress sold one of my sisters; took cotton for pay. I remember hearing them tell about the big price she brought because cotton was so high. Old mistress got 15 bales of cotton for sister, and it was only a few days till freedom came and the man who had traded all them bales of cotton lost my sister, but old mistress kept the cotton. She was smart, wasn't she? She knew freedom was right there. Sister came right back to my parents.

"Just give me time, miss, and I'll tell you the whole story. This woman what had me hired tried to run away and take all her slaves along. I don't remember just how many, but a dozen or more. Lots of white folks tried to run away and hide their slaves until after the Yankee soldiers had been through the town searching for them what had not been set free. She was trying to get to the woods country. But she got nervous and scared and done the worst thing she could. She run right into a Yankee camp. Course they asked where we all belonged and sent us where we belonged. They had always taught us to be scared of the Yankees. I remember just as well when I got back to where my mother was she asked me: "Boy, why you come here? Don't you know old mistress got you rented out? You're goin' be whipped for sure." I told her, no, now we got freedom. That was the first they had heard. So then she had to tell my father and mother. She tole them how they have no place to go, no money,—nothing to start life on; they better stay on with her. So my father and mother kept on with her; she let them have a part of what they made; she took some for board, as was right. The white ladies what had me between them fixed it up that I would serve out the time I was rented out for. It was about six months more. My parents saved money and we all went to a farm. I stayed with them till I was 19 years old. Of course they got all the money I made. I married when I was 20, still living in Georgia. We tried to farm on shares. A man from Arkansas came there, getting up a colony of colored to go to Arkansas to farm. Told big tales of fine land with nobody to work it. Not half as many Negroes in Arkansas as in Georgia. Me and my wife joined up to go.

"Well, ma'am, I didn't get enough education to be what you call a educated man. My father paid for a six months night course for me after peace. I learned to read and write and figure a little. I have used my tablespoon full of brains ever since, always adding to that start. I learned everything I could from the many white friends I have had. Any way, miss, I have known enough to make a good living all these years.

"Now I'll get on with the story. First work I got in Arkansas was working on a farm; me and her both; we always tried to stay together. We could not make anything on the Garner farm, and it was mighty unhealthy down in Fourche bottoms. I carried her back to Little Rock and I got work as house man in the Bunch home. From there I went to the home of Dudley E. Jones and stayed there 28 years. That was the beginning of my catering. I just naturally took to cooking and serving. White folks was still used to having colored wait on them and they liked my style. Mr. Jones was so kind. He told his friends about how I could plan big dinners and banquets; then cook and serve them. Right soon I was handling most of the big swell weddings for the society folks. Child, if I could call off the names of the folks I have served, it would be mighty near everybody of any consequence in Little Rock for more than 55 years. Yes ma'am, I'm now being called on to serve the grandchildren of my first customers.

"During the 28 years I lived in Mr. Jones' family I was serving banquets, big public dinners, all kinds of big affairs. I have had the spring and fall banquets for the Scottish Rite Masons for more than 41 years. I have served nearly all the Governor's banquets, college graduation and reunion parties; I took care of President Roosevelt—not this one, but Teddy----. Served about 600 that day. Any big parties for colored people?... Yes ma'am! Don't you remember when Booker T. Washington was here?... No ma'am. White folks didn't have a thing to do with it, excepting the city let us have the new fire station. It was just finished but the fire engines ain't moved in yet. I served about 600 that time. Yes ma'am, there was a lot of white folks there. Then, I have been called to other places to do the catering. Lonoke, Benton, Malvern, Conway—a heap of places like that.

"No miss, I didn't always have all the catering business; oh, no. There was Mr. Rossner. He was a fine man. White gentleman. I used to help him a lot. But when he sold out to Bott, I got a lot of what business Mr. Rossner had had, Mr. Bott was a Jew. All that time my wife was my best helper. I took a young colored fellow named Freeling Alexander and taught him the business. He never been able to make it go on his own, but does fine working on salary. He has a cafeteria now.

"Well thank you miss, speaking about my home like that. Yes ma'am, I sure do own it. Fifty-two years I been living right here. First I bought the lot; it took me two years to pay for it. Next I build a little house. The big pin oak trees out front was only saplings when I set them out. Come out in the back yard and see my pecan tree.... It is a giant, ain't it? Yes ma'am, it was a tiny thing when I set it out fifty-two years ago. Our only child was born in this house,—a dear daughter—and her three babies were born here too. After my wife and daughter died, me and the children kept on trying to keep the home together. I have taught them the catering business. Both granddaughters are high school graduates. The boy is in Mexico. Before he went he signed his name to a check and said: "Here, grandpa. You ain't going to want for a thing while I'm gone. If something happens to your catering business, or you get so you can't work, fill this in for whatever you need." But thank the good Lord, I'm still going strong. Nobody has ever had to take care of H.K. Miller. Now let me tell you something else about this place. For more than ten years I have been paying $64.64 every year for my part of that asphalt paving you see out in front. Yes ma'am, the lot is 50 foot front, and I am paying for only half of it; from my curb line to the middle of the street. Maybe if I live long enough I'll get it paid for sometime.

"I haven't tried to lay by much money. I don't suppose there is any other colored man—uneducated like me—what has done more for his community. I have given as high as $80 and $100 at one time to help out on the church debt or when they wanted to build. I always help in times of floods and things like that. I've helped many white persons in my lifetime.

"Well, now, I'll tell you what I think about the voting system. I think this. Of course we are still in subjection to the white people; they are in the majority and have most of the government on their side. But I think that, er,—er,—well I'll tell you, while it is all right for them to be at the head of things, they ought to do what is right. Being educated, they ought to know right from wrong. I believe in the Bible, miss. Look here. This little book—Gospel of St. John—has been carried in my pocket every day for years and years. And I never miss a day reading it. I don't see how some people can be so unjust. I guess they never read their Bible. The reason I been able to make my three-score years and ten is because I obeys what the Good Book says.

"Now, let me see. I can remember that I been voting mighty near ever since I been here. I never had any trouble voting. I have never been objected from voting that I remember of.

"Now you ask about what I think of the young people. Well, I tell you. I think really that the young people of today had better begin to check up, a little. They are going too fast. They don't seem to have enough consideration. When I see so many killed in automobile accidents, and know that drinking is the cause of so many car accidents,—well, yes ma'am, drinking sure does have a lot to do with it. I think they should more consider the way they going to make a living. Make a rule to look before they act. Another thing—the education being given them—they are not taking advantage of it. If they would profit by what they learn they could benefit theirselves. A lot of them now spend heap of time trying to get to be doctors and lawyers and like that. That is a mistake. There is not enough work among colored people to support them. I know. Negroes do not have confidence in their race for this kind of business. No ma'am. Colored will go for a white doctor and white lawyer 'cause they think they know more about that kind of business. I would recommend as the best means of making a living for colored young people is to select some kind of work that is absolutely necessary to be done and then do it honestly. The trades, carpentering, paper hanging, painting, garage work. Some work that white people need to have done, and they just as soon colored do it as white. White folks ain't never going to have Negro doctors and lawyers, I reckon. That's the reason I took up catering—even that long ago. Fifty-five years ago I knew to look around and find some work that white folks would need done. There's where your living comes from.

"Yes, miss, my business is slack—falling off, as you say. Catering is not what it used to be. You see, 30 or 40 years ago, people's homes were grand and big; big dining rooms, built for parties and banquets. But for the big affairs with 500 or 600 guests, they went to the hotels. Even the hotels had to rent my dishes, silver and linens.... Oh, lord, yes, miss. I always had my own. It took me ten years to save enough money to start out with my first 500 of everything.... You want to see them?... Sure, I keep them here at home.... Look. Here's my silver chests, all packed to go. I have them divided into different sizes. This one has fifty of every kind of silver, so if fifty guests are to be provided for. I keep my linens, plates of different sizes, glasses and everything the same way. A 200-guest outfit is packed in those chests over there. No, ma'am, I don't have much trouble of losing silver, because it all has my initials on; look: H.K.M. on every piece. Heap of dishes are broken every time I have a big catering. I found one plate yesterday—the last of a full pattern I had fifteen years ago. About every ten years is a complete turnover of china. Glassware goes faster, and of course, the linen is the greatest overhead. Yes ma'am, as I was telling you, catering is slack because of clubs. So many women take their parties to clubs now. Another thing, the style of food has changed. In those old days, the table was loaded with three four meats, fish, half dozen vegetable dishes, entrees, different kinds of wine, and an array of desserts. Now what do they have? Liquid punch, frozen punch and cakes. In June I had a wedding party for 400, and that's all they served. I had to have 30 punch bowls, but borrowed about half from my white friends.

"You have got that wrong about me living with my grandchildren. No ma'am! They are living with me. They make their home with me. I don't expect ever to marry again. I'm 86. In my will I am leaving everything I have to my three grandchildren.

"Well, miss, you're looking young and blooming. Guess your husband is right proud of you? Say you're a widow? Well, now, my goodness. Some of these days a fine man going to find you and then, er—er, lady, let me cater for the wedding?"

Interviewer: Samuel S. Taylor
Person interviewed: Henry Kirk Miller [HW: Same as H.K. Miller]
1513 State Street, Little Rock, Arkansas
Age 87 [HW: 86]

H.K MILLER

"I am eighty-six years old-eighty-six years and six months. I was born July 25, 1851. I was a slave. Didn't get free till June 1865. I was a boy fifteen years old when I got free.

"I have been living in this house fifty years. I have been living in Arkansas ever since 1873. That makes about sixty-five years.

"The engineer who got killed in that wreck the other day (a wreck which occurred February 7, 1938, Monday morning at three and in which the engineer and five other people were killed) came right from my town, Fort Valley, Georgia. I came here from there in 1873. I don't know anybody living in Fort Valley now unless it's my own folks. And I don't 'spect I'd know them now. When I got married and left there, I was only twenty-one years old.

Parents and Relatives

"My mother and father were born in South Carolina. After their master and missis married they came to Georgia. Back there I don't know. When I remember anything they were in Georgia. They said they came from

South Carolina to Georgia. I don't know how they came. Both of my parents were Negroes. They came to Arkansas ahead of me. I have their pictures." (He carried me into the parlor and showed me life-sized bust portraits of his mother and father.)

"There were eighteen of us: six boys and twelve girls. They are all dead now but myself and one sister. She lives in Atlanta, Georgia. I am older than she is.

Occupation

"I am a caterer. I have been serving the Scottish Rite Masons in their annual reunion every six months for forty-one years. We are going to the Seventh Street Entrance this Friday. One of the orders will have a dinner and I am going down to serve it. I served the dinner for Teddy Roosevelt there, thirty years ago. This Roosevelt is a cousin of his.

Masters

"My parents' master was named Wade. When he died, I was so little that they had to lift me up to let me see into the coffin so I could look at him. I went to his daughter. My name is after my father's father. My grandfather was named Miller. I took his name. He was a white man.

"Wade's daughter was named Riley, but I keep my grandfather's name. My mother and father were then transferred to the Rileys too, and they took the name of Riley. It was after freedom that I took the name Miller from my original people. Haven Riley's father was my brother." (Haven Riley lives in Little Rock and was formerly an instructor at Philander Smith College. Now he is a public stenographer and a private teacher.)

"Wade owned all of my brothers and sisters and parents and some of my kin—father's sister and brother. There might have been some more I can't remember. Wade was a farmer.

"I remember once when my mother and father were going to the field to work, I went with them as usual. That was before Wade died and his daughter drew us.

"My wife died six years ago. If she had lived till tomorrow, she would have been married to me sixty years. She died on the tenth of February and we were married on the sixth. We just lacked five years of being married sixty years when she died.

Food

"For food, I don't know anything more than bread and meat. Meal, meat, molasses were the only rations I saw. In those times the white people had what was known as the white people's house and then what was known as nigger quarters. The children that weren't big enough to work were fed at the white people's house. We got milk and mush for breakfast. When they boiled cabbage we got bread and pot-liquor. For supper we got milk and bread. They had cows and the children were fed mostly on milk and mush or milk and bread. We used to bake a corn cake in the ashes, ash cake, and put it in the milk.

"The chickens used to lay out in the barn. If we children would find the nests and bring the eggs in our missis would give us a biscuit, and we always got biscuits for Christmas.

Houses in the Negro Quarters

"In the nigger quarters there were nothing but log houses. I don't remember any house other than a log house. They'd just go out in the woods and get logs and put up a log house. Put dirt and mud or clay in the cracks to seal it. Notch the logs in the end to hitch them at corners. Nailed planks at the end of the logs to make a door frame.

"My people all ate and cooked and lived in the same room. Some of the slaves had dirt floors and some of them had plank floors.

"Food was kept in the house in a sort of box or chest, built in the wall sometimes. Mostly it was kept on the table.

"In cooking they had a round oven made like a pot only the bottom would be flat. It had an iron top. The oven was a bought oven. It was shaped like a barrel. The top lifted up. Coal was placed under the oven and a little on top.

Tables and Chairs

"Tables were just boards nailed together. Nothing but planks nailed together. I don't remember nothing but homemade benches for chairs. They sometimes made platted or split-bottom chairs out of white oak. Strips of oak were seven feet long. They put them in water so they would bend easily and wove them while they were flexible and fresh. The whole chair bottom was made out of one strip just like in caning. Those chairs were stouter than the chairs they make now."

(To be continued) [TR: No continuation found.]

Interviewer: Mrs. Annie L. LaCotts
Person interviewed: Matilda Miller
Humphrey, Ark.
Age: 79

MATILDA MILLER

The day of the interview Matilda, a nice clean-looking Negro woman, was in bed, suffering from some kind of a pain in her head. She lives in a little two-room unpainted boxed house beside the highway in Humphrey. Her house is almost in the shadow of the big tank which was put up recently when the town acquired its water system.

When told that the visitor wanted to talk with her about her early life, Matilda said, "Well, honey, I'll tell you all I can, but you see, I was just a little girl when the war was, but I've heard my mother tell lots of things about then.

"I was born a slave; my mother and daddy both were owned by Judge Richard Gamble at Crockett's Bluff. I was born at Boone Hill—about twelve miles north of De-Witt—and how come it named Boone Hill, that farm was my young mistress's. Her papa give it to her, just like he give me to her when I was little, and after she married Mr. Oliver Boone and lived there the farm always went by the name of 'Boone Hill.' The house is right on top of a hill, you know, it shure was a pretty place when Miss Georgia lived there, with great big Magnolia trees in the front yard. I belonged to Miss Georgia, my young mistress, and when the niggers were freed my mamma staid on with her. She was right there when both of his chillun were born, Mr. John Boone and Miss Mary, too. I nursed both of them chillun. You know who Miss Mary is now, don't you? Yes'um, she's Mr. Lester Black's wife and he's good, too.

"I was de oney child my mother had till twelve years after the surrender. You see, my papa went off with Yankees and didn't come back till twelve years after we was free, and then I had some brothers and sisters. Exactly nine months from the day my daddy come home, I had a baby brother born. My mother said she knew my daddy had been married or took up with some other woman, but she hadn't got a divorce and still counted him her husband. They lived for a long time with our white folks, for they were good to us, but you know after the boys and girls got grown and began to marry and live in different places, my parents wanted to be with them and left the white folks.

"No mam, I didn't see any fighting, but we could hear the big guns booming away off in the distance. I was married when I was 21 to Henry Miller and lived with him 51 years and ten months; he died from old age and hard work. We had two chillun, both girls. One of them lives here with me in that other room. Mamma said the Yankees told the Negroes when they got em freed they'd give em a mule and a farm or maybe a part of the plantation they'd been working on for their white folks. She thought they just told em that to make them dissatisfied and to get more of them 'to join up with em' and they were dressed in pretty blue clothes and had nice horses and that made lots of the Negro men go with them. None of em ever got anything but what their white folks give em, and just lots and lots of em never come back after the war cause the Yankees put them in front where the shooting was and they was killed. My husband Henry Miller died four years ago. He followed public work and made plenty of money but he had lots of friends and his money went easy too. I don't spect I'll live long for this hurtin' in my head is awful bad sometime."

Interviewer: Miss Irene Robertson
Person interviewed: Nathan Miller, Madison, Arkansas
Age: Born in 1868

NATHAN MILLER

"Lady, I'll tell you what I know but it won't nigh fill your book.

"I was born in 1862 south of Lockesburg, Arkansas. My parents was Marther and Burl Miller.

"They told me their owners come here from North Carolina in 1820. They owned lots of slaves and lots of land. Mother was medium light—about my color. See, I'm mixed. My hair is white. I heard mother say she never worked in the field. Father was a blacksmith on the place. He wasn't a slave. His grandfather willed him free at ten years of age. It was tried in the Supreme Court. They set him free. Said they couldn't break the dead man's will.

"My father was a real bright colored man. It caused some disturbance. Father went back and forth to Kansas. They tried to make him leave if he was a free man. They said I would have to be a slave several years or leave the State. Freedom settled that for me.

"My great grandmother on my mother's side belong to Thomas Jefferson. He was good to her. She used to tell me stories on her lap. She come from Virginia to Tennessee. They all cried to go back to Virginia and their master got mad and sold them. He was a meaner man. Her name was Sarah Jefferson. Mariah was her daughter and Marther was my mother. They was real dark folks but mother was my color, or a shade darker.

"Grandmother said she picked cotton from the seed all day till her fingers nearly bled. That was fore gin day. They said the more hills of tobacco you could cultivate was how much you was worth.

"I don't remember the Ku Klux. They was in my little boy days but they never bothered me.

"All my life I been working hard—steamboat, railroad, farming. Wore clean out now.

"Times is awful hard. I am worn clean out. I am not sick. I'm ashamed to say I can't do a good day's work but I couldn't. I am proud to own I get commodities and $8 from the Relief."

Interviewer: Thomas Elmore Lacy
Person interviewed: Sam Miller, Morrilton, Arkansas
Age: 98

SAM MILLER

"I is ninety-eight years old, suh. My name's Sam Miller, and I was born in Texas in 1840—don't know de month nor de day. My parents died when I was jes' a little chap, and we come to Conway County, Arkansas fifty years ago; been livin' here ever since. My wife's name was Annie Williamson. We ain't got no chillun and never had none. I don't belong to no chu'ch, but my wife is a Baptis'.

"Can't see to git around much now. No, suh, I can't read or write, neither. My memory ain't so good about things when I was little, away back yonder, but I sure members dem Ku Klux Klans and de militia. They used to ketch people and take em out and whup em.

"Don't rickolleck any of de old songs but one or two—oh, yes, dey used to sing 'Old time religion's good enough for me' and songs like dat.

"De young people! Lawzy, I jest dunno how to take em. Can't understand em at all. Dey too much for me!"

NOTE: The old fellow chuckled and shook his head but said very little more. He could have told much but for his faulty memory, no doubt. He was almost non-committal as to facts of slavery days, the War between the States, and Reconstruction period. Has the sense of humor that seems to be a characteristic of most of the old-time Negroes, but aside from a whimsical chuckle shows little of the interest that is usually associated with the old generation of Negroes.

Interviewer: Miss Irene Robertson
Person interviewed: W.D. Miller, West Memphis, Arkansas
Age: 65?

W.D. MILLER

"Grandpa was sold twice in Raleigh, North Carolina. He was sold twice to the same people, from the Millers to the Robertsons (Robersons, Robinsons, etc.?). He said the Robertsons were not so very good to him but the Millers were. Grandma was washing when a Yank come and told them they had been sot free. They quit washing and went from house to house rejoicing. My parents' names was Jesse and Mary Miller, and Grandma Agnes and Grandpa Peter Miller. The Robertsons was hill wheat farmers. The Millers had a cloth factory. Dan Miller owned it and he raised wheat. Mama was a puny woman and they worked her in the factory. She made cloth and yarn.

"I was born in Raleigh, North Carolina or close by there. My father's uncle John House brought about one hundred families from North Carolina to Quittenden County, Mississippi. I was seven years old. He said they rode mules to pick cotton, it growed up like trees. We come in car boxes. I came to Heath and Helena eleven years ago. Papa stayed with his master Dan Miller till my uncle tolled him away. He died with smallpox soon after we come to Mississippi.

"It is a very good country but they don't pick cotton riding on mules, at least I ain't seed none that way."

El Dorado District
FOLKLORE SUBJECTS
Name of Interviewer: Pernella Anderson
Subject: Slavery Customs
Story:—Information

Information given by: Mose Minser—Farmer—Age—78
Place of Residence: 5 miles from El Dorado—Section 8

[TR: Information moved from bottom of first page.]

MOSE MINSER

Ah use ter could tawk an tell a thing plum well but ah been broke up by a cah. Cah run ovah mah haid an ah couldn' tawk fuh 30 days. So now ah aint no good fuh nothin. Ah recollect one night ah dream a dream. De dream at ah dreamt, next morning dat dream come true. Jes like ah dreamt hit. Yes hit did. Ah wuz heah in slavery time. Ah membuh when dey freed us niggers. Se here, ah wuz a purty good size kid when dey free us. Ah kin membuh our house. Sot dis way. An ole Marster called all his niggers up. Dey all come along roun in a squad on de porch. Ah did not heah whut he said tuh em. But mah step-pa wuz dere an tole us we wuz free. Ah atter dey freed mah step-pa ah recollect he went on home and fried some aigs (eggs) in de ubben. Know we didn have no stove we cooked on de fiuhplace. As ah said cook dem aigs, gimme some uv hit, an he lef' den. Went east and ah aint nevah seed dat man since. Ah membuhs once ah got a whoopin bout goin tuh de chinquepin tree. Some uv um tole me ole master wuz gwianter let us quit at dinnuh an so in place uv me goin ter dinnuh ah went on by de chinquepin tree tuh git some chanks. Ah had a brothuh wid me. So ah come tuh fine out dat dey gin tuh callin us. Dey hollered tuh come on dat we wuz gointer pick cotton. So in place uv us goin on tuh de house we went on back tuh de fiel'. Our fiel wuz bout a mile fum de house. Ole Moster waited down dere at de gate. He call me when ah got dere an wanted tuh know why ah didn come and git mah dinnah sos ah could pick cotton. So he taken mah britches down dat day. Mah chinks all run out on de groun' an he tole mah brothah tuh pick um up. Ah knocked mah brothuh ovah fuh pickin um up an aftuh ah done dat ole moster taken his red pocket han'cher out and tied hit ovah mah eyes tuh keep me fum seein mah brothuh pick um up.

So when he got through wid me and put mah britches back on me ah went on tuh de fiel and went tuh pickin cotton. Dat evenin when us stop pickin cotton ah took mah brothah down and taken mah chinquapins.

Interviewer: Miss Irene Robertson
Person interviewed: Gip Minton, Des Arc, Arkansas
Age: 84

GIP MINTON

"I was born at Jackson, Alabama on the Tennessee River. It was sho a putty river. I never did know my grandfolks. I think my father was a soldier. My master was a soldier, I think. He was in de war. I do remember the Civil War. I remember the last battle at Scottsboro. There was several but one big battle and they got to Belfontain. That is where it seemed they were trying to go. I don't recollect who won the battle. I heard them fighting and saw the smoke and after they went on saw the bodies dead and all that was left was like a cyclone had swept by. There was a big regiment stationed at Scottsboro. It was just like any war fought with guns and they lived in tents. They took everything they could find. Looked like starvation was upon de land.

"I had two sisters and one brother and my mother died when I was a baby. I come out here to Arkansas with my mothers old master and mistress and never did see nor hear of none of them. No I never did hear from none of them. I come out here when I was ten or twelve years old. It was, it was right after the war. I recken I was freed, but I was raised by white folks and I stayed right on wid em. Dat freedom ain't never bothered me.

"My master and mistress names was Master Alfred

Minton. Dey call me Gip for him. Gip Minton is what they always called me. My mistress was Miss Annie Minton. I stayed right wid em. They raised me and I come on here wid em. I don't know nothin about that freedom.

"I recken they was good to me. I et in de kitchen when they got through or on a table out in de back yard sometimes. I slept in an outhouse they fixed up mostly, when I got up big.

"We come on the train to Memphis and they come on thater way to Lonoke whar we settled. Don Shirley was the man I come on horseback with from Memphis to Lonoke. He was a man what dealt in horses. Sure he was a white man. He's where we got some horses. I don't remember if he lived at Lonoke or not.

"I have voted, yes ma'am, a heap of times. I don't remember what kind er ticket I votes. I'm a Democrat, I think so. I ain't voted fur sometime now. I don't know if I'll vote any more times or not. I don't know what is right bout votin and what ain't right.

"When I was a boy I helped farm. We had what we made. I guess it was plenty. I had more to eat and I didn't have as many changes of clothes as folks has to have nowdays bout all de difference. They raised lots more. They bought things to do a year and didn't be allus goin to town. It was hard to come to town. Yes mam it did take a long time, sometimes in a ox wagon. The oxen pulled more over muddy roads. Took three days to come to town and git back. I farmed one-half-for-the-other and on shear crop. Well one bout good as the other. Bout all anybody can make farmin is plenty to eat and a little to wear long time ago and nows the same way. The most I reckon I ever did make was on Surrounded Hill (Biscoe) when I farmed one-half-fur-de-udder for Sheriff Reinhardt. The ground was new and rich and the seasons hit just fine. No maam I never owned no farm, no livestock, no home. The only thing I owned was a horse one time. I worked 16 or 17 years for Mr. Brown and for Mr. Plunkett and Son. I drayed all de time fur em. Hauled freight up from the old depot (wharf) down on the river. Long time fore a railroad was thought of. I helped load cotton and hides on the boats. We loaded all day and all night too heap o'nights. We worked till we got through and let em take the ship on.

"The times is critical for old folks, wages low and everything is so high. The young folks got heap better educations but seems like they can't use it. They don't know how to any avantage. I know they don't have as good chances at farmin as de older folks had. I don't know why it is. My son works up at the lumber yard. Yes he owns this house. That's all he owns. He make nough to get by on, I recken. He works hard, yes maam. He helps me if he can. I get $4 a month janitor at the Farmers and Merchants Bank (Des Arc). I works a little garden and cleans off yards. No maam it hurts my rheumatism to run the yard mower. I works when I sho can't hardly go. Nothin matter cept I'm bout wo out. I plied for the old folks penshun but I ain't got nuthin yet. I signed up at the bank fur it agin not long ago. I has been allus self sportin. Didn't pend on no livin soul but myself."

Interviewer: Mrs. Bernice Bowden
Person interviewed: A.J. Mitchell
419 E. 11th Avenue, Pine Bluff, Arkansas
Age: 78
Occupation: Garbage hauler

A.J. MITCHELL

"I was 'bout seven when they surrendered. I can remember when my old master sold Aunt Susan. She raised me. I seen old master when he was tryin' to whip old Aunt Susan. She was the cook. She said, 'I ain't goin' let you whip me' and I heard my sister say next day he done sold Aunt Susan. I ain't seed her since. I called her ma. My mother died when I was two years old. She was full Injun. My father was black but his hair was straight. His face was so black it shined. Looked like it was greased. My father said he was freeborn and I've seen stripes on his back look like the veins on back of my hand where they whipped him tryin' to make him disown his freedom.

"Old Jack Clifton was my master. Yes ma'm, that was his name.

"I 'member when they had those old looms—makin' cloth and old shuttle to put the thread on. I can see 'em now.

"I can 'member when this used to be a Injun place. I've seen old Injun mounds. White folks come and run 'em out and give 'em Injun Territory.

"I heered the guns in the war and seed the folks comin' home when the war broke. They said they was fitin' 'bout freedom, tryin' to free the people. I 'member when they was fitin' at Marks Mill. I know some of the people said that was where they was sot free.

"I don't know as I seed any Ku Klux when they was goin' round. Hearin' 'bout 'em scared me. I have a good recollection. I can remember the first dream I ever had and the first time I whistled. I can remember when I was two or three years old. Remember when they had a big old conch shell. Old master would blow it at twelve o'clock for 'em to come in.

"Old master was good to us but I 'member he had a leather strap and if we chillun had done anything he'd make us younguns put our head 'tween his legs and put that strap on us. My goodness! He called me Pat and called his own son Bug—his own son Junie. We played together. Old master had nicknames for everybody.

"My first mistress was named Miss Mary but she died. I 'member when old master married and brought Miss Becky home.

"Marse John (he was old master's oldest son) he used to tote me about in his saddle bags. He was the overseer.

"I 'member old master's ridin' hoss—a little old bay pony—called him Hardy. I never remember nobody else bein' on it—that was his ridin' hoss.

"Old master had dogs. One was Gus and one named Brute (he was a red bone hound). And one little dog they called Trigger. Old master's head as white as cotton.

"I do remember the day they said the people was free—after the war broke. My father come and got me.

"Now I'm givin' you a true statement. I've been stayin' by myself twenty-three years. I been here in Pine Bluff—well I jest had got here when the people was comin' back from that German war.

"My God, we had the finest time when we killed hogs—make sausage. We'd eat cracklin's—oh, we thought they wasn't nothin' like cracklin's. The Lord have mercy, there was an old beech tree set there in my master's yard. You could hear that old tree pop ever' day bout the same time, bout twelve o'clock. We used to eat beech mass. Good? Yes ma'm! I think about it often and wonder why it was right in old master's yard.

"I've cast a many a vote. Not a bit of trouble in the world. Hope elect most all the old officers here in town. I had a brother was a constable under Squire Gaines. Well of course, Miss, I don't think it's right when they disfranchised the colored people. I tell you, Miss, I read the Bible and the Bible says every man has his rights—the poor and the free and the bound. I got good sense from the time I leaped in this world. I 'member well I used to go and cast my vote just that quick but they got so they wouldn't let you vote unless you could read.

"I've had 'em to offer me money to vote the Democrat ticket. I told him, no. I didn't think that was principle. The colored man ain't got no represetive now. Colored men used to be elected to the legislature and they'd go and sell out. Some of 'em used to vote the Democrat ticket. God wants every man to have his birthright.

"I tell you one thing they did. This here no fence law was one of the lowest things they ever did. I don't know what the governor was studyin' 'bout. If they would let the old people raise meat, they wouldn't have to get so much help from the government. God don't like that, God wants the people to raise things. I could make a livin' but they won't let me.

"The first thing I remember bout studyin' was Junie, old master's son, studyin' his book and I heard 'em spell the word 'baker'. That was when they used the old Blue Back Speller.

"I went to school. I'm goin' tell you as nearly as I can. That was, madam, let me see, that was in sixty-nine as near as I can come at it. Miss, I don't know how long I went. My father wouldn't let me. I didn't know nothin' but work. I weighed cotton ever since I was a little boy. I always wanted to be weighin'. Looked like it was my gift—weighin' cotton.

"I'm a Missionary Baptist preacher. Got a license to preach. You go down and try to preach without a license and they put you up.

"Madam, you asked me a question I think I can answer with knowledge and understanding. The young people is goin' too fast. The people is growin' weaker and wiser. You take my folks—goin' to school but not doin' anything. I don't think there's much to the younger generation. Don't think they're doin' much good. I was brought up with what they called fireside teachin'."

STATE—Arkansas
NAME OF WORKER—Bernice Bowden
ADDRESS—1006 Oak Street, Pine Bluff, Arkansas
DATE—November 2, 1938
SUBJECT—Exslaves

[TR: Repetitive information deleted from subsequent pages.]

GRACIE MITCHELL

Circumstances of Interview

1. Name and address of informant—Gracie Mitchell

2. Date and time of interview—November 1, 1938, 3:00 p.m.

3. Place of interview—117 Worthen Street

4. Name and address of person, if any, who put you in touch with informant—Bernice Wilburn, 101 Miller Street, Pine Bluff, Arkansas

5. Name and address of person, if any, accompanying you—None

6. Description of room, house, surroundings, etc.—A frame house (rented), bare floors, no window shades; a bed and some boxes and three straight chairs. In an adjoining room were another bed, heating stove, two trunks, one straight chair, one rocking chair. A third room the kitchen, contained cookstove and table and chairs.

Text of Interview

"They said I was born in Alabama. My mother's name was Sallie and my father was Andrew Wheeler. I couldn't tell when I was born—my folks never did tell me that. Belonged to Dr. Moore and when his daughter married he give my mother to her and she went to Mobile. They said I wasn't weaned yet. My grandmother told me that. She is dead now. Don't know nothin' bout nary one o' my white folks. I don't recollect nothin' bout a one of 'em 'cept my old boss. He took us to Texas and stayed till the niggers was all free and then he went back. Good to me? No ma'm—no good there. And if you didn't work he'd see what was the matter. Lived near Coffeyville in Upshaw county. That's whar my husband found me. I was living with my aunt and uncle. They said the reason I had such a good gift makin' quilts was cause my mother was a seamstress.

"I cooked 'fore I married and I could make my own dresses, piece quilts and quilt. That's mostly what I done. No laundry work. I never did farm till I was married. After we went to Chicago in 1922, I took care of other folks chillun, colored folks, while they was working in laundries and factories. I sure has worked. I ain't nobody to what I was when I was first married. I knowed how to turn, but I don't know whar to turn now—I ain't able.

"I use to could plow just as good as any man. I could put that dirt up against that cotton and corn. I'd mold it up. Lay it by? Yes ma'm I'd lay it by, too.

"They didn't send me to school but they learned me how to work.

"I had a quilt book with a lot o' different patterns but I loaned it to a woman and she carried it to Oklahoma. Mighty few people you can put confidence in nowdays.

"I don't go out much 'cept to church—folks is so critical.

> "You have to mind how you walk on the cross;
> If you don't, your foot will slip,
> And your soul will be lost."

"I was a motherless chile but the Lord made up for it by givin' me a good husband and I don't want for anything."

Interviewer's Comment

According to her husband, Gracie spends every spare moment piecing quilts. He said they use to go fishing and that Gracie always took her quilt pieces along and if the fish were not biting she would sew. She showed me twenty-two finished quilt tops, each of a different design and several of the same design, or about thirty quilts in all. Two were entirely of silk, two of applique design which called "laid work". They were folded up in a trunk and as she took them out and spread them on the bed for me to see she told me the name of the design. The following are the names of the designs:

1. Breakfast Dish
2. Sawtooth (silk)
3. Tulip design (Laid work)
4. "Prickle" Pear
5. Little Boy's Breeches

6. Birds All Over the Elements
7. Drunkard's Path
8. Railroad Crossing
9. Cocoanut Leaf ("That's Laid Work")
10. Cotton Leaf
11. Half an Orange
12. Tree of Paradise
13. Sunflower
14. Ocean Wave (silk)
15. Double Star
16. Swan's Nest
17. Log Cabin in the Lane
18. Reel
19. Lily in de Valley (Silk)
20. Feathered Star
21. Fish Tail
22. Whirligig

Gracie showed me her winter coat bought in Chicago of fur fabric called moleskin, and with fur collar and cuffs.

She sells the quilt tops whenever she can. Many are made of new material which they buy.

Personal History of Informant

1. Ancestry—Father, Andrew Wheeler; Sallie Wheeler, mother.

2. Place and date of birth—Alabama. No date known, about 80 years old.

3. Family—Husband and one grown son.

4. Places lived in, with dates—Alabama, Texas till 1897, Arkansas 1897-1922, Chicago, 1922 to 1930. Arkansas 1930 to date.

5. Education, with dates—No education.

6. Occupations and accomplishments, with dates—Cooked before marriage at 16; farmed after marriage; home sewing.

7. Special skills and interests—Quilt making and knitting.

8. Community and religious activities—Assisted husband in ministry.

9. Description of informant—Hair divided into many pigtails and wrapped with rags. Skin, dark. Medium height, slender, clothing soiled.

10. Other points gained in interview—Spends all her time piecing quilts, aside from housework.

United States. Work Projects Administration

Interviewer: Miss Irene Robertson
Person interviewed: Hettie Mitchell (mulatto)
Brinkley, Arkansas
Age: 69

HETTIE MITCHELL

"I am sixty-nine years old. I was raised in Dyersburg, Tennessee. I can tell you a few things mother told us. My own grandma on mother's side was in South Carolina. She was stole when a child and brought to Tennessee in a covered wagon. Her mother died from the grief of it. She was hired out to nurse for these people. The people that stole her was named Spence. She was a house woman for them till freedom. She was never sold. Spences was not cruel people. Mother was never sold. She was the mother of twelve and raised nine to a good age—more than grown. The Spences seemed to always care for her children. When I go to Dyersburg they always want us to come to see them and they treat us mighty well.

"Mother was light. She said she had Indian strain (blood) but father was very light and it was white blood but he never discussed it before his children. So I can't tell you excepting he said he was owned by the Brittians in South Carolina. He said his mother died soon after he was sold. He was sold to a nigger trader and come in the gang to Memphis, Tennessee and was put on the block and auctioned off to the highest bidder. He was a farm hand.

"Mother married father when she was nineteen years old. She was a house girl. She lived close to her old mistress. She was very, very old before she died she nearly stayed at my mother's house. Her mind wasn't right and mother understood how to take care of her and was kind to her. The Spences heard about grandma. They wrote and visited years after when mother was a girl.

"The way that father found out about his kin folks was this: One day a creek was named and he told the white man, 'I was born close to that creek and played there in the white sand and water when I was a little boy.' The white man asked his name, said he knew the creek well too. Father told him he never was named till he was sold and they named him Sam—Sam Barnett. He was sold to Barnett in Memphis. But his dear own mother called him 'Candy.' The white man found out about his people for him and they found out his own dear mother died that same year he was taken from South Carolina from grief. He heard from some of his people from that time on till he died.

"I worked on the farm in Tennessee till I married. I ironed, washed, and have kept my own house and done the work that goes along with raising a small family. We own our home. We have saved all we could along. I have never had a real hard time like some I know. I guess my time is at hand now. I don't know which way to turn since my husband got down sick.

"I don't vote. Seem like it used to not be a nice place for women to go where voting was taking place. Now they go mix up and vote. That is one big change. Time is changing and changing the people. Maybe it is the people is changing up the world as time goes by. We colored folks look to the white folks to know the way to do. We have always done it."

United States. Work Projects Administration

Interviewer: Miss Irene Robertson
Person interviewed: Mary Mitchell, Hazen, Arkansas
Age: 60

MARY MITCHELL

"I was born in Trenton, Tennessee. My parents had five children. They were named William and Charlotte Wells. My father ran away and left my mother with all the children to raise. By birth mother was a Mississippian. She had been a nurse and my father was a timber man and farmer. My mother said she had her hardest time raising her little children. She was taken from her parents when a small girl and put on a block and sold. She never said if her owners was bad to her, but she said they was rough on Uncle Peter. He would fight. She said they would tie Uncle Peter and whoop him with a strap. From what she said there was a gang of slaves on Mr. Wade's place. He owned her. I never heard her mention freedom but she said they had a big farm bell on a tall post in the back yard and they had a horn to blow. It was a whistle made of a cow's horn.

"She said they was all afraid of the Ku Klux. They would ride across the field and they could see that they was around, but they never come up close to them."

STATE—Arkansas
NAME OF WORKER—Bernice Bowden
ADDRESS—1006 Oak Street, Pine Bluff, Arkansas
DATE—November 3, 1938
SUBJECT—Exslaves

[TR: Repetitive information deleted from subsequent pages.]

MOSES MITCHELL

Circumstances of Interview

1. Name and address of informant—Moses Mitchell, 117 Worthen Street

2. Date and time of interview—November 1, 1938, 1:00 p.m.

3. Place of interview—117 Worthen Street, Pine Bluff, Arkansas

4. Place and address of person, if any, who put you in touch with informant—Bernice Wilburn, 101 Miller Street, Pine Bluff, Arkansas

5. Name and address of person, if any, accompanying you—None

6. Description of room, house, surroundings, etc.—A frame house (rented), bare floors, no window shades; a bed and some boxes and three straight chairs. In an adjoining room were another bed, heating stove, two trunks, one straight chair, one rocking chair. A third

room, the kitchen, contained cookstove and table and chairs.

Text of Interview

"I was born down here on White River near Arkansas Post, August, 1849. I belonged to Thomas Mitchel and when they (Yankees) took Arkansas Post, our owners gathered us up and my young master took us to Texas and he sold me to an Irishman named John McInish in Marshall for $1500. $500 in gold and the rest in Confederate money. They called it the new issue.

"I was twelve years old then and I stayed in Texas till I was forty-eight. I was at Tyler, Texas when they freed us. When they took us to Texas they left my mother and baby sister here in Arkansas, down here on Oak Log Bayou. I never saw her again and when I came back here to Arkansas, they said she had been dead twenty-eight years. Never did hear of my father again.

"I'm supposed to be part Creek Indian. Don't know how much. We have one son, a farmer, lives across the river. Married this wife in 1873.

"My wife and I left Texas forty-one years ago and came back here to Arkansas and stayed till 1922. Then we went to Chicago and stayed till 1930, and then came back here. I'd like to go back up there, but I guess I'm gettin' too old. While I was there I preached and I worked all the time. I worked on the streets and the driveways in Lincoln Park. I was in the brick and block department. Then I went from there to the asphalt department. There's where I coined the money. Made $6.60 in the brick and block and $7.20 a day in the asphalt. Down here they don't know no more about asphalt than a pig does about a holiday. A man that's from the South and never been nowhere, don't know nothin', a woman either.

"Yes ma'm, I'm a preacher. Just a local preacher, wasn't ordained. The reason for that was, in Texas a man over forty-five couldn't join the traveling connection. I was licensed, but of course I couldn't perform marriage ceremonies. I was just within one step of that.

"I went to school two days in my life. I was privileged to go to the first free school in Texas. Had a teacher named Goldman. Don't know what year that was but they found out me and another fellow was too old so they wouldn't let us go no more. But I caught my alphabet in them two days. So I just caught what education I've got, here and there. I can read well—best on my Bible and Testament and I read the newspapers. I can sorta scribble my name.

"I've been a farmer most of my life and a preacher for fifty-five years. I can repair shoes and use to do common carpenter work. I can help build a house. I only preach occasionally now, here and there. I belong to the Allen Temple in Hoboken (East Pine Bluff).

"I think the young generation is gone to naught. They're a different cut to what they was in my comin' up."

Interviewer's Comment

This man and his wife live in the outskirts of West pine Bluff. They receive a small sum of money and commodities from the County Welfare Department. He has a very pleasant personality, a good memory and intelligence above the ordinary. Reads the Daily Graphic and Arkansas Gazette. Age 89. He said, "Here's the idea, freedom is worth it all."

Personal History of Informant

1. Ancestry—Father, Lewis Mitchell; Mother, Rhoda Mitchell

2. Place and date of birth—Oak Log Bayou, White River, near Arkansas Post, Ark.

3. Family—Wife and one grown son.

4. Places lived in, with dates—Taken to Texas by his young master and sold in Marshall during the war. Lived in Tyler, Texas until forty-eight years of age; came back to Arkansas in 1897 and stayed until 1922; went to Chicago and lived until 1930; back to Jefferson County, Arkansas.

5. Education, with dates—Two days after twenty-one years of age. No date.

6. Occupations and accomplishments, with dates—Farmer, preacher, common carpenter, cobbler, public work on streets in Chicago, farmed and preached until he went to Chicago in 1922. The he worked in the maintenance department of city streets of Chicago and of Lincoln Park, Chicago.

7. Special skills and interests—Asphalt worker

8. Community and religious activities—Licensed Methodist Preacher. No assignment now.

9. Description of informant—Five feet eight inches tall;

weight, 165 pounds, nearly bald. Very prominent cheek bones. Keen intelligence. Neatly dressed.

10. Other points gained in interview—Reads daily papers; knowledge of world affairs.

United States. Work Projects Administration

Pine Bluff District
FOLKLORE SUBJECTS
Name of Interviewer: Martin - Barker
Subject: Negro Customs

Information by: Ben Moon
[TR: Information moved from bottom of second page.]

BEN MOON

I was born on the Walker place, in 1869. My father was a slave to Mr. Bob. I used to drive Miss Lelia (Eulalie) to the Catholic church here in Pine Bluff. She used to let me go barefooted, and bare headed.

Miss Lelia was the daughter of Col. Creed Taylor. All during slavery time I drove her gins. We had eight mules. Eight at a time hitched to each lever, they would weave in an out but they was so hitched that they never got in any body's way. They just walked around and round like they did in those days. We had herds of sheep, we sheared them and wove yarn for socks. We raised wheat, when it was ripe we laid a canvas cloth on the ground and put wheat on it, then men and women on horse back rode over it, and thrashed it that way. They called it treading it. Then we took it to the mill and ground it and made it into flour. For breakfast, (we ate awful soon in the morning), about 4 AM, then we packed lunch in tin buckets and eat again at daylight. Fat meat, cornbread and molasses. Some would have turnip greens for breakfast.

Summertime, Miss Lelia would plant plenty of fruit,

and we would have fried apples, stewed peaches and things.

Sunday mornings we would have biscuit, butter, molasses, chicken, etc.

For our work they paid us seventy-five cents a day and when come cotton picking time old rule, seventy five cents for pickin cotton. Christmas time, plenty of fireworks, plenty to eat, drink and everything. We would dance all Christmas.

All kind of game was plentiful, plenty of coon, possum, used up everything that grew in the woods. Plenty of corn, we took it to the grist mill every Saturday.

Ark. riv. boats passed the Walker place, and dey was a landing right at dere place, and one at the Wright place, that is where the airport is now.

All de white folks had plenty of cattle den and in de winter time dey was all turned in on the fields and with what us niggers had, that made a good many, and you know yorself dat was good for de ground.

Mother was a slave on the Merriweather place, her marster was Mick[TR: name not clear] Merriweather. My granma was Gusta Merriweather, my mother Lavina and lived on the Merriweather place in what was then Dorsey county, near Edinburg, now Cleveland Co. My grandfather was Louis Barnett, owned by Nick Barnett of Cleveland co., then Dorsey co. Fathers people was owned by Marse Bob Walker. Miss Lelia (Eulalie) was mistis. Miss Maggie Benton was young mistis.

I dont believe in ghosts or spirits.

Interviewer: Mrs. Bernice Bowden
Person interviewed: Emma Moore
3715 Short West Second, Pine Bluff, Arkansas
Age: 80
Occupation: Laundry work

EMMA MOORE

"I'se born in slavery times. When my daddy come back from the War, he said I was gwine on seven or eight.

"He stayed in the War three years and six months. I know that's what he always told us. He went with his master, Joe Horton. Looks like I can see old Marse Joe now. Had long sandy whiskers. The las' time I seed him he come to my uncle's house. We was all livin' in a row of houses. Called em the quarters. I never will fergit it.

"I was born on Horton's Island here in Arkansas. That's what they told me.

"I know when my daddy went to war and when he come back, he put on his crudiments (accoutrements) to let us see how he looked.

"I seed the soldiers gwine to war and comin' back. Look like to me I was glad to see em till I seed too many of em.

"Yankees used to come down and take provisions. Yes, 'twas the Yankees!

"My granddaddy was the whippin' boss. Had a white boss too named Massa Fred.

"Massa Joe used to come down and play with us chillun. His name was Joe Horton. Ever'body can tell you that was his name. Old missis named Miss Mary. She didn't play with us much.

"Yes ma'am, they sure did take us to Texas durin' of the War—in a ox wagon. Stayed down there a long time.

"We didn't have plenty to eat but we had to eat what we did. I member they wouldn't give us chillun no meat, jus' grease my mouf and make my mother think we had meat.

"Now my mother told me, at night some of the folks used to steal one of old massa's shoats and cook it at night. I know when that pot was on the rack but you better not say nothin' bout it.

"All us chillun stayed in a big long log house. Dar is where us chillun stayed in the daytime, right close to Miss Mary.

"I used to sit on the lever at the gin. You know that was glory to me to ride. I whipped the old mule. Ever' now and then I'd give him a tap.

"When they pressed the cotton, they wet the press and I member one time they wet it too much. I don't say they sont it back but I think they made em pay for it. And they used to put chunks in the bale to make it weigh heavy. Right there on that lake where I was born.

"Used to work in the field. These white folks can tell you I loved to work. I used to get as much as the men. My mammy was a worker and as the sayin' is, I was a chip off the old block.

"The first teacher I went to school to was named Mr. Cushman. Didn't go only on rainy days. That was the first school and you might say the las' one cause I had to nuss them chillun.

"You know old massa used to keep all our ages and my daddy said I was nineteen when I married, but I don't know what year 'twas—honest I don't.

"I been married three times.

"I member one time I was goin' to a buryin'. I was hurryin' to get dressed. I wanted to be ready when they come by for me cause they say it's bad luck to stop a corpse. If you don't know that I do—you know if they had done started from the house.

"My mama and daddy said they was born in Tennessee and was bought and brought here.

"I been goin' to one of these gov'ment schools and got my eyes so weak I can't hardly see to thread a needle. I'se crazy bout it I'm tellin' you. I sit up here till God knows how long. They give me a copy to practice and they'd brag on me and that turned me foolish. I jus' thought I was the teacher herself almos'. That's the truf now.

"I can't read much. I don't fool with no newspaper. I wish I could, woman—I sure do.

"I keep tellin' these young folks they better learn somethin'. I tell em they better take this chance. This young generation—I don't know much bout the whites—I'm tellin' you these colored is a sight.

"Well, I'm gwine away from here d'rectly—ain't gwine be here much longer. If I don't see you again I'll meet you in heaven."

Interviewer: Miss Irene Robertson
Person interviewed: Patsy Moore, Madison, Arkansas
Age: 74

PATSY MOORE

"My mother was sold in Jamestown, Virginia to Daphney Hull. Her white folks got in debt. My papa was born in Georgia. Folks named Williams owned him. Ma never seen her ma no more but William Hull went to Virginia and bought her two sisters.

"I was named Patsy after grandma in Virginia. She had twenty-one children to ma's knowing. Ma was a light color. Pa was a Molly Glaspy man. That means he was Indian and African. Molly Glaspy folks was nearly always free folks. Ma was named Mattie. If they would have no children they got trafficked about.

"Daphney Hull was good but William Hull and his wife was both mean. They lived on the main road to Holly Springs. Daphney Hull was a Methodist man, kind-hearted and good. He was a bachelor I think. He kept a woman to cook and keep his house. Auntie said the Yankees was mean to Mr. William Hull's wife. They took all their money and meat. They had their money hid and some of the black folks let the Yankees find out where it was. They got it.

"Papa was a soldier. He sent for us. We come to Memphis, Tennessee in a wagon. We lived there five or six years. Pa got a pension till he died. Both my parents was field hands in slavery. Ma took in washing and ironing in Memphis.

"I was born in De Sota County, Mississippi. I remember Forrest's battle in Memphis. I didn't have sense to be scared. I seen black and white dead in the streets and alleys. We went to the magazine house for protection, and we played and stayed there. They tried to open the magazine house but couldn't.

"When freedom come, folks left home, out in the streets, crying, praying, singing, shouting, yelling, and knocking down everything. Some shot off big guns. Den come the calm. It was sad then. So many folks done dead, things tore up and nowheres to go and nothing to eat, nothing to do. It got squally. Folks got sick, so hungry. Some folks starved nearly to death. Times got hard. We went to the washtub onliest way we all could live. Ma was a cripple woman. Pa couldn't find work for so long when he mustered out.

"I do recollect the Civil War well.

"I live with my daughter. I have a cough since I had flu and now I have chills and fever. My daughter helps me all I get. She lives with me.

"Some of the young folks is mighty good. I reckon some is too loose acting. Times is hard. Harder in the winter than in summer time. We has our garden and chickens to help us out in summer."

Interviewer: Mrs. Bernice Bowden
Person interviewed: Ada Moorehead
2300 E. Barraque, Pine Bluff, Arkansas
Age: 82?

ADA MOOREHEAD

"I was here in slavery times, honey, but I don't know exactly how old I am. I was born in Huntsville, Alabama but you know in them days old folks didn't tell the young folks no thin' and I was so small when they brought me here. I don't know what year I was born but I believe I'm about eighty-two. You know when a person ain't able to work and dabble out his own clothes, you know he's gone a long ways.

"My white folks was Ad White what owned me. Called him Marse Ad. Don't call folks marse much now-days.

"My father was sold away from us in Alabama and we heard he was here in Pine Bluff so Aunt Fanny brought us here. She just had a road full of us and brought us here to Arkansas. We walked. We was a week on the road. I know we started here on Monday morning and we got here to the courthouse on the next Monday round about noon. That was that old courthouse. I reckon that ground is in the river now.

"When we got here I saw my father. He took me to his sister—that was my Aunt Savannah—and dropped me down.

"Mrs. Reynolds raised me. She come to Aunt Savannah's house and hired me the very same day I got here. I nursed Miss Katie. She was bout a month old. You know—a little long dress baby. Don't wear then long dresses now—gettin' wiser.

"Mrs. Reynolds she was good to me. And since she's gone looks like I'm gone too—gone to the dogs. Cause when Mrs. Reynolds got a dress for Miss Katie—got one for me too.

"My father was a soldier in the war. Last time I heard from him I know he was hauling salt to the breastworks. Yes, I was here in the war. That was all right to me but I wished a many a time I wasn't here.

"I went to school two or three days in a week for about a term. But I didn't learn to read much. Had to hire out and help raise my brother and sister. I'm goin' to this here government school now. I goes every afternoon.

"Since I got old I can think bout the old times. It comes to me. I didn't pay attention to nothin' much when I was young.

"Oh Lord, I don't know what's goin' to become of us old folks. Wasn't for the Welfare, I don't know what I'd do.

"I was sixteen when I married. I sure did marry young. I married young so I could see my chillun grown. I never married but once and I stayed a married woman forty-nine years to the very day my old man died. Lived with one man forty-nine years. I had my hand and heart full. I had a home of my own. How many chillun? Me? I had nine of my own and I raised other folks' chillun. Oh,

I been over this world right smart—first one thing and then another. I know a lot of white folks. They all been pretty good to me."

United States. Work Projects Administration

Interviewer: Mary D. Hudgins
Person Interviewed: Mrs. Mary Jane (Mattie) Mooreman
Home: with son
Age: 90

MRS. MARY JANE (MATTIE) MOOREMAN

"Yes, ma'am. I've been in Hot Springs, been in Hot Springs 57 years. That's a long time. Lots of changes have come—I've seen lots of changes here—changed from wooden sidewalks and little wood buildings.

"Your name's Hudgins? I knew the Hudginses—knew Miss Nora well. What's that? Did I know Adeline? Did I know Adeline! Do you mean to tell me she's still alive? Adeline! Why Miss Maud," (addressing Mrs. Eisele, for whom she works—and who sat nearby to help in the interview) "Miss Maude, I tell you Adeline's WHITE, she's white clean through!" (see interview with Adeline Blakeley, who incidentally is as black as "the ace of spades"—in pigmentation.) "Miss Maude, you never knew anybody like Adeline. She bossed those children and made them mind—just like they was hers. She took good care of them." (Turning to the interviewer) "You know how the Hudgins always was about their children. Adeline thought every one of 'em was made out of gold---made out of pure GOLD.

"She made 'em mind. I remember once, she was down

on Central Avenue with Ross and he did southing or other that, wasn't nice. She walked over to the umbrella stand, you remember how they used to have umbrellas for sale out in front of the stores. She grabbed an umbrella and she whipped Ross with it--she didn't hurt him. Then she put it back in the stand and said to the man who ran the store, 'If that umbrella's hurt, just charge it to Harve Hudgins.' That's the way Adeline was. So she's still alive. Law how I'd like to see her. Bring me a picture of her. Oh Miss Mary, I'd love to have it.

"Me? I was born on Green river near Hartford, Kentucky. Guess I was about a year and a half, from what they told me when my mistress married. Don't know how she ever met my master. She was raised in a convent and his folks lived a long way from hers. But anyhow she did. She was just 13 when she married. The man she married was named Charles Mooreman M-O-O-R-E-M-A-N. They had a son called Charles Wycliff Mooreman. He was named for his mother's people. I got a son I called Charles Wycliff too. He works at the Arlington. He's a waiter. They say he looks just like me. Mr. Charles Wycliff Mooreman--back in Kentucky. I still gets letters from him.

"Miss Mary I guess I had a pretty easy time in slavery days. They was good to us. Besides I was a house niggah." (Those who have been "house niggahs" never quibble at the word slave or negro. A subtle social distinction brewed in the black race to separate house servants from field hands as far as wealthy planters from "poor white trash.".) "Once I heard a man say of my mother, 'You could put on a white boiled shirt and lie flat down on the floor in her kitchen and not get dirty.'"

"Cook? No, ma'am!" (with dignity and indignation) "I never cooked until after I was married, and I never washed, never washed so much as a rag. All I washed was the babies and maybe my mistress's feet. I was a lady's maid. I'd wait on my mistress and I'd knit sox for all the folks. When they would sleep it was our duty—us maids—to fan 'em with feathers made out of turkey feathers—feather fans. Part of it was to keep 'em cool. Then they didn't have screens like we have today. So part of it was to keep the flies off. I remember how we couldn't stomp our feet to keep the flies from biting for fear of waking 'em up.

"No, Miss Mary, we didn't get such, good food. Nobody had all the kinds of things we have today. We had mostly buttermilk and cornbread and fat meat. Cake? 'Deed we didn't. I remember once they baked a cake and Mr. Charles Wycliff—he was just a little boy—he got in and took a whole fistful out of the cake. When Miss found out about it, she give us all doses of salts—enough to make us all throw up. She gave it to all the niggahs and the children—the white children. And what did she find out? It was her own child who had done it.

"Yes ma'am we learned to read and write. Oh, Miss Maude now—I don't want to recite. I don't want to." (But she did "Twinkle, Twinkle Little Star" and "The Playful Kitten"—the latter all of 40 lines.) "I think, I think they both come out of McGuffey's second Reader. Yes ma'am I remember's McGuffey's and the Blueback speller too.

"No, Miss Mary, there wasn't so much of the war that was fought around us. I remember that old Master used to go out in the front yard and stand by a locust tree and put his ear against it. He said that way he could hear the cannon down to Bowling Green. No, I didn't never hear any shooting from the war myself.

"Yes ma'am, the Confederates used to come through lots. I remember how we used to go to the spring for water for 'em. Then we'd stand with the buckets on our heads while they drank—drank out of a big gourd. When the buckets was empty we'd go back to the spring for more water.

"Once the Yankees come by the place. It was at night. They went out to the quarters and they tried to get 'em to rise up. Told 'em to come on in the big house and take what they wanted. Told 'em to take anything they wanted to take, take Master's silver spoons and Miss' silk dress. 'If they don't like it, we'll shoot their brains out,' they said. Next morning they told Master. He got scared and moved. At that time we was living at Cloverport.

"It was near the end of the war and we was already free, only we didn't know it. He moved on up to Stephensport. That's on the Ohio too. He took me and a brother of mine and another black boy. While we was there I remember he took me to a circus. I remember how the lady—she was dressed in pink come walking down a wire—straight on down to the ground. She was carrying a long pole. I won't never forget that.

"Not long afterwards I was married. We was all free then. My husband asked my master if he could marry me. He told him 'You're a good man. You can come and live on my farm and work for me, but you can't have Mattie.' So we moved off to his Master's farm.

"A little while after that his Master bought a big farm

in Arkansas. He wanted to hire as many people as he could. So we went with him. He started out well, but the first summer he died. So everything had to be sold. A man what come down to bid on some of the farm tools and stock—come to the auction, he told us to come on up to Woodruff county and work for him. We was there 7 years and he worked the farm and I took care of myself and my babies. Then he went off and left me.

"I went in to Cotton Plant and started working there. Finally he wrote me and tried to get me to say we hadn't never been married. Said he wanted to marry another woman. The white folks I worked for wouldn't let me. I'd been married right and they wouldn't let me disgrace myself by writing such a letter.

"Finally I came on to Hot Springs. For a while I cooked and washed. Then I started working for folks, regular. For 9 years, tho, I mostly washed and ironed.

"I came to Hot Springs on the 7th of February—I think it was 57 years ago. You remember Miss Maud—it was just before that big hail storm. You was here, don't you remember—that hail storm that took all the windows out of all the houses, tore off roofs and swept dishes and table-cloths right off the tables. Can't nobody forget that who's seen it.

"Miss Mary, do you know Miss Julia Huggins? I worked for her a long time. Worked for her before she went away and after she came back. Between times I cooked for Mrs. Button (Burton—but called Button by everyone) Housley. When Miss Julia come back she marches right down to Mrs. Housley's and tells me she wants me to work for her again. 'Can't get her now,' says Mrs. Housley, 'Mattie's done found out she's black.' But anyhow I went to see her, and I went back to work for her, pretty foxy Miss Julia was.

"I been working for Mrs. Eisele pretty near twenty five years. Saw her children grow up and the grand children. Lancing, he's my heart. Once when Mr. and Mrs. Eisele went to see Mrs. Brown, Lancing's mother, they took me with them. All the way to Watertown, Wisconsin. There wasn't any more niggas in the town and all the children thought I was somthing to look at. They'd come to see me and they'd bring their friends with 'em. Once while we was there, a circus come to town. The children wanted me to see it. Told me there was a negro boy in it. Guess they thought it would be a treat to me to see another niggah. I told 'em, 'Law, don't you think I see lots, lots more than I wants, everyday when I is at home?'

"It used to scare me. The folks would go off to a party or a show and leave me alone with the baby. No, Miss Mary, I wasn't scared for myself. I thought somebody might come in and kidnap that baby. No matter how late they was I'd sit on the top step of the stairs leading upstairs—just outside the door where Lansing was asleep. No matter what time they come home they'd find me there. 'Why don't you go on in your bedroom and lie down?' they'd ask me. 'No,' I'd tell 'em, 'somebody might come in, and they would have to get that baby over my dead body.'

"Jonnie, that's my daughter" (Mrs. D.G. Murphy, 338 Walnut Street, a large stucco house with well cared for lawn) "she wants me to quit work. I told her, 'You put that over on Mrs. Murphy—you made her quit work and took care of her. What happened to her? She died! You're not going to make me old.'

"Twice she's got me to quit work. Once, she told me it was against the law. Told me there was a law old folks couldn't work. I believed her and I quit. Then I come on down and I asked Mr. Eisele" (an important business executive and prominent in civic affairs, [HW: aged 83]) "He rared back and he said, 'I'd like to see anybody stop me from working.' So I come on back.

"Another time, it was when the old age pensions come in. They tried to stop me again. Told me I had to take it. I asked Mr. Eisele if I could work just the same. 'No,' he says 'if you take it, you'll have to quit work.' So I stamped my foot and I says, 'I won't take nobody's pension.'

"The other day Jonnie called up here and she started to crying. Lots of folks write her notes and say she's bad to let me work. Somebody told her that they had seen me going by to work at 4 o'clock in the morning. It wasn't no such. I asked a man when I was on the way and it was 25 minutes until 5. Besides, my clock had stopped and I couldn't tell what time it was. Yes, Miss Mary, I does get here sort of early, but then I like it. I just sit in the kitchen until the folks get up.

"You see that picture over there, it's Mr. Eisele when he was 17. I'd know that smiling face anywhere. He's always good to me. When they go away to Florida I can go to the store and get money whenever I need it. But it's always good to see them come back. Miss Maud says I'm sure to go to Heaven, I'm such a good worker. No, Miss Mary, I'm not going to quit work. Not until I get old."

Interviewer: Samuel S. Taylor
Person interviewed: Evelina Morgan
1317 W. Sixteenth Street, Little Rock, Arkansas
Age: App. 81

[TR: Original first page moved to follow second page per HW: Insert this page before Par. 1, P. 3]

EVELINA MORGAN

"I was born in Wedgeboro, North Carolina, on the plantation of—let me see what that man's name was. He was an old lawyer. I done forgot that old white man's name. Old Tom Ash! Senator Ash—that's his name. He was good to his slaves. He had so many niggers he didn't know them all.

"My father's name was Alphonso Dorgens and my mother's name was Lizzie Dorgens. Both of them dead. I don't know what her name was before she married. My pa belonged to the Dorgens' and he married my ma. That is how she come to be a Dorgen. Old Man Ash never did buy him. He just visited my mother. They all was in the same neighborhood. Big plantations. Both of them had masters that owned lots of land. I don't know how often he visited my mother after he married her. He was over there all the time. They were right adjoining plantations.

"I was born in a frame house. I don't know nothin' about it no more than that. It was j'ined to the kitchen. My mother had two rooms j'ined to the kitchen. She was the old mistress' cook. She could come right out of the kitchen and go on in her room.

"My father worked on the farm. They fed the slaves meat and bread. That is all I remember—meat and bread and potatoes. They made lots of potatoes. They gave 'em what they raised. You could raise stuff for yourself if you wanted to.

"My mother took care of her children. We children was on the place there with her. She didn't have nobody's children to take care of but us.

"I was six years old during of the War. My ma told me my age, but I forgot it; I never did have it put down. The only way I gits a pension, I just tells 'em I was six years old during of the War, and they figures out the age. Sorta like that. But I know I was six years old when the Rebels and the Yankees was fighting.

"I seed the Yankees come through. I seed that. They come in the time old master was gone. He run off—he run away. He didn't let 'em git him. I was a little child. They stayed there all day breaking into things—breaking into the molasses and all like that. Old mistress stayed upstairs hiding. The soldiers went down in the basement and throwed things around. Old master was a senator; they wanted to git him. They sure did cuss him: 'The ----, ----, ----, old senator,' they would say. He took his finest horses and all the gold and silver with him somewheres. They couldn't git 'im. They was after senators and high-ups like that.

"The soldiers tickled me. They sung. The white people's yard was jus' full of them playing 'Yankee Doodle' and 'Hang Jeff Davis on a Sour Apple Tree.'

"All the white people gone! Funny how they run away

like that. They had to save their selves. I 'member they took one old boss man and hung him up in a tree across a drain of water, jus' let his foot touch—and somebody cut him down after 'while. Those white folks had to run away.

Patrollers

"I used to hear them all talk about the patrollers. I used to hear my mother talking about them. My ma said my master wouldn't let the patrollers come on his place. They could go on anybody else's place but he never did let them come on his place. Some of the slaves were treated very bad. But my ma said he didn't allow a patroller on the place and he didn't allow no other white man to touch his niggers. He was a big white man—a senator. He didn't know all his Negroes but he didn't allow nobody to impose on them. He didn't let no patroller and nobody else beat up his niggers.

How Freedom Came

"I don't know how freedom came. I know the Yankees came through and they'd pat we little niggers on the head and say, 'Nigger, you are just as free as I am.' And I would say, 'Yes'm.'

Right After Freedom

"Right after the War my mother and father moved off the place and went on another plantation somewheres—I don't know where. They share cropped. I don't know how long. Old mistress didn't want them to move at all. I never will forget that.

Present Occupation and Opinions

"I used to cook out all the time when I got grown. I couldn't tell you when I married. You got enough junk down there now. So I ain't giving you no more. My husband's been dead about seven years. I goes to the Methodist church on Ninth and Broadway. I ain't able to do no work now. I gets a little pension, and the Lord takes care of me. I have a hard time sometime.

"I ain't bothered about these young folks. They is somethin' awful. It would be wonderful to write a book from that. They ought to git a history of these young people. You could git a wonderful book out of that.

"The colored folks have come a long way since freedom. And if the white folks didn't pin 'em down they'd go further. Old Jeff Davis said when the niggers was turned loose, 'Dive up your knives and forks with them.' But they didn't do it.

"Some niggers was sharp and got something. And they lost it just like they got it. Look at Bush. I know two or three big niggers got a lot and ain't got nothin' left now. Well, I ain't got no time for no more junk. You got enough down there. You take that and go on."

Interviewer's Comment

During the interview, a little "pickaninny" came in with his mother. His grandmother and a forlorn little dog were also along. "Tell grandma what you want," his mother prompted. "Is that your grandson?" I interrupted. "No," she said, "He ain't no kin to me, but he calls me 'ma' and acts as if I was his grandma." The little fellow hung back. He was just about twenty-two months old, but large and mature for that age.

"Tell 'ma' what you want," his grandmother put in. Finally, he made up his mind and stood in front of her and said, "Buh—er." His mother explained, "I've done made him some corn bread, but he ain't got no butter to put on it and he wants you to give him some."

Sister Morgan sat silent awhile. Then she rose deliberately and went slowly to the ancient ice-box, opened it and took out a tin of butter which she had evidently churned herself in some manner and carefully cut out a small piece and wrapped it neatly and handed it to the little one. After a few amenities, they passed out.

Even with her pitiful and meagre lot, the old lady evidently means to share her bare necessities with others.

The manner of her calculation of her age is interesting. She was six years old when the War was going on. She definitely remembers seeing Sherman's army and Wheeler's cavalry after she was six. Since they were in her neighborhood in 1864, she is undoubtedly more than eighty. Eighty-one is a fair estimate.

Interviewer: Samuel S. Taylor
Person interviewed: James Morgan
819 Rice Street, Little Rock, Arkansas
Age: 65

JAMES MORGAN

"During the slave time, the pateroles used to go from one plantation to the other hunting Negroes. They would catch them at the door and throw hot ashes in their faces. You could go to another plantation and steal or do anything you wanted if you could manage to get back to your old master's place. But if you got caught away from your plantation, they would get you. Sometimes a nigger didn't want to get caught and beat, so he would throw a shovel of hot ashes in the pateroles' faces and beat it away.

"My daddy used to tell lots of stories about slavery times. He's been dead forty-three years and my mother has been dead forty-one years—forty-one years this May. I was quite young and lots of the things they told me, I remember, and some of them, I don't.

"I was born in 1873. That was eight years after the War ended. My father's name was Aaron and my mother's name was Rosa. Both of them was in slavery. [TR: sentence lined out.] I got a brother that was a baby in her lap when the Yankee soldiers got after a chicken. The chicken flew up in her lap and they never got that one. The white folks lost it, but the Yankees didn't get it. I have heard my mother tell all sorts of things. But they just come to me at times. The soldiers would take chickens or anything they could get their hands on—those soldiers would.

"My mother married the first time in slavery. Her first husband was sold in slavery. That is the onliest brother I'm got living now out of ten—that one that was settin' in her lap when the soldiers come through. He's in Boydell, Arkansas now. It used to be called Morrell. It is about one hundred twenty-one miles from here, because Dermott is one hundred nine and Boydell is about twelve miles further on. It's in Nashville[HW:?] County. My brother was a great big old baby in slavery times. He was my mother's child by her first husband. All the rest of them is dead and he is the onliest one that is living.

"I was a section foreman for the Missouri Pacific for twenty-two years. I worked there altogether for thirty-five years, but I was section foreman for twenty-two years. There's my card. Lots of men stayed on the job till it wore them out. Lewis Holmes did that. It would take him two hours to walk from here to his home—if he ever managed it at all.

"It's warm today and it will bring a lot of flies. Flies don't die in the winter. Lots of folks think they do. They go up in cracks and little places like that under the weatherboard there—any place where it is warm—and there they huddle up and stay till it gets warm. Then they come out and get something to eat and go back again when it cools off. They live right on through the winter in their hiding places.

"Both of my parents said they always did their work whatever the task might be. And my daddy said he never got no whipping at all. You know they would put a task on you and if you didn't do it, you would get a whipping. My daddy wouldn't stand to be whipped by a paterole, and he didn't have to be whipped by nobody else, because he always did his work.

"He was one of the ones that the pateroles couldn't catch. When the pateroles would be trying to break in some place where he was, and the other niggers would be standing 'round frightened to death and wonderin' what to do, he would be gettin' up a shovelful of ashes. When the door would be opened and they would be rushin' in, he would scatter the ashes in their faces and rush out. If he couldn't find no ashes, he would always have a handful of pepper with him, and he would throw that in their faces and beat it.

"He would fool dogs that my too. My daddy never did run away. He said he didn't have no need to run away. They treated him all right. He did his work. He would get through with everything and sometimes he would be home before six o'clock. My mother said that lots of times she would pick cotton and give it to the others that couldn't keep up so that they wouldn't be punished. She had a brother they used to whip all the time because he didn't keep up.

"My father told me that his old master told him he was free. He stayed with his master till he retired and sold the place. He worked on shares with him. His old master sold the place and went to Monticello and died. He stayed with him about fifteen or sixteen years after he was freed, stayed on that place till the Government donated him one hundred sixty acres and charged him only a dollar and sixty cents for it. He built a house on it and cleared it up. That's what my daddy did. Some folks don't believe me when I tell 'em the Government gave him a hundred and sixty acres of land and charged him only a dollar and sixty cents for it—a penny a acre.

"I am retired now. Been retired since 1938. The Government took over the railroad pension and it pays me now. That is under the Security Act. Each and every man on the railroad pays in to the Government.

"I have been married right around thirty-nine years.

"I was born in Chicot County, Arkansas.[TR: sentence lined out.] My father was born in Georgia and brought here by his master. He come here in a old covered ox wagon. I don't know how they happened to decide to come here. My mother was born in South Carolina. She met my father here in Arkansas. They sold her husband and she was brought here. After peace was declared she met my daddy. Her first husband was sold in South Carolina and she never did know that became of him. They put him up on the block and sold him and she never did know which way he went. He left her with two boys right then. She had a sister that stayed in South Carolina. Somebody bought her there and kept her and somebody bought my mother and brought her here. My father's master was named McDermott. My mother's last master was named Belcher or something like that.

"I don't belong to any church. I have always lived decent and kept out of trouble."

Interviewer's Comment

When Morgan said "there is my record", he showed

me a pass for the year 1938-39 for himself and his wife between all stations on the Missouri Pacific lines signed by L.W. Baldwin, Chief Executive Officer.

He is a good man even if he is not a Christian as to church membership.

United States. Work Projects Administration

Interviewer: Miss Irene Robertson
Person Interviewed: Olivia Morgan
Hazen, Ark.
Age: 62

OLIVIA MORGAN

"I am 62 years old. I was born in Lafayette County close to New Lewisville. I heard mama say many a time she was named after her state—North Carolina. Her name was Carolina Alexandria. They brought her a slave girl to this new country. She and papa must of met up toreckly after freedom. She had some children and I'm one of my papa's oldest children.

"Papa come here long fore the war started. The old master in Atlanta, Georgia—Abe Smith—give his son three boys and one girl. He emigrated to Arkansas.

"Mama said her first husband and the young master went off and he never come back as she knowed of. Young master played with mama's second girl a whole heap. One day they was playing hiding round. Just as she come running to the base from round the house, young master hit her on the forehead with a rock. It killed her. Old master tried to school him but he worried so they sent him off—thought it would do his health good to travel. I don't think they ever come back.

"After freedom mama married and went over to papa's master's. Papa stayed round there a long time. They got news some way they was to get forty acres land and a mule to start out with but they said they never got nothing.

"My papa said he knowed it to be a fact, the Ku Klux cut a colored woman's breast off. I don't recollect why he said they got after her. The Jayhawkers was bad too. They all went wild; some of em left men hanging up in trees. They needed a good master to protect em worse after the war than they needed em before. They said they had a Yankee government then was reason of the Ku Klux. They run the Jayhawkers out and made the Yankees go on home. Everybody had a hard time. Bread was mighty scarce when I was a child. Times was hard. Men that had land had to let it lay out. They had nothin' to feed the hands on, no money to pay, no seed, no stock to work. The fences all went to rack and all the houses nearly down. When I was a child they was havin' hard times.

"I'm a country woman. I farmed all my life. I been married two times; I married Holmes, then Morgan. They dead. I washed, ironed, cooked, all at Mr. Jim Buchannan's sawmill close to Lewisville two years and eight months; then I went back to farmin' up at Pine Bluff. My oldest sister washed and ironed for Mrs. Buchannan till she moved from the sawmill to Texarkana. He lived right at the sawmill ground.

"My papa voted a Republican ticket. I don't vote. My husbands have voted along. If the women would let the men have the business I think times would be better. I don't believe in women voting. The men ought to make the livings for the families, but the women doing too much. They crowding the men out of work.

"Some folks is sorry in all colors. Seems like the young

folks ain't got no use for quiet country life. They buying too much. They say they have to buy everything. I ain't had no depression yet. I been at work and we had crop failures but I made it through. Some folks good and some ain't. Times is bout to run away with some of the folks. They all say times is better than they been since 1928. I hope times is on the mend."

Interviewer: Miss Irene Robertson
Person interviewed: Tom Morgan, Madison, Arkansas
Age: 71

TOM MORGAN

"My mother was the mother of fourteen of us children. Their names was Sarah and Richard Morgan.

"My great-grandfather b'long to Bill Woods. They had b'long to the Morgans and when freedom come they changed their names back. Some of them still owned by Morgans.

"Mother's owners was Auris and Lucella Harris. They had a boy named Harley Harris and a girl. He had a small farm.

"Mother said her master wasn't bad, but my father said his owner was tough on him—tough on all of them. They was all field hands. They had to git up and be doing. He said they fed by torch morning and night and rested in the heat of the day two or three hours. Feed the oxen and mules. In them days stock and folks all et three times a day. I does real well now to get two meals a day, sometimes but one. They done some kind of work all the year 'round. He said they had tasks. They better git the task done or they would get a beating.

"I haven't voted in so long a time. I voted Republican. I thought I did.

"I worked at the railroad till they put me off. They put me off on disability. Trying to git my papers fixed up to work or get something one. Back on the railroad job. I farmed when I was young."

El Dorado District
FOLKLORE SUBJECTS
Name of Interviewer: Pernella Anderson
Subject: Slavery Days—Cruel Master Murdered by Slaves
Story:—Information

This Information given by: Charity Morris
Place of Residence: Camden, Arkansas
Age: 90
[TR: Information moved from bottom of first page.]

CHARITY MORRIS

Ah wuz born in Carolina uh slave an ah was de eldest daughtuh of Christiana Webb whose owner wuz Master Louis Amos. Mah mammy had lots uv chillun an she also mammied de white chillun, whut wuz lef' mammyless. When ah wuz very small dey rented me out tuh some very po' white fokes. Dey wuzn use tuh slaves so mah marster made him promise [HW: not] tuh beat me or knock me bout. Dey promise dey wouldn. Dey cahried me home an ah clare dey wuz so mean tuh me till ah run off an tried tuh fin' de way back tuh mah marster. Night caught me in de woods. Ah sho' wuz skeered. Ah wuz skeered uv bears an panthers so ah crawled up in a ole bandoned crib an crouched down gainst de loft. Ah went off tuh sleep but wuz woke by somethin scratchin on de wall below. Ah stayed close as ah could tuh de wall an 'gin er prayin. Dat things scratched all night an ah prayed all night. De nex' mawnin dese white fokes sent word tuh Marster dat ah had lef' so Marster foun' me an took me home and let me stay dar too. Ah didn' work in de fiel' ah worked in de house. We lived in uh log cabin. Evah Sunda mawnin Marster Louis would have all us slaves tuh de house while he would sing an pray an read de Bible tuh us all.

De people dat owned de plantation near us had lots of slaves. Dey owned lots uv mah kin fokes. Dey marster would beat dem at night when dey come fum de fiel' an lock em up. He'd whoop um an sen' um tuh de fiel'. Dey couldn' visit no slaves an no slaves was 'lowed tuh visit em. So mah cousin Sallie watched him hide de key so she moved dem a li'l further back so dat he had tuh lean ovah tuh reach dem. Dat mawnin soon when he come tuh let em out she cracked him in de haid wid de poker an made little Joe help put his haid in de fiuh place. Dat day in de fiel' Little Joe made er song; "If yo don' bleave Aunt Sallie kilt Marse Jim de blood is on huh under dress". He jes hollered hit. "Aunt Sallie kilt Marse Jim." Dey zamined Aunt Sallie's under dress so dey put huh in jail till de baby come den dey tried huh an sentenced huh tuh be hung an she wuz.

Our Marster use tuh tell us if we left de house de patarollers would catch us. One night de patarollers run mah two brothers home, Joe an Henry.

When de ole haid died out dey chillun got de property. Yo see we slaves wuz de property. Den we got separated. Some sent one way an some nother. Hit jes happent dat Marse Jim drawed me.

When de Wah broke out we could heah li'l things bein said. We couldn' make out. So we begin tuh move erbout. Later we learnt we wuz runnin fum de wah. In runnin we run intuh a bunch uv soldiers dat had got kilt. Oh dat wuz terrible. Aftuh mah brudders foun out dat dey wuz fightin tuh free us dey stole hosses an run erway tuh keep fum bein set free. Aftuh we got tuh Morris Creek hit wuz bloody an dar wuz one uv de hosses turnin roun an roun in de watuh wid his eyes shot out. We nevah saw nuthin else uv Joe nor Henry nor de othuh horse from dat day tuh dis one. But we went on an on till we come tuh a red house and dat red house represented free. De white fokes wouldn go dat way cause dey hated tuh give us up. Dey turnt an went de othuh way but hit wuz too late. De news come dat Mr. Lincoln had signed de papuhs dat made us all free an dere wuz some 'joicing ah tells yo. Ah wuz a grown woman at dat time. Ole Moster Amos brought us on as fur as Fo'dyce an turnt us a loose. Dat's wha' dey settled. Some uv de slaves stayed wid em an some went tuh othuh places. Me an mah sistuh come tuh Camden an settled. Ah mahried George Morris. We havn' seen our pa an ma since we wuz 'vided and since we wuz chillun. When we got tuh Camden and settled down we went tuh work an sont back tuh de ole country aftuh ma an pa. Enroute tuh dis country we come through Tennessee an ah membuh comin through Memphis an Pine Bluff to Fordyce.

As we wuz comin we stopped at de Mississippi Rivuh. Ah wuz standin on de bank lookin at de great roll uv watuh high in de air. Somebody snatched me back and de watuh took in de bank wha ah wuz standin. Yo cound'n stand too close tuh de rivuh 'count uv de waves.

Der wuz a col' wintuh and at night we would gather roun a large camp fire an play sich games as "Jack-in-de-bush cut him down" an "Ole gray mule-out ride him." Yaul know dem games ah know. An in de summer times at night we played Julands. On our way tuh Arkansas we drove ox-teams, jinnie teams, donkey teams, mule teams an horse teams. We sho had a good time.

Interviewer: Miss Irene Robertson
Person interviewed: Emma Morris, Forrest City, Arkansas
Age: 71

EMMA MORRIS

"My parents was Jane and Sam McCaslin. They come from close to Atlanta, Georgia to Hernando, Mississippi after slavery. Ma was heired and they bought pa before they left North Carolina. They bought pa out of a nigger drove after he was grown. He raised tobacco and corn. Pa helped farm and they raised hogs. He drove hogs to sell. He didn't say where they took the hogs, only they would have to stay up all night driving the hogs, and they rode horses and walked too and had shepherd dogs to keep them in a drove.

"Pa was a Böwick (B(our)ick) but I never heard him say nothing bout Master Bowick, so I don't know his other name. He said they got in a tight [TR: missing word?] and had to sell some of the slaves and he being young would bring more than one of the older men. He was real black. Ma was lighter but not very light.

"McCaslin was a low heavy set man and he rented out hacks and horses in Atlanta and pa drove, greased the harness and curried and sheared the horses. Master McCaslin brought them in town and rented them out. He didn't have a livery stable. He just furnished conveyances. I heard him tell about a good hitching post where he could more than apt rent out his rig and how he always stopped and fed the horses when eating time come. He took a feed box all the time. Master McCaslin would tell him to not drive too hard when he had to make long drives. He never would let him take a whoop.

"He had some girls I heard him say. May and Alice was their names. He didn't say much about the family. He took a basket of provision with him to eat Miss May and Miss Alice fixed up. The basket was close wove and had a lid. The old man farmed. He drove too. He drove a hack. Ma worked in the field. I heard her tell about the cockleburs. Well, she said they would stick on your dress and stick your legs and you would have to pick them off and sometimes the beggar's-lice would be thick on their clothes and they would pick them off.

"When they would clean out the fence corners (rail fence) they would leave every little wild plum tree and leave a whole lot of briers so they would have wild plums and berries. They raised cotton. Sometime during the War old Master McCaslin took all his slaves and stock way back in the bottoms. The cane was big as ma's wrist she said. They put up some cabins to live in and shelter the stock. Pa said some of em went in the army. He didn't want to go. They worked a corn crop over in there.

"They left soon as they was freed. I don't know how they found it out. They walked to way over in Alabama and pa made terms with a man, to come to Mississippi. Then they come in a wagon and walked too. She had three little children. I was [HW: born] close to Montgomery, Alabama in September but I don't know how long it was after the War. I was the first girl. There was two more boys and three more girls after me. Ma had children born in three states.

"Ma died with the typhoid fever. Then two sisters and a brother died. Pa had it all summer and he got well. Miss (Mrs.) Betty Chamlin took us children to a house and fed us away from ma and the sick girls and boy. We was on her place. She had two families then. We got water from a spring. It was a pretty spring under a big hill. We would wade where the spring run off. She moved us out of that house.

"Miss Betty was a widow. She had several boys. They worked in the field all the time. We stayed till the boys left and she sold her place. She went back to her folks. I never did see her no more. We scattered out. Pa lived about wid us till he died. I got three girls living. I got five children dead. I got one girl out here from town and one girl at Meridian and my oldest girl in Memphis. I takes it time around wid em.

"I seen the Ku Klux but they never bothered us. I seen them in Alabama, I recken it was. I was so small I jes' do remember seeing them. I was the onliest child born in Alabama. Pa made one crop. I don't know how they got along the rest of the time there. We started share cropping in Mississippi. Pa was always a good hand with stock. If they got sick they sent for him to tell them what to do. He never owned no land, no home neither.

"I farmed all my life. I used to make a little money along during the year washing and ironing. I don't get no help. I live with the girls. My girl in Memphis sends me a little change to buy my snuff and little things I have to have. She cooks for a lawyer now. She did take care of an lady. She died since I been here and she moved. I rather work in the field than do what she done when that old lady lived. She was like a baby to tend to. She had to stay in that house all the time.

"The young folks don't learn manners now like they used to. Times is better than I ever seen em. Poor folks have a hard time any time. Some folks got a lot and some ain't got nothing everywhere."

Interviewer: Samuel S. Taylor
Person interviewed: Claiborne Moss
1812 Marshall Street, Little Rock, Arkansas
Age: 81

CLAIBORNE MOSS

"I was born in Washington County, Georgia, on Archie Duggins' plantation, fifteen miles from Sandersville, the county-seat, June 18, 1857.

"My mother's name was Ellen Moss. She was born in Georgia too, in Hancock County, near Sparta, the county-seat. My father was Fluellen Moss. He, too, was born in Hancock County. Bill Moss was his owner. Jesse Battle was my mother's owner before she married. My mother and father had ten children, none of them living now but me, so far as I know. I was the fifth in line. There were four older than I. The oldest was ten years older than I.

"Bill Moss' and Jesse Battle's plantations ware not far apart. I never heard my father say how he first met my mother. I was only eight years old when he died. They were all right there in the same neighborhood, and they would go visiting. Battle and Moss and Evans all had plantations in the same neighborhood and they would go from one place to the other.

"When Bill Moss went to Texas, he gave my mother and father to Mrs. Beck. Mrs. Beck was Battle's daughter and Mrs. Beck bought my father from Moss and that kept them together. He was that good. Moss sold out and went to Texas and all his slaves went walking while he went on the train. He had about a hundred of them. When he got there, he couldn't hear from them. He didn't know where they was—they was walking and he had got on the train—so he killed hisself. When they got there, just walking along, they found him dead.

"Moss' nephew, Whaley, got two parts of all he had. Another fellow—I can't call his name—got one part. His sister, they sent her back five—three of my uncles and two of my aunties.

"Where I was raised, Duggins wasn't a mean man. His slaves didn't get out to work till after sunup. His brother, who lived three miles out from us, made his folks get up before sunup. But Duggins didn't do that. He seemed to think something of his folks. Every Saturday, he'd give lard, flour, hog meat, syrup. That was all he had to give. That was extra. War was going on and he couldn't get nothing else. On Wednesday night he'd give it to them again. Of course, they would get corn-meal and other things from the kitchen. They didn't eat in the kitchen or any place together. Everybody got what there was on the place and cooked it in his cabin.

"Before I was born, Beck sold my mother and father to Duggins. I don't know why he sold them. They had an auction block in the town, but out in the country they didn't have no block. If I had seen a nigger and wanted to buy him, I would just go up to the owner and do business with him. That was the way it was with Beck and Duggins. Selling my mother and father was just a private transaction between them.

Rations

"Twice a week, flour, syrup, meat, and lard were given to the slaves. you got other food from the kitchen. Meat, vegetables, milk, —all the milk you wanted—bread.

A Mean Owner

"Beck, Moss, Battle, and Duggins, they was all good people. But Kenyon Morps, now talk about a mean man, there was one. He lived on a hill a little off from the Duggins plantation. His women never give birth to children in the house. He'd never let 'em quit work before the time. He wanted them to work—work right up to the last minute. Children were all born in the field and in fence corners. Then he had to let 'em stay in about a week. Last I seen him, he didn't have nothin', and was ragged as a jay bird.

Houses

"Our house was a log house. It had a large room, and then it had another room as large as that one or larger built on to it. Both of these rooms were for our use. My mother and father slept in the log cabin and the kids slept back in the other room. My sister stayed with Joe Duggins. Her missis was a school-teacher, and she loved sister. My master gave my sister to Joe Duggins. Mrs. Duggins taught my sister, Fannie, to read and spell but not to write. If there was a slave man that knowed how to write, they used to cut off his thumb so that he couldn't write.

"There was some white people wouldn't have the darkies eating butter; our white people let us have butter, biscuits, and ham every day. They would put it up for me.

"I had more sense than any kid on the plantation. I would do anything they wanted done no matter how hard it was. I walked five miles through the woods once on an errand. The old lady who I went to said:

"'You walk way down here by yourself?'

"I told her, 'yes'.

"She said, 'Well, you ain't going back by yo'self because you're too little,' and she sent her oldest son back with me. He was white.

"My boss was sick once, and he wanted to get his mail. The post office was five miles away. He said to me:

"'Can't you get my mail if I let you ride on my horse?'

"I said, 'Yes sir.' I rode up to the platform on the horse. They run out and took me off the horse and filled up the saddle bags. Then they put me back on and told me not to get off until I reached my master. When I got back, everybody was standing out watching for me. When my boss heard me coming, he jumped out the bed and ran out and took me off the horse and carried me and the sacks and all back into the house.

Soldiers

"I saw all of Wheeler's cavalry. Sherman come through first. He came and stayed all night. Thousands and thousands of soldiers passed through during the night. Cooper Cuck was with them. He was a fellow that used to peddle around in all that country before the War. He went all through the South and learned everything. Then he joined up with the Yankees. He come there. Nobody seen him that night. He knowed everybody knowed him. He went and hid under something somewhere. He was under the hill at daybreak, but nobody seen him. When the last of the soldiers was going out in the morning, one fellow lagged behind and rounded a corner. Then he galloped a little ways and motioned with his arms. Cooper Cuck come out from under the hill, and he and Cooper Cuck both came back and stole everything that they could lay their hands on—all the gold and silver that was in the house, and everything they could carry.

"Wheeler's cavalry was about three days behind Sherman. They caught up with Sherman, but it would have been better if they hadn't, 'cause he whipped 'em and drove 'em back and went right on. They didn't have much fighting in my country. They had a little scrimmage once—thirty-six men was all they was in it. One of the Yankees got lost from his company. He come back and inquired the way to Louisville. The old boss pointed the way with his left hand and while the fellow was looking that way, he drug him off his horse and cut his throat and took his gun off'n him and killed him.

"Sherman's men stayed one night and left. I mean, his officers stayed. We had to feed them. They didn't pay nothing for what they was fed. The other men cooked and ate their own grub. They took every horse and mule we had. I was sitting beside my old missis. She said:

"'Please don't let 'em take all our horses.'

"The fellows she was talking to never looked around. He just said: 'Every damn horse goes.'

"The Yankees took my Uncle Ben with them when

they left. He didn't stay but a couple of days. They got in a fight. They give Uncle Ben five horses, five sacks of silverware, and five saddles. The goods was taken in the fight. Uncle Ben brought it back with him. The boss took all that silver away from him. Uncle Ben didn't know what to do with it. The Yankees had taken all my master's and he took Ben's. Ben give it to him. He come back 'cause he wanted to.

"When Wheeler's cavalry came through they didn't take nothing—nothing but what they et. I heard a fellow say, 'Have you got anything to eat?'

"My mother said, 'I ain't got nothin' but some chitlins.'

"He said, 'Gimme some of those; I love chitlins.' "Mother gave 'em to me to carry to him. I didn't get half way to him before the rest of the men grabbed me and took 'em away from me and et 'em up. The man that asked for them didn't get a one.

Slave Money

"The slaves would sometimes have five or six dollars. Mostly, they would make charcoal and sell it to get money.

Patrollers

"I seen patrollers. They come to our house. They didn't whip nobody. Our folks didn't care nothin' about 'em. They come looking for keys and whiskey. They couldn't whip nobody on my master's plantation. When they would come there, he would be sitting up with 'em.

He would sit there in his back door and look at 'em. Wouldn't let 'em hit nobody.

"Them colored women had more fun that enough—laughing at them patrollers. Fool 'em and then laugh at 'em. Make out like they was trying to hide something and the patrollers would come running up, grab 'em and try to see what it was. And the women would laugh and show they had nothing. Couldn't do nothin' about it. Never whipped anybody 'round there. Couldn't whip nobody on our place; couldn't whip nobody on Jessie Mills' place; couldn't whip nobody on Stephen Mills' place; couldn't whip nobody on Betsy Geesley's place; couldn't whip nobody on Nancy Mills' place; couldn't whip nobody on Potter Duggins' place. Potter Duggins was a cousin to my master. Nobody run them peoples' plantations but theirselves.

Social Life

"When slaves wanted to, they would have dances. They would have dances from one plantation to the other. The master didn't object. They had fiddles, banjo and quills. They made the quills and blowed 'em to beat the band. Good music. They would make the quills out of reeds. Those reeds would sound just like a piano. They didn't have no piano. They didn't serve nothing. Nothing to eat and nothing to drink except them that brought whiskey. The white folks made the whiskey, but the colored folks would get it.

"We had church twice a month. The Union Church was three miles away from us. My father and I would go when they had a meeting. Bethlehem Church was five miles away. Everybody on the plantation belonged to that church. Both the colored and the white belonged and went there. They had the same pastor for Bethlehem, Union, and Dairy Ann. His name was Tom Adams. He was a white man. Colored folks would go to Dairy Ann sometimes. They would go to Union too.

"Sometimes they would have meetings from house to house, the colored folks. The colored folks had those house to house meetings any time they felt like it. The masters didn't care. They didn't care how much they prayed.

"Sometimes they had corn shuckings. That was where they did the serving, and that was where they had the big eatings. They'd lay out a big pile of corn. Everybody would get down and throw the corn out as they shucked it. They would have a fellow there they would call the general. He would walk from one person to another and from one end of the pile to the other and holler and the boys would answer. His idea was to keep them working. If they didn't do something to keep them working, they wouldn't get that corn shucked that night. Them people would be shucking corn! There would be a prize to the one who got the most done or who would be the first to get done. They would sing while they were shucking. They had one song they would sing when they were getting close to the finish. Part of it went like this:

> 'Red shirt, red shirt
> Nigger got a red shirt.'

After the shucking was over, they would have pies, beef, biscuits, corn bread, whiskey if you wanted it. I believe that was the most they had. They didn't have any ice-cream. They didn't use ice-cream much in those days. Didn't have no ice down there in the country. Not a bit of ice there. If they had anything they wanted to save, they would let it down in the well with a rope and keep it cool down there. They used to do that here until they stopped them from having the wells.

"Ring plays too. Sometimes when they wanted to amuse themselves, they would play ring plays. They all take hands and form a ring and there would be one in the center of the ring. Now he is got to get out. He would come up and say, 'I am in this lady's garden, and I'll bet you five dollars I can get out of here.' And d'reckly he would break somebody's hands apart and get out.

How Freedom Came

"The old boss called 'em up to the house and told 'em, 'You are free as I am.' That was one day in June. I went on in the house and got something to eat. My mother and father, he hired them to stay and look after the crop. Next year, my mother and father went to Ben Hook's place and farmed on shares. But my father died there about May. Then it wasn't nobody working but me and my sister and mother.

What the Slaves Got

"The slaves never got nothing. Alexander Stephens, the Vice-President of the Confederacy, divided his plantation up and gave it to his darkies when he died. I knew him and his brother too. Alexander[HW: *] never did walk. He was deformed. Big headed rascal, but he had sense! His brother was named Leonard[HW: *]. He was a lawyer. He really killed himself. He was one of these die-hard Southerners. He did something and they arrested him. It made him so mad. He'd bought him a horse. He got on that horse and fell off and broke his neck. That was right after the War. They kept garrisons in all the counties right after the War.

"I was in Hancock County when I knew Vice-President Stephens. I don't know where he was born but he had a plantation in Toliver [HW: Taliaferro] County. Most of the Stephenses was lawyers. He was a lawyer too, and he would come to Sparta. That is where I was living then. There was more politics and political doings in Sparta than there was in Crawfordville where he lived. He lived between Montgomery and Richmond during the War, for the capital of the Confederacy was at Montgomery one time and Richmond another.

"After the War, the Republicans nominated Alexander Stephens for governor. The Democrats knew they couldn't beat him, so they turned 'round and nominated him too. He had a lot of sense. He said, 'What we lost on the battle-field, we will get it back at the ballot box.' Seeb Reese, United States Senator from Hancock County, said, 'If you let the nigger have four or five dollars in his pocket he never will steal.'

Life Since Freedom

"After my father died, my mother stayed where she was till Christmas. Then she moved back to the place she came from. We went to farming. My brother and my uncle went and farmed up in Hancock County; so the next year we moved up there. We stayed there and farmed for a long while. My mother married three years afterwards. We still farmed. After awhile, I got to be sixteen years old and I wouldn't work with my stepfather, I told my mother to hire me out; if she didn't I would be gone. She hired me out all right. But the old man used all my money. The next year I made it plain to her that I wanted her to hire me out again but that nobody was to use a dollar of my money. My mother could get as much of it as she wanted but he couldn't. The first year I bought a buggy for them. The old man didn't want me to use it at all. I said, 'Well then, he can't use my money no more.' But I didn't stop helping him and giving him things. I would buy beef and give it to my mother. I knew they would all eat it. He asked me for some wheat. I wouldn't steal it like he wanted me to but I asked the man I was working for for it. He said, 'Take just as much as you want.' So I let him come up and get it. He would carry it to the mill.

Ku Klux Klan

"The Ku Klux got after Uncle Will once. He was a brave man. He had a little mare that was a race horse. Will rode right through the bunch before they ever realized that it was him. He got on the other side of them. She was gone! They kept on after him. They went down to his house one night. He wouldn't run for nothing. He shot two of them and they went away. Then he was out of ammunition. People urged him to leave, for they knew he didn't have no more bullets; but he wouldn't and they came back and killed him.

"They came down to Hancock County one night and the boys hid on both sides of the bridge. When they got in the middle of the bridge, the boys commenced to fire on them from both sides, and they jumped into the river. The darkies went on home when they got through shooting at them; but there wasn't no more Ku Klux in Hancock County. The better thinking white folks got together and stopped it.

"The Ku Klux kept the niggers scared. They cowed them down so that they wouldn't go to the polls. I stood there one night when they were counting ballots. I belonged to the County Central Committee. I went in and stood and looked. Our ballot was long; theirs was short. I stood and seen Clait Turner calling their names from our ballots. I went out and got Rube Turner and then we both went back. They couldn't call the votes that they had put down they had. Rube saw it.

"Then they said, 'Are you going to test this?'

"Rube said, 'Yes.' But he didn't because it would have cost too much money. Rube was chairman of the committee.

"The Ku Klux did a whole lot to keep the niggers away from the polls in Washington and Baldwin counties. They killed a many a nigger down there.

"They hanged a Ku Klux for killing his wife and he said he didn't mind being hung but he didn't want a damn nigger to see him die.

"But they couldn't keep the niggers in Hancock County away from the polls. There was too many of them.

Work in Little Rock

"I came to Little Rock, November 1, 1903. I came here

with surveyors. They wanted to send me to Miami but I wouldn't go. Then I went to the mortar box and made mortar. Then I went to the school board. After that I ain't had no job. I was too old. I get a little help from the government.

Opinions of the Present

"I think that the young folks ought to make great men and women. But I don't see that they are making that stride. Most of them is dropping below the mark. I think we ought to have some powerful men and women but what I see they don't stand up like they should.

Own Family

"I have three daughters, no sons. These three daughters have twelve grandchildren."

Interviewer: Miss Irene Robertson
Person interviewed: Frozie Moss (dark mulatto), Brinkley, Arkansas
Age: 69

FROZIE MOSS

"When my grandma whut raised me got free she and grandpa come to Memphis and didn't stay there long till they went to Crittenden County on a man's farm. My grandma was born in Alabama and my grandpa in Virginia. I know he wasn't in the Nat Turner rebellion, for my mother had nine children and all but me at Holly Grove, Mississippi. I was born up in Crittenden County. She died. I remember very little about my father. I jes' remember father a little. He died too. My grand parents lived at Holly Grove all during the war. They used to talk about how they did. She said hardest time she ever lived through was at Memphis. Nothing to do, nothing to eat and no places to stay. I don't know why they left and come on to Memphis. She said her master's name was Pig'ge. He wasn't married. He and his sisters lived together. My grandmother was a slave thirty years. She was a field hand. She said she would be right back in the field when her baby was two weeks old. They didn't wont the slaves to die, they cost too much money, but they give them mighty hard work to do sometimes. Grandma and grandpa was heap stronger I am at my age. They didn't know how old they was. Her master told her how long he had her when they left him and his father owned her before he died. I think they had a heap easier time after they come to Arkansas from what she said. I can't answer yo questions because I'm just tellin' you what I remembers and I was little when they used to talk so much.

"If the young generation would save anything for the time when they can't work I think they would be all right. I don't hear about them saving. They buys too much. That their only trouble. They don't know how to see ahead.

"I owns this house is all. I been sick a whole heap, spent a lot on my medicines and doctor bill. I worked on the farm till after I come to Brinkley. We bought this place here and I cooks. I cooked for Miss Molly Brinkkell, Mr. Adams and Mrs. Fowler. I washes and irons some when I can get it. Washing and ironing 'bout gone out of fashion now. I don't get no moneys. I get commodities from the Sociable Welfare. My son works and they don't give me no money."

Interviewer: Thomas Elmore Lucy
Person interviewed: Mose Moss, Russellville, Arkansas
Age: 65

MOSE MOSS

"Mose Moss is my name, suh, and I was born in 1875 in Yell County. My father was born in old Virginny in 1831 and died in Yell County, Arkansas, eight miles from Dardanelle, in 1916. Yes suh, I've lived in Pope County a good many years. I recollects some things pretty well and some not so good.

"Yes suh, my father used to talk a heap about the Ku Klux Klan, and a lot of the Negroes were afraid of em and would run when they heard they was comin' around.

"My father's name was Henry Moss. He run away from the plantation in Virginia before the War had been goin' on very long, and he j'ined the army in Tennessee—yes suh, the Confedrit army. Ho suh, his name was never found on the records, so didn't never draw no pension.

"After he was freed he always voted the Republican ticket till he died.

"After the War he served as Justice of the Peace in his township in Yell County. Yes suh, that was the time they called the Re-con-struc-tion.

"I vote the Republican ticket, but sometimes I don't

vote at the reg'lar elections. No, I've never had any trouble with my votin'.

"I works at first one thing and another but ain't doin' much now. Work is hard to get. Used to work mostly at the mines. Not able to do much of late years.

"Oh, yes, I remember some of the old songs they used to sing when my parents was living: 'Old-Time Religion' was one of em, and 'Swing Low, Sweet Chariot' was another one we liked to sing."

Interviewer: Miss Irene Robertson
Person interviewed: S.O. Mullins, Clarendon, Arkansas
Janitor for Masonic Hall
He wears a Masonic ring
Age: 80

S.O. MULLINS

"My master was B.F. Wallace—Benjamin Franklin Wallace and Katie Wallace. They had no children to my recollection.

"I was born at Brittville, Alabama. My parents' names was George W. Mullins and Millie. They had, to my recollection, one girl and three boys. Mr. Wallace moved to Arkansas before the Civil War. They moved to Phillips County. My mother and father both farm hands and when my grandmother was no longer able to do the cookin' my mother took her place. I was rally too little to recollect but they always praised Wallace. They said he never whipped one of his slaves in his life. His slaves was about free before freedom was declared. They said he was a good man. Well when freedom was declared all the white folks knowed it first. He come down to the cabins and told us. He said you can stay and finish the crops. I will feed and clothe you and give you men $10 and you women $5 apiece Christmas. That was more money then than it is now. We all stayed on and worked on shares the next year. We stayed around Poplar Grove till he died. When I was nineteen I got a job, porter on the railroad. I brought my mother to Clarendon to live with me. I was in the railroad service at least fifteen years. I was on the passenger train. Then I went to a sawmill here and then I farmed, I been doing every little thing I find to do since I been old. All I owns is a little house and six lots in the new addition. I live with my wife. She is my second wife. Cause I am old they wouldn't let me work on the levy. If I been young I could have got work. My age knocks me out of 'bout all the jobs. Some of it I could do. I sure don't get no old age pension. I gets $4 every two months janitor of the Masonic Hall.

"I have a garden. No place for hog nor cow.

"My boys in Chicago. They need 'bout all they can get. They don't help.

"The present conditions seem good. They can get cotton to pick and two sawmills run in the winter (100 men each) where folks can get work if they hire them. The stay (stave) mill is shut down and so is the button factory. That cuts out a lot of work here. The present generation is beyond me. Seems like they are gone hog wild."

Interviewer's Note

The next afternoon he met me and told me the following story:——

"One night the servants quarters was overflowin' wid Yankee soldiers. I was scared nearly to death. My mother left me and my little brother cause she didn't wanter sleep in the house where the soldiers was. We slept on the floor and they used our beds. They left next mornin'. They camped in our yard under the trees. Next morning they was ridin' out when old mistress saw 'em. She said they'd get it pretty soon. When they crossed the creek—Big Creek—half mile from our cabins I heard the guns turn in on 'em. The neighbors all fell out wid my master. They say he orter go fight too. He was sick all time. Course he wasn't sick. They come and took off 25 mules and all the chickens and he never got up. They took two fine carriage horses weighed 2,000 pounds apiece I speck. One named Lee and one Stone Wall. He never went out there. He claimed he was sick all time. One of the carriage horses was a fine big white horse and had a bay match. Folks didn't like him—said he was a coward. When I went over cross the creek after the fightin' was over, men just lay like dis[A] piled on top each other."

[A: # He used his fingers to show me how the soldiers were crossed.]

Interviewer: Miss Irene Robertson
Person interviewed: Alex Murdock, Edmondson, Arkansas
Age: 65

ALEX MURDOCK

"My owner or least my folks was owned by Dr. [HW: 'Murder'] (Murdock). He had a big farm. He was a widower. He had no children as ever I knowed of. Dr. 'Murder' raised my father's mother. He bought her at Tupelo, Mississippi. He raised mother too. She was bright color. I'm sure they stayed on after freedom 'cause I stayed there till we come to Arkansas. Father was a teamster. He followed that till he died. He owned a dray and died at Brinkley. He was well-known and honorable.

"I worked in the oil mill at Brinkley-American Oil Company.

"Mother was learned durin' slavery but I couldn't say who done it. She taught school 'round Buena Vista and Okolona, Mississippi. She learned me. I was born 1874— November 25, 1874. I heard her say she worked in the field one year. They give her some land and ploughed it so she could have a patch. It was all she could work. I don't know how much. It was her patch. Our depot was Prairie Station, Mississippi. My parents was Monroe [HW: 'Murder'] Murdock [TR: lined out] and Lucy Ann Murdock [TR: lined out] [HW: Murder]. It is spelled M-u-r-d-o-c-k.

"I farmed all my whole life. Oil milling was the surest, quickest living but I likes farmin' all right.

"I never contacted the Ku Kluxes. They was 'bout gone when I come on.

"I voted off an' on. This is the white folks' country and they going to run their gov'mint. The thing balls us up is, some tells us one way and some more tells us a different way to do. And we don't know the best way. That balls us up. Times is better than ever I seen them, for the man that wants to work.

"I get $8 a month. I work all I can."

Interviewer: Miss Irene Robertson
Person interviewed: Bessie Myers, Brassfield, Arkansas
Age: 50? didn't know

BESSIE MYERS

"My mother was named Jennie Bell. She was born in North Ca'lina (Carolina). She worked about the house. She said there was others at the house working all the time with her.

"She said they daresn't to cross the fence on other folks' land or go off up the road 'lessen you had a writing to show. One woman could write. She got a pass and this woman made some more. She said couldn't find nothing to make passes on. It happened they never got caught up. That woman didn't live very close by. She talked like she was free but was one time a slave her own self.

"Mother said she would run hide every time the Yankee men come. She said she felt safer in the dark. They took so many young women to wait on them and mother was afraid every time they would take her.

"She said she had been at the end of a corn row at daylight ready to start chopping it over, or pull fodder, or pull ears either. She said they thought to lie in bed late made you weak. Said the early fresh air what made children strong.

"On wash days they all met at a lake and washed. They had good times then. They put the clothes about on the bushes and briers and rail fences. Some one or two had to stay about to keep the clothes from a stray hog or goat till they dried. And they would forage about in the woods. It was cool and pleasant. They had to gather up the clothes in hamper baskets and bring them up to iron. Mother said they didn't mind work much. They got used to it.

"Mother told about men carried money in sacks. When they bought a slave, they open up a sack and pull out gold and silver.

"The way she talked she didn't mind slavery much. Papa lived till a few years ago but he never would talk about slavery at all. His name was Willis Bell."

Interviewer: Miss Sallie C. Miller
Person interviewed: Mary Myhand, Clarksville, Arkansas
Age: 85

MARY MYHAND

"My mammie died when I was a little girl She had three children and our white folks took us in their house and raised us. Two of us had fever and would have died if they hadn't got us a good doctor. The doctor they had first was a quack and we were getting worse until they called the other doctor, then we commence to get well. I don't know how old I am. Our birthdays was down in the mistress' Bible and when the old war come up, the house was burned and lost everything but I know I am at least 83 or 84 years old. Our white folks was so good to us. They never whipped us, and we eat what they eat and when they eat. I was born in White County, Tennessee and moved to Missouri but the folks did not like it there so we come to Benton County, Arkansas. One side of the road was Benton County and the other side was Washington County but we always had to go to Bentonville, the county seat, to tend to business. I was a little tod of a girl when the war come up. One day word come that the 'Feds' were coming through and kill all of the old men and take all the boys with them, so master took my brother and a grandson of his and started South. I was so scared. I followed them about a half mile before they found me and I begged so hard they took me with them. We went to Texas and was there about one year when the Feds gave the women on our place orders to leave their home. Said they owned it now. They had just got to Texas where we was when the South surrendered and we all come back home.

"We stayed with our white folks for about twenty years after the war. They shore was good to me. I worked for them in the house but never worked in the field. I came across the mountain to Clarksville with a Methodist preacher and his family and married here. My husband worked in a livery stable until he died, then I worked for the white folks until I fell and hurt my knee and got too old. I draws my old age pension.

"I do not know about the young generation. I am old and crippled and don't go out none."

Interviewer: Mrs. Bernice Bowden
Person interviewed: Griffin Myrax
913 Missouri Street, Pine Bluff, Arkansas
Age 77?

GRIFFIN MYRAX

"I don't know my age exactly. You know in them days people didn't take care of their ages like they do now. I couldn't give you any trace of the war, but I do remember when the Ku Klux was runnin' around.

"Oh Lord, so much of the time I heard my mother talk about the slavery. I was born in Oklahoma and my grandfather was a full-blooded Crete Indian. He was very much of a man and lived to be one hundred thirty years old. All Crete Indians named after some herb—that's what the name Myrax means.

"I heard my mother say that in slavery times the man worked all day with weights on their feet so when night come they take them off and their feet feel so light they could outran the Ku Klux. Now I heard her tell that.

"My parents moved from Oklahoma to Texas and I went to school in Marshall, Texas. All my schoolin' was in Texas—my people was tied up there. My last schoolin' was in Buchanan, Texas. The professor told my mother she would have to take me out of school for awhile, I studied too hard. I treasured my books. When other children was out playin' I was studyin'.

"There was some folks in that country that didn't get along so well. I remember there was a blind woman that the folks sent something to eat by another colored woman. But she eat it up and cooked a toadfrog for the old blind woman. That didn't occur on our place but in the neighborhood. When the people found it out they whipped her sufficient.

"When my grandfather died he didn't have a decayed tooth in his head. They was worn off like a horse's teeth but he had all of them.

"I always followed sawmill work and after I left that I followed railroading. I liked railroading. I more or less kept that in my view.

"About this slavery—I couldn't hardly pass my sentiments on it. The world is so far gone, it would be the hardest thing to put the bridle on some of the people that's runnin' wild now."

Name of Interviewer: Irene Robertson
Subject: Ex-slaves—Dreams—Herbs: Cures and Remedies
Story:—

This information given by: Tom Wylie Neal
Place of Residence: Hazen, Arkansas—Near Green Grove
Occupation: Farmer—Feeds cattle in the winter for a man in Hazen.
Age: 85
[TR: Information moved from bottom of first page.]

TOM WYLIE NEAL

His father and mother belonged to Tom Neal at Calhoun, Georgia. He remembers the big battle at Atlanta Ga. He was eight years old. He saw the lights, [saw the bullets in the air at night] and heard the boom, boom of guns and cannons. They passed along with loaded wagons and in uniforms. The horses were beautiful, and he saw lots of fine saddles and bridles. His mistress' name was Mrs. Tom Neal. She had the property and married Tom Neal. She had been married before and her first husband died but her first husband's name can't be recalled. She had two children—girls—by her first husband. Her second husband just married her to protect them all he could. He didn't do anything unless the old mistress told him to do it and how to do it. Wylie Neal was raised up with the old mistress' children. He was born a slave and lived to thirteen years. "The family had some better to eat and lots more to wear, but they gave me plenty and never did mistreat me. They had a peafowl. That was good luck, to keep some of them about on the place." They had guineas, chickens and turkeys. They never had a farm bell. He never saw one till he came to Arkansas. They blew a big "Conch shell" instead. Mistress had cows and she would pour milk or pot-liquor out in a big pewter bowl on a stump and the children would come up there from the cabins and eat [till the field hands had time to cook a meal.][HW:?] Wylie's mother was a field hand. They drank out of tin cans and gourds. The master mated his hands. Some times he would ask his young man or woman if they knew anybody they would like to marry that he was going to buy more help and if they knew anybody he would buy them if he could. The way they met folks they would get asked to corn shuckings and log rollings and Mrs. Neal always took some of her colored people to church to attend to the stock, tie the horses and hitch up, maybe feed and to nurse her little girls at church. The colored folks sat on the back seats over in a corner together. If they didn't behave or talked out they got a whipping or didn't go no more. "They kept the colored people scared to be bad."

The colored folks believed in hoodoo and witches. Heard them talking lots about witches. They said if they found anybody was a witch they would kill them. Witches took on other forms and went out to do meaness. They said sometimes some of them got through latch holes. They used buttons and door knobs whittled out of wood, and door latches with strings.

People married early in "Them days"—when Mistress' oldest girl married she gave her Sumanthy, Wylie's oldest sister when they come home [they would let her come.] They sent their children to school some but the colored folks didn't go because it was "pay school." Every year they had "pertracted meeting." Looked like a thousand people come and stayed two or three weeks along in August, in tents. "We had a big time then and some times we'd see a colored girl we'd ask the master to buy. They'd preach to the colored folks some days. Tell them the law. How to behave and serve the Lord." When Wylie was twelve years old the "Yanks" came and tore up the farm. "It was just like these cyclones that is [TR: illegible word] around here in Arkansas, exactly like that."

His mistress left and he never saw her again. General [HW: John Bell] Hood was the [TR: illegible word] he thinks, but he was given to Captain Condennens to wait on him. They went to Marietta, Ga., and Kingston, Ga. "Rumors came about that we were free and everybody was drifting around. The U.S. Government gave us food then like they do now and we hunted work. Everybody nearly froze and starved. We wore old uniforms and slept anywhere we could find, an old house or piece of a house. In 1865-1869—the Ku Klux was miserable on the colored folks. Lots of folks died out of consumption in the spring and pneumonia all winter.

"There wasn't any doctors seeing after colored folks for they had no money and they used herbs—only medicine they could get."

Only herbs he remembers he used is: chew black snake roots to settle sick stomach. Flux weed tea for disordered stomach. People eat so much "messed up food" lot of them got sick.

Wylie Neal wandered about and finally came to Chattanooga. They got old uniforms and victuals from the "Yanks" about a year.

Colonel Stocker come and got up a lot of hands and paid their way to Memphis on the train. From there they were put on the Molly Hamilton boat and went to Linden, Arkansas, on the St. Francis River. "He fared fine" there. In 1906[TR: ?] he came to Hazen and since then he has owned small farms at Biscoe and forty acres near Hazen. It was joining the old Joe Perry place. Dr. ---- got a mortgage on it and took it. Wylie Neal lives with his niece and she is old too so they get relief and a pension.

"He don't believe in dreams but some dreams like when you dream of the dead there's sho' goner be falling weather." He "don't dream much" he says.

He has a birthmark on his leg. It looks like a bunch of berries. He never heard what caused it. It has always been there.

Interviewer: Mrs. Bernice Bowden
Person interviewed: Sally Nealy
105 Mulberry Street, Pine Bluff, Arkansas
Age: 91

SALLY NEALY

"Yes mam, I was a slave! I was sixteen years old when the war begun. I was born in Texas.

"My old master was John Hall and my young master was Marse Dick. Marse John went to war the 5th day of May in 1861 and he was killed in June. They wasn't nothin' left to bring home but his right leg and his left arm. They knowed it was him cause his name was tattooed on his leg.

"He was a mean rascal. He brought us up from the plantation and pat us on the head and give us a little whisky and say 'Your name is Sally or Mary or Mose' just like we was dogs.

"My old mistress, Miss Caroline, was a mean one too. She was the mother of eight children—five girls and three boys. When she combed her hair down low on her neck she was all right but when she come down with it done up on the top of her head—look out.

"It was my job to scrub the big cedar churns with brick dust and Irish potato and polish the knives and forks the same way. Then every other day I had to mold twelve dozen candles and sweep the yard with a dogwood bresh broom.

"She didn't give us no biscuits or sugar 'cept on Christmas. Jest shorts and molasses for our coffee. When the Yankee soldiers come through old mistress run and hide in the cellar but the Yankees went down in the collar too and took all the hams and honey and brandied peaches she had.

"They didn't have no doctors for the niggers then. Old mistress just give us some blue mass and castor oil and they didn't give you nothin' to take the taste out your mouth either.

"Oh lord, I know 'bout them Ku Klux. They wore false faces and went around whippin' people.

"After the surrender I went to stay with Miss Fulton. She was good to me and I stayed with her eleven years. She wanted to know how old I was so my father went to Miss Caroline and she say I 'bout twenty now.

"Some white folks was good to their slaves. I know one man, Alec Yates, when he killed hogs he give the niggers five of 'em. Course he took the best but that was all right.

"After freedom the Yankees come and took the colored folks away to the marshal's yard and kept them till they got jobs for 'em. They went to the white folks houses and took things to feed the niggers.

"I ain't been married but once. I thought I was in love but I wasn't. Love is a itchin' 'round the heart you can't get at to scratch.

"I 'member one song they sung durin' the war

    'The Yankees are comin' through
    By fall sez I
    We'll all drink stone blind
    Johnny fill up the bowl.'"

United States. Work Projects Administration

Slave Narratives

FOLKLORE SUBJECTS
Name of interviewer: Mrs. Bernice Bowden
Subject: Songs of Civil War Days
Story:—Information

This information given by: Sally Neeley
Place of residence: 105 N. Mulberry, Pine Bluff, Arkansas
Occupation: None
Age: 90

[TR: Information moved from bottom of first page.]
[TR: Same as previous informant (Sally Nealy).]

SALLY NEELEY

(1)
"In eighteen hundred and sixty-one
Football (?) sez I;
In eighteen hundred and sixty-one
That's the year the war begun
We'll all drink stone blind,
Johnny, come fill up the bowl.

(2)
"In eighteen hundred and sixty-two
Football (?) sez I;
In eighteen hundred and sixty-two
That's the year we put 'em through
We'll all drink stone blind,
Johnny, come fill up the bowl.

(3)
"In eighteen hundred and sixty-three

Football (?) sez I;
In eighteen hundred and sixty-three
That's the year we didn't agree
We'll all drink stone blind.
Johnny, come fill up the bowl.

(4)
"In eighteen hundred and sixty-four
Football (?) sez I;
In eighteen hundred and sixty-four
We'll all go home and fight no more
We'll all drink stone blind.
Johnny, come fill up the bowl.

(5)
"In eighteen hundred and sixty-five
Football (?) sez I;
In eighteen hundred and sixty-five
We'll have the Rebels dead or alive
We'll all drink stone blind,
Johnny, come fill up the bowl.

(6)
"In eighteen hundred and sixty-six
Football (?) sez I;
In eighteen hundred and sixty-six
We'll have the Rebels in a helava fix
We'll all drink stone blind,
Johnny, come fill up the bowl.

(7)
"In eighteen hundred and sixty-seven
Football (?) sez I;

In eighteen hundred and sixty-seven
We'll have the Rebels dead and at the devil
We'll all drink stone blind.
Johnny, came fill up the bowl."

Interviewer's Comment

The word "football" doesn't sound right in this song, but I was unable to find it in print, and Sally seemed to think it was the right word.

Sally is a very wicked old woman and swears like a sailor, but she has a remarkable memory.

She was "bred and born" in Rusk County, Texas and says she came to Pine Bluff when it was "just a little pig."

Says she was sixteen when the Civil War began.

I have previously reported an interview with her.

Interviewer: Miss Irene Robertson
Person interviewed: Wylie Nealy [HW: Biscoe Arkansas?]
Age: 85

WYLIE NEALY

I was born in 1852. I am 85 years old. I was born in Gordon County. The closest town was Calhoun, South Carolina. My sister died in '59. That's the first dead, person I ever saw. One of my sisters was give away and another one was sold before the Civil War started. Sister Mariah was give to the young mistress, Miss Ella Conley. I didn't see her sold. I never seed nobody sold but I heard 'em talking about it. I had five sisters and one brother. My father was a free man always. He was a Choctaw Indian. Mother was part Cherokee Indian. My mother's mistress was Mrs. Martha Christian. He died and she married Tom Nealy, the one they call me fur, Wylie Nealy.

Liberty and Freedom was all I ever heard any colored folks say dey expected to get out of de war, and mighty proud of dot. Nobody knowed they was goin to have a war till it was done broke out and they was fightin about it. Didn't nobody want land, they jess wanted freedom. I remembers when Lincoln was made the President both times and when he was killed. I recollects all that like yesterday.

The army had been through and swept out everything. There wasn't a chicken or hog nowhere to be had, took the stock and cattle and all the provisions. So de slaves jess had to scatter out and leave right now. And after de army come through. I was goin back down to the old place and some soldiers passed riding along and one said "Boy where you goin? Said nothing up there." I says, "I knows it." Then he say "Come on here, walk along back there" and I followed him. I was twelve years old. He was Captain McClendenny. Then when I got to the camp wid him he say "You help around here." I got sick and they let me go back home then to Resacca, Georgia and my mother died. When I went back they sent me to Chattanooga with Captain Story. I was in a colored regiment nine months, I saw my father several times while I was at Chattanooga. We was in Shermans army till it went past Atlanta. They burned up the city. Two of my masters come out of the war alive and two dead. I was mustered out in August 1865. I stayed in camp till my sisters found a cabin to move in. Everybody got rations issued out. It was a hard time. I got hungry lots times. No plantations was divided and the masters didn't have no more than the slaves had when the war was done. After the Yankees come in and ripped them up old missus left and Mr. Tom Nealy was a Home Guard. He had a class of old men. Never went back or seen any more of them. Everybody left and a heap of the colored folks went where rations could be issued to them and some followed on in the armies. After I was mustered out I stayed around the camps and went to my sister's cabin till we left there. Made anything we could pick up. Men come in there getting people to go work for them. Some folks went to Chicago. A heap of the slaves went to the northern cities. Colonel Stocker, a officer in the Yankee army, got us to come to a farm in Arkansas. We wanted to stay together is why we all went on the farm. May 1866, when we come to Arkansas is the first farmin I had seen done since I left Tom Nealy's place. Colonel Stocker is mighty well known in St. Francis County. He brought lots of families, brought me and my brother, my two brothers and a nephew. We come on the train. It took four or five days. When we got to Memphis we come to Linden on a boat "Molly Hamilton" they called it. I heard it was sunk at Madison long time after that. Colonel Stocker promised to pay $6 a month and feed us. When Christmas come he said all I was due was $12.45. We made a good crop. That wasn't it. Been there since May. Had to stay till got all the train and boat fare paid. There wasn't no difference in that and slavery 'cept they couldn't sell us.

I heard a heap about the Ku Klux but I nebber seed them. Everybody was scared of them.

The first votin I ever heard of was in Grant's election. Both black and white voted. I voted Republican for Grant. Lot of the southern soldiers was franchised and couldn't vote. Just the private soldiers could vote at tall. I don't know why it was. I was a slave for thirteen years from birth. Every slave could vote after freedom. Some colored folks held office. I knew several magistrates and sheriffs. There was one at Helena (Arkansas) and one at Marianna. He was a High Sheriff. I voted some after that but I never voted in the last Presidento election. I heard 'em say it wasn't no use, this man would be elected anyhow. I sorter quit off long time ago.

In 1874 and 1875 I worked for halves and made nough to buy a farm in St. Francis County. It cost $925. I bought it in 1887. Eighty acres to be cleared down in the bottoms. My family helped and when my help got shallow, the children leaving me, I sold it for $2,000, in 1904. I was married jess once and had eight children; five livin and three dead. Me and the old woman went to Oklahoma. We went in January and come back to Biscoe (Arkansas) in September. It wasn't no place for farming. I bought 40 acres from Mr. Aydelott and paid him $500. I sold it and come to Mr. Joe Perry's place, paid $500 for 40 acres of timber land. We cleared it and I got way in debt and lost it. Clear lost it! Ize been working anywhere I could make a little since then. My wife died and I been doing little jobs and stays about with my children. The Welfare gives me a little check and some supplies now and then.

No maam, I can't read much. I was not learnt. I could figure a little before my eyes got bad. The white folks did send their children to pay schools but we colored children had to stay around the house and about in the field to work. I never got no schoolin. I went with old missus to camp meeting down in Georgia one time and got to go to white church sometimes. At the camp meeting there was a big tent and all around it there was brush harbors and tents where people stayed to attend the meetins. They had four meetins a day. Lots of folk got converted and shouted. They had a lot of singings They had a lots to eat and a big time.

I don't think much about these young folks now. It seems lack everybody is having a hard time to live among us colored folks. Some white folks has got a heap and fine cars to get about in. I don't know what go in to become of 'em.

People did sing more than I hear them now but I never could sing. They sing a lot of foolish songs and mostly religious songs.

I don't recollect of any slave uprising. I never heard of any. We didn't know they was going to have a war till they was fighting. Yes maam, they heard Lincoln was going to set 'em free, but they didn't know how he was going to do it. Everybody wanted freedom. Mr. Hammond (white) ask me not long ago if I didn't think it best to bring us from Africa and be slaves than like wild animals in Africa. He said we was taught about God and the Gospel over here if we was slaves. I told him I thought dot freedom was de best anywhere.

We had a pretty hard time before freedom. My mother was a field woman. When they didn't need her to work they hired her out and they got the pay. The master mated the colored people. I got fed from the white folks table whenever I curried the horses. I was sorter raised up with Mr. Nealy's children. They didn't mistreat me. On Saturday the mistress would blow a cone shell and they knowed to go and get the rations. We got plenty to eat. They had chickens and ducks and geese and plenty milk. They did have hogs. They had seven or eight guineas and a lot of peafowls. I never heard a farm bell till I come to Arkansas. The children et from pewter bowls or earthen ware. Sometimes they et greens or milk from the same bowl, all jess dip in. The Yankees took me to General Hood's army and I was Captain McCondennen's helper at the camps. [HW: ?] We went down through Marietta and Atlanta and through Kingston. Shells come over where we lived. I saw 'em fight all the time. Saw the light and heard the roaring of de guns miles away. It looked like a storm where the army went along. They tramped the wheat and oats and cotton down and turned the horses in on the corn. The slaves show did hate to see the Yankees waste everything. They promised a lot and wasn't as good as the old masters. All dey wanted was to be waited on too. The colored folks was freed when the Yankees took all the stock and cattle and rations. Everybody had to leave and let the government issue them rations. Everybody was proud to be free. They shouted and sung. They all did pretty well till the war was about to end then they was told to scatter and no whars to go. Cabins all tore down or burned. No work to do. There was no money to pay. I wore old uniforms pretty well till I come to Arkansas. I been here in Hazen since 1906. I come on a boat from Memphis to Linden. Colonel Stocker brought a lot of us on the train. The name of the boat was Molly Hamilton. It was a big boat and we about filled it. I show was glad to get back on a farm.

I don't know what is goin to become of the young folks. Everything is so different now and when I was growin up I don't know what will become of the younger generation.

Interviewer: Miss Irene Robertson
Person interviewed: Emaline Neland, Marianna, Arkansas
Age: Born 1859

EMALINE NELAND

"I was born two years before the War. I was born in Murray County, Tennessee. It was middle Tennessee. When I come to remembrance I was in Grant County, Arkansas. When I remember they raised wheat and corn and tobacco. Mother's master was Dr. Harrison. His son was married and me and my brother Anderson was give to him. He come to Arkansas 'fore ever I could remember. He was a farmer but I never seen him hit a lick of work in my life. He was good to me and my brother. She was good too. I was the nurse. They had two children. Brother was a house boy. Me and her girl was about the same size but I was the oldest. Being with the other children I called her mother too. I didn't know no other mother till freedom.

"Freedom! Well, here is the very way it all was: Old master told her (mother) she was free. He say, 'Go get your children, you free as I is now.' Ain't I heard her say it many a time? Well, mother come in a ox wagon what belong to him and got us. They run me down, caught me and got me in the wagon. They drove twenty-five miles. Old Dr. Harrison had moved to Arkansas. Being with the other children I soon learnt to call her ma. She had in all ten or eleven children. She was real dark.

"Pa was a slave too. He was a low man. He was a real bright man. He was brighter than I is. He belong to a widow woman named Tedford. He renamed his self after freedom. He took the name Brown 'stead of Tedford. I never heard him say why he wasn't satisfied with his own name. He was a soldier. He worked for the Yankees.

"After the War pa and ma got back together and lived together till she died. There was five days' difference in their deaths. They died of pneumonia. He was 64 years old and she was 54 years old. I was at home when pa come from the War. All my sisters was light, one sister had sandy hair like pa. She was real light. Ma was a good all 'round woman. She cooked more than anything else. She nursed. Dr. Harrison told her to stay till her husband come back or all the time if he didn't ever come back. Ma never worked in the field. When pa come he moved us on a place to share crop. Ma never worked in the field. He was buying a home in Grant County. He started to Mississippi and stopped close to Helena and ten or twelve miles from Marianna. He had a soldier friend wouldn't let him go. He told him this was a better country. He decided to stay down in here.

"I heard a whole heap about the Ku Klux. One time when a crowd was going to church, we heard horse's feet coming; sound like they would run over us. We all got clear out of reach so they wouldn't run over us. They had on funny caps was all I could see, they went so fast. We give them the clear road and they went on. That is all I ever seen of the Ku Klux.

"I seen Dr. Harrison's wife. She was a little old lady but we left after I went there.

"I used to sew for the public. Yes, white and colored folks. I learnt my own self to sew. I never had but one boy in my life. He died at seven weeks old. I raised a stepson. I married twice. I married at home both times. Just a quiet marriage and a colored preacher married me both times.

"The present conditions is hard. I want things and can't get 'em. If I had the strength to hold out to work I could get along.

"The present generation—young white and black—blinds me. They turns corners too fast. They going so fast they don't have time to take advice. They promise to do better but they don't. They do like they want to do and don't tell nobody till they done it. I say they just running way with their selves.

"I get $8 and a little help along. I'm thankful for it. It is a blessing I tell you."

United States. Work Projects Administration

Interviewer: Samuel S. Taylor
Person interviewed: Henry Nelson
904 E. Fifth Street, Little Rock, Arkansas
Age: About 70

HENRY NELSON

"My name is Henry Nelson. I was born in Arkansas—Crittenden County near Memphis, Tennessee. I was born not far from Memphis but on this side.

"My mother's name was Adeline Taylor. That was her old slavery folks' name. She was a Taylor before she married my father—Nelson. My father's first name was Green. I don't remember none of my grandparents. My father's mother died before I come to remember and I know my mother's mother died before I could remember.

"My father was born in Mississippi—Sardis, Mississippi—and my mother was a Tennesseean—Cartersville[HW:?] Tennessee, twenty-five miles above Memphis. [HW: Carter, in Carter County, about 35 m. north of Memphis, but no Cartersville.] [TR: moved from bottom of following page.]

"After peace was declared, they met in Tennessee. That was where my mother was born, you know. They fell in love with one another in Shelby County, and married there. My mother had been married once before during slavery time. She had been made to marry by her master. Her first husband was named Eli. He was my oldest sister's father. Him and my mother had the same master and missis. She was made to marry him. She was only thirteen years old when she married him. She was fine and stout and her husband was fine and stout, and they wanted more from that stock. I don't know how old he was but he was a lot older than she was. He was a kind of an elderly man. She had just one child by him—my oldest sister, Georgia. She was only married a short time before freedom came.

"My father farmed. He was always a farmer—raised cotton and corn. My mother was a farmer too. Both of them—that is both of her husbands—were farmers.

"My mother and father used to go off to places to dance and the pateroles would get after them. You had to have a pass to go off your place and if you didn't have a pass, they would make you warm. Some of them would get caught sometimes and the pateroles would whip them. They would sure got whipped if they didn't have a pass.

"The old master come out and told them they were free when peace was declared. He said, 'You are free this morning—free as I am.'

"Right after the War, my mother come further down in Tennessee, and that is how she met my father where she was when she was married. They went farming. They farmed on shares—sharecropped. They were on a big place called Ensley place. The man that owned the place was called Nuck Ensley.

"My mother and father didn't have no schooling. I never heard that they were bothered by the Ku Klux.

"She didn't live with her first husband after slavery. She left him when she was freed. She never did intend to marry him. She was forced to that."

Interviewer's Comment

Nelson evidently rents rooms. A yellow sallow-faced, cadaverous, and dissatisfied looking "gentleman" went into the house eyeing me suspiciously as he passed. In a moment he was out again interrupting the old man with pointless remarks. In—out again—standing over me—peering on my paper in the offensive way that ill-bred people have. He straightened up with a disgusted look on his face. He couldn't read shorthand.

"What's that you're writin'?"

"Shorthand."

"What's that about?"

"History."

"History uv whut?"

"Slavery."

"He don't know nothin' about slavery."

"Thank you. However, if he says he does, I'll just continue to listen to him if you don't mind."

"Humph," and the "yellow gentleman" passed in.

Out again—eyeing both the old man and me with disgust that was unconcealed. To him, "You don't know whutchu're doin'."

Deep silence by all. Exit the yellow brother.

To the old man, I said, "Is that your son?"

"Lawd, no, that's jus' a roomer."

Out came the yellow brother again. "See here, Uncle, if you want me to fix that fence you'd bettuh come awn out heah now. It's gettin' dark."

I closed my notebook and arose. "Don't let me interfere with your program, Brother Nelson."

The old man settled back in his chair. His eyes inspected the sky, his jaw "sorta" set. The yellow brother looked at him a minute and passed on.

Five minutes later. Enter, the Madam. She also was of the yellow variety with the suspicious and spiteful look of an undersized black Belgian police dog. A moment of silence—a word to him.

"You don't know whutchu're doin'." Silence all around. To me, "You're upsettin' my work."

I arose. "Madam, I'm sorry."

The old man spoke, "You ain't keepin' me from nothin'."

"Well, I said, you've given me a nice start; I'll come again and get the rest."

Interviewer: Miss Irene Robertson
Person interviewed: Henry Nelson, Edmondson, Arkansas
Age: 70
[TR: Appears to be same as last informant despite different address.]

HENRY NELSON

"My mother belong to the Taylors close to Carterville, Tennessee. My father never was sold. He belong to the Nelsons. My parents married toreckly after the surrender and come on to this state. I was born ten miles from Edmondson. Their names was Adeline and Green Nelson. They didn't get nothing after freedom like land or a horse. I'm seventy years old and I would have known.

"I was at Alton, Illinois in the lead works thirteen years ago and I had a stroke. I been cripple ever since.

"My folks never spoke of being nothing but field hands. Folks used to be proud of their crops, go look over them on Sunday when company come. Now if they got a garden they hide it and don't mention it. Times is changed that way.

"Clothes ain't as lasty as they used to be. People has a heap more money to spend and don't raise and have much at home as they did when I was a child. Times is all turned around and folks too. I always had plenty till I couldn't do hard work. I farmed my early life. We didn't have much money but we had rations and warm clothes. I cleared new ground, hauled wood, big logs. I steamboated on the Sun, Kate Adams, and One Arm John. I helped with the freight. I railroaded with pick and shovel and in the lead mines. I worked from Memphis to Helena on boats a good while. I come back here to farm. Time is changed and I'm changed.

"It has been so long since I heard my parents tell about slavery I couldn't tell you straight. She told till she died, talked about how the Yankees done when they come through. They took axes and busted up good furniture. They et up and wasted the rations, then humor up the black folks like they was in their favor when they was settin' out wasting their living. They done made it to live on. Some followed them and some stayed on. They wanted freedom but it wasn't like they thought it would be. They didn't know how it would be. They didn't know it meant set out. Seem like they left. In some ways times was better and some ways it was worse. They had to work or starve is what they told me. That's the way I found freedom. 'Course their owners made them work and he looked out for the ration and in slavery.

"I keeps up my own self all I can. I don't get help."

Interviewer: Mrs. Bernice Bowden
Person interviewed: Iran Nelson
603 E. Fourteenth Ave., Pine Bluff, Ark.
Age: 77

IRAN NELSON

"Yes ma'm, they fotch me from Mississippi to Arkansas on the steamboat—you know they didn't have railroads then. They fotch my mother and they went back after grandfather and grandmother too.

"Dr. Noell was our master and he had us under mortgage to his brother-in-law. They fotched us here till he could get straight from that debt, but fore that could be, we got free.

"I knowed slavery times. I member seem' em lash some of the rest but you know I wasn't big enough to put in the fields. Old mistress say when I got big enough, she goin' take me for a house girl. When they fotched mama and grandmother here they had eighty some odd head of niggers. They was gwine carry em back home after they got that mortgage paid but the war come.

"I member when the Yankees come, my white folks would run and hide and hide us colored folks too. Boss man had the colored folks get all the meat out of the smokehouse and hide it in the peach orchard in the grass.

"I used to play with old mistress daughter Addie. We

would play in the parlor and after we moved to town some of the little girls would pick up and go home. You know these town folks didn't believe in playin' with the colored folks.

"After mama was free she stayed right there on the place and made a crop. Raised eight hundred bales and the average was nine. Mama plowed and hoed too. I had to work right with her too.

"I never went to school but once. I learned my ABC's but couldn't read. My next ABC's was a hoe in my hand. Mama had a switch right under her belt. I worked but I couldn't keep up. Just seein' that switch was enough. I had a pretty good time when I was young, but I had to go all the time."

Interviewer: Mrs. Bernice Bowden
Person interviewed: James Henry Nelson
1103 Orange, Pine Bluff, Arkansas
Age: 82
Occupation: Gardener

JAMES HENRY NELSON

"I member all about the war—why of cose. I saddled many a cavalry hoss. I tell you how I know how old I am. Old master, Henry Stanley of Athens, Alabama, moved to Palaski, Tennessee and left me with young mistress to take care of things. One day we was drivin' up some stock and I said, 'Miss Nannie, how old is you?' And she said, 'I'm seventeen.' I was old enough to have the knowledge she would know how old I was and I said, 'How old am I?' And she said, 'You is seven years old.' That was durin' the war.

"I remember the soldiers comin' and stoppin' at our building—Yankees and Southern soldiers, too. They fit all around our plantation.

"The Yankees taken me when I was a little fellow. About two years after the war started, young Marse Henry went to war and took a colored man with him but he ran away—he wouldn't stay with the Rebel army. So young Marse Henry took me. I reckon I was bout ten. I know I was big enough to saddle a cavalry hoss. We carried three horses—his hoss, my hoss and a pack hoss. You know chillun them days, they made em do a man's work. I studied bout my mother durin' the war, so they let me go home.

"One day I went to mill. They didn't low the chillun to lay around, and while I was at the mill a Yankee soldier ridin' a white hoss captured me and took me to Pulaski, Tennessee and then I was in the Yankee army. I wasn't no size and I don't think he would a took me if it hadn't been for the hoss.

"We come back to Athens and the Rebels captured the whole army. Colonel Camp was in charge and General Forrest captured us and I was carried south. We was marchin' along the line and a Rebel soldier said, 'Don't you want to go home and stay with my wife?' And so I went there, to Millville, Alabama. Then he bound me to a friend of his and I stayed there till the war bout ended. I was getting along very well but a older boy 'suaded me to run away to Decatur, Alabama.

"Oh I seen lots of the war. Bof sides was good to me. I've seen many a scout. The captain would say 'By G----, close the ranks.' Captains is right crabbed. I stayed back with the hosses.

"After the war I worked about for this one and that one. Some paid me and some didn't.

"I can remember back to Breckenridge; and I can remember hearin' em say 'Hurrah for Buchanan!' I'm just tellin' you to show how fur back I can remember. I used to have a book with a picture of Abraham Lincoln with an axe on his shoulder and a picture of that log cabin, but somebody stole my book.

"I worked for whoever would take me—I had no

mother then. If I had had parents to make me go to school, but I got along very well. The white folks taught me not to have no bad talk. They's all dead now and if they wasn't I'd be with them.

"I'm a natural born farmer—that's all I know. The big overflow drownded me out and my wife died with pellagra in '87. She was a good woman and nice to white folks. I'm just a bachin' here now. I did stay with my daughter but she is mean to me, so I just picked up my rags and moved into this room where I can live in peace. I'm a christian man, and I can't live right with her. When colored folks is mean, they's meaner than white folks.

"I'm gettin' along very well now. I been with white folks all my day—and it's hard for me to get along with my folks.

"In one way the world is crueler than they used to be. They don't appreciate things like they used to. They have no feelin's and don't care nothin' bout the olden people.

"Well, good-bye, I'm proud of you."

Interviewer: Miss Irene Robertson
Person interviewed: John Nelson, Holly Grove, Arkansas
Age: 76

JOHN NELSON

"My parents was Jazz Nelson and Mahaney Nelson. He come from Louisiana durin' slavery. She come from Richmond, Virginia. I think from what they said he come to Louisiana from there too. They was plain field hands.

"My folks belong to Miss Mary Ann Richardson and Massa Harve Richardson. They had five children and every one dead now. They lived at Duncan Station.

"The white folks told em they was free. They had no place to go and they been workin' the crop. White folks glad for em to stay and work on. And the truth is they was glad to git to stay on cause they had no place to go. They kept stayin' on a long time.

"I was so small I don't know if the Ku Klux ever did come bout our place at tall."

United States. Work Projects Administration

Interviewer: Miss Irene Robertson
Person interviewed: Lettie Nelson
St. Marys Street, Helena, Arkansas
Age: 55 or 56?

LETTIE NELSON

"Grandma was Patsy Smith. She said in slavery they had a certain amount of cotton to pick. If they didn't have that amount they would put their heads between the rails of the fences and whoop them. They whooped them in the ebenin' when they weighed up the cotton. Grandma was raised in Virginia. She was light. Mama was light. They was carried from Virginia to Louisiana in wagons. They found clothes along the road people had lost. She said several bundles of good clothes. They thought they had dropped off of wagons ahead of them. They washed and wore the clothes. Some of 'em fit so they wore them. Mama left her husband and brother in Virginia. Ed Smith was her second husband. He was a light man. My grandpa was a field man. I never heard if grandpa was sold. Jimmie Stansberry was the man that bought or brought mama and grandma to Louisiana. Mama cooked and worked in the field both. Grandma did too. She cooked in Louisiana more than mama. They belong to Lou and Jimmie Stansberry and they had two boys. They lived close to Minden, Louisiana. I don't know so much about my parents and grandma talked but we didn't pay enough attention to remember it all. She was old and got things confused.

"They was glad when freedom come but they lived on with Jimmie Stansberry. I remember them. Grandma raised me after my parents died. Then she lived with me till she died. She was awful old when she died. They would talk about how different Virginia and Louisiana was. It took them a long time to make that trip."

Interviewer: Mrs. Bernice Bowden
Person interviewed: Mattie Nelson
710 E. Fourth Street, Pine Bluff, Arkansas
Age: 72

MATTIE NELSON

"I was born in Chicot County, Arkansas in '65. They said I was born on the roadside while we was on our way here from Texas. They had to camp they said. Some people called it emigrate. Now that's the straightest way I can tell it.

"Our mistress and master was named Chapman. I member when I was a child mistress used to be so good to us. After surrender my parents stayed right on there with the Chapmans, stayed right on the place till they died.

"My mudder and pappy neither one of em could read or write, but I went to school. I always was apt. I am now. I always was one to work—yes ma'm—rolled logs, hope clean up new ground—yes ma'm. When we was totin' logs, I'd say, "Put the big end on me" but they'd say, "No, you're a woman." Yes ma'm I been here a long time. I do believe in stirrin' work for your livin', yes ma'm, that's what I believe in.

"I been workin' ever since I was six years old. My daughter was just like me—she had a gift, but she died. I seen all my folks die and that lets me know I got to die too.

"White folks used to come along in buggies, and hoss back too, and stop and watch me plow. Seem like the hotter the sun was the better I liked it.

"Yes ma'm, I done all kinds a work and I feels it now, too."

Interviewer: Mrs. Bernice Bowden
Person interviewed: Dan Newborn
1000 Louisiana, Pine Bluff, Arkansas
Age: 78

DAN NEWBORN

"I was born in 1860. Born in Knoxville, Tennessee. I suppose it was in the country.

"Solomon Walton was my mother's owner and my father belonged to the Newborns. My grandmother belonged to the Buggs in Richmond, Virginia and she was sold to the Waltons. When my mother died in '65 my grandmother raised me. After she was freed she went to the Powell Clayton place. Her daughter lived there and she sent up the river and got her. I went too. Me and two more boys.

"I never went to school but about thirty days. Hardly learned my alphabet.

"In '66, my grandmother bound two of us to Powell Clayton for our 'vittils' and clothes and schoolin', but I didn't get no schoolin'. I waited in the house. Stayed there three years, then we come back to the Walton place.

"My grandmother said the Waltons treated her mean. Beat her on the head and that was part of her death. Every spring her head would run. She said they didn't get much of somethin' to eat.

"I was married 'fore my grandmother died—to this

wife that died two months ago. We stayed together fifty-seven years.

"To my idea, this younger generation is too wild—not near as settled as when I was comin' up. They used to obey. Why, I slept in the bed with my grandmother till I was married. She whipped me the day before I was married. It was 'cause I had disobeyed her. Children will resist their mothers now.

"I think the colored people is better off now 'cause they got more privilege, but the way some of 'em use their privilege, I think they ought to be slaves.

"My grandmother taught me not to steal. My white folks here have trusted me with two and three hundred dollars. I don't want nothin' in the world but mine.

"I been workin' here for Fox Brothers thirty-eight years and they'll tell you there's not a black mark against me.

"I used to be a mortar maker and used to sample cotton. Then I worked at the Cotton Belt Shops eight years.

"I've bought me a home that cost $780.

"I don't mind tellin' about myself 'cause I've been honest and you can go up the river and get my record.

"Out of all due respect to everybody, the Yankees is the ones I like.

"Vote? Oh yes, Republican ticket. I like Roosevelt's administration. If I could vote now, I'd vote for him. He has done a whole lot of good."

Interviewer: Miss Irene Robertson
Person Interviewed: Sallie Newsom
Brinkley, Ark.
Age 75?

SALLIE NEWSOM

"Miss, I don't know my age, but I know I is old. I'm sick now.

"My grandma's mistress and mama's mistress and my mistress was Miss Jennie Brawner at Thomasville, Georgia. Me and my oldest sister was born in Atlanta. Then freedom come on. My own papa wanted mama to follow him to Mississippi. He had a wife there. She wouldn't go. She stayed on a while with Mr. Acy and Miss Jennie. They come from Virginia. Her name was Catherine.

"Grandma toted her big hoop dresses about and carried her trains up off the floor. Combed her long glossy hair. Mama was a house girl too, but then grandma took to the kitchen. She was the cook then.

"Old Miss Jennie wanted mama to give her my oldest sister Lulu, so mama gave her to her. Then when we started to come to Holly Grove, Mississippi, Miss Jennie still wanted her. Mama didn't want to part from her. She was married again and brought me but my aunts told mama to leave her there, she would have a good home and be educated, so she 'greed to leave her two years. She sent back for her at the end of two years; she wrote and didn't want to come. She was still at Miss Jennie's. I haben seen her from the day we left Atlanta till this very day. A woman, colored woman, was here in Brinkley once seen her. Said she was so fine and nice. Had nice soft skin and was well to do. I have wrote but my letters come back. I know Miss Jennie is dead, and my sister may be by now.

"My papa was Abe Brooks. His master was Mars Jonas Brooks. Old master give him to the young master. He was rich, rich, and traveled all time. His pa give him a servant. He cooked for him, drove his carriage—they called it a brake in them days—followed him to the hotels and barrooms. He drink and give him a dram. When he was freed he come to Mississippi with the Brooks to farm for them. I went to see my papa at Waterford, Miss.

"When we was at Holly Springs, Mississippi my cousin was a railroad man so he helped me run away. He paid my way. I come to Clarendon. I cooked, washed and ironed. In two or three years I went back to see mama. They was glad to see me. They had eight children.

"I couldn't guarantee you about the eight younger children, but there ain't a speck of no kind of blood about me and Lulu Violet but African. We are slick black Negroes. (She is very black, large and bony.)

"Miss Jennie Brawner had one son—Gus Brawner—and he may be living now in Atlanta.

"My uncle said he seen the Yankees come through Thomasville, Georgia. I never seen an army of them. I seen soldiers, plenty of em. None of the Brooks or Brawners went to war that I heard of. I was kept close and too young to know much of what happened. I heard about the Ku Klux but I never seen them.

"I know Miss Jennie Brawner come from Virginia but I don't brought grandma with her or bought her. She never did say.

"I don't vote. My husband voted, I don't know how he voted.

"Since I been sick, I get a check and commodities."

United States. Work Projects Administration

Interviewer: Miss Sallie C. Miller
Person interviewed: Pete Newton, Clarksville, Arkansas
Age: 83 [TR: 85?]
Occupation: Farmer and day laborer

PETE NEWTON

"My white folks was as good to me as they could be. I ain't got no kick to make about my white people. The boys was all brave. I was raised on the farm. I staid with my boss till I was nearly grown. When the war got so hot my boss was afraid the 'Feds' would get us. He sent my mammy to Texas and sent me in the army with Col. Bashom, to take care of his horses. I was about eleven or twelve years old. Col. Bashom was always good to me. He always found a place for me to sleep and eat. Sometimes after the colonel left the folks would run as off and not let me stay but I never told the colonel. I went to Boston, Texas with the colonel and his men and when he went on the big raid into Missouri he left me in Sevier County, Arkansas with his horses 'Little Baldy' and 'Orphan Boy'. They was race horses. The colonel always had race horses. He was killed at Pilot Knob, Missouri. After the colonel was killed his son George (I shore did think a lot of George) come after me and the horses and brough' us home.

"While I was in Arkadelphia with Col. Bashom's horses, I went down to the spring to water the horses. The artillery was there cleaning a big cannon they called 'Old Tom'. Of course I went up to watch them. One of the men saw me and hollered, 'Stick his head in the cannon.' It liked to scared me to death. I jumped on that race horse and run. I reconed I would have been killed but my uncle was there and saw me and stopped the horse.

"Another time we went to a place and me and another colored boy was taking care of the horses while our masters eat dinner. I saw some watermelons in the garden with a paling fence around it. I said if the other boy would pull a paling off I would crawl through and get us a watermelon. He did but the man who owned the place saw me just as I got the melon and whipped us and told us if we hollered he would kill us. We didn't holler and we never told Col. Bashom either.

"After the war my mammie come back from Texas and took me over to Dover to live but my old boss told her if she would let him have me he would raise and educate me like his own children. When I got back the old boss already had a boy so I went to live with one of his sons. He told me it was time for me to learn how to work. My boss was rough but he was good to me and taught me how to work. The old boss had five sons in the army and all was wounded except one. One of them was shot through and through in the battle of Oak Hill. He got a furlough and come back and died. I left my white folks in 1869 and went to farming for myself up in Hartman bottom. I married when I was about seventeen years old.

"They though' a house near us was hainted. Nobody wanted to live in it so they went to see what the noise was. They found a pet coon with a piece of chain around his neck. The coon would run across the floor and drag the chain.

"The children now are bad. No telling that will be in the next twenty or thirty years everything is so changed now.

"I learnt to sing the hymns but never sang in the choir. We sang 'Dixie', 'John Brown's Body Lies, etc.', 'Juanita', 'Just Before the Battle, Mother', 'Old Black Joe'."

Interviewer: Mrs. Bernice Bowden
Person interviewed: Charlie Norris
122 Miller Street, Pine Bluff, Arkansas
Age: 81

CHARLIE NORRIS

"Born in slavery times? That's me, I reckon. I was born October 1, 1857 in Arkansas in Union County. Tom Murphy was old master's name.

"Yes ma'am, I remember the first regiment left Arkansas—went to Virginia. I member our white folks had us packin' grub out in the woods cause they was spectin' the Yankees.

"I member when the first regiment started out. The music boat come to the landin' and played 'Yankee Doodle.' They carried all us chillun out there.

"After they fit they just come by from daylight till dark to eat. They was death on bread. My mother and Susan Murphy, that was the old lady herself, cooked bread for em.

"I stayed with the Murphys—round on the plantation amongst em for five or six years after freedom. Andrew Norris, my father's old master, was the first sheriff of Ouachita County.

"My mother belonged to the Murphys and my father belonged to the Norrises and after freedom they never did go back together.

"My mother told me that Susan Murphy would suckle me when my mother was out workin' and then my mother would suckle her daughter.

"I was raised up in the house you might say till I was a big nigger. Had plenty to eat. That's one thing they did do. I lived right amongst a settlement of what they called free niggers cause they was treated so well.

"Sometimes Susan Murphy got after me and whipped me and old Marse Tom would tell me to run and not let her whip me. You see, I was worth $1,500 to him and he thought a lot of us black kids.

"Old man Tom Murphy raised me up to a big nigger and never did whip me but twice and that was cause I got drunk on tobacco and turned out his horse.

"Yes ma'am, I voted till bout two or three years ago. Oh Lawd, the colored used to hold office down in the country. I've voted for white and black.

"Some of the colored folks better off free and some not. That's what I think but they don't."

Interviewer: Miss Irene Robertson
Person Interviewed: Emma Oats (Mulatto)
Holly Grove, Ark.
Age: 90 or older

EMMA OATS

"I was born in St. Louis. My mother died when I was little. I never knowed no father. (He was probably a white man.) Jack Oats raised me. Jim Oats at Helena was his son. He is still living. He come through here (Holly Grove) not long ago. I was raised on the Esque place.

"I was fraid of my grandma. I wouldn't live with her. I know'd her. She was a big woman, big white eyes, big thick lips, and had 'Molly Glaspy hair,' long straight soft hair. She was a African woman. She made my clothes. I was fraid of her. I never lived with her. My folks was all free folks. When my mother died my uncle took us— me and brother. He hired us out and we got stole. Gene Oglesby stole us and brought us to Memphis to Joe Nivers. I recken he sold us then. Then they stood me up in the parlor and sold me to Jack Oats. They said I was 'good pluck.' Joe Nivers sold me to Jack Oats for $1,150.00 when I was four years old. My brother was name Milton Smith. I ain't seen him from that day till this. Joe Nivers kept him, I recken. I come here on a 'legal tender'—name of the boat I recken. I know that. I recken it was name of a boat. I got off and Thornton Walls, old colored man, toted me cross every mud hole we come to. He belong to Bud

Walls' (white man at Holly Grove) daddy. When we got home Jack Oats and all of em was there.

"I slept on a pallet and lounge and took care of their children. I played round. Done bout as I pleased. They had a cook they called Aunt Joe—Joe Oats. We had plenty to eat and wear. They dressed me like one their children. We had good flannel clothes. When she washed her children she washed me too. When she combed their hair she combed mine too. She kept working with it till I had pretty hair. Some of her children died. It hurt me bad as it did them. All I done was play with em and see after em. Their names was Sam, John, Dixie, Sallie, Jim. I went in the hack to church; if she took the children, she took me. I was a good size girl when she died. The last word she spoke was to me; she said, 'Emma, take care of my children.' Dr. John Chester was her doctor.

"Oats come here from North Alabama. Will Oats, Wyatt Oats, and Jack Oats—all brothers.

"When mistress living we took a bath every Friday in a sawed-intwo barrel (wooden tub). The cook done our washing. We had clean fresh clothes. We had to dress up every few days. If we get dirty she say she would give us lashes. She never give me none, I never was sassy (saucy). That what most of em got 10 lashes, 25, 50 lashes for.

"When I was bout grown I went to school a little bit to James A. Kerr here at Holly Grove. I was good and grown too.

"I was settin' on the gate post—they had a picket fence. I seen some folks coming to our house. I run in the house and says, 'Miss Mai Liza, the Yankees coming here!' She told her husband to get in the bed. He says, 'Oh God, what she know bout Yankees?' Miss Mai Liza say, 'I don't know; she's one of em, I speck she knows em.' One of the officers come in and asked him what was the matter. He said he was sick. He had boils bout on him. He had a Masonic pin on his shirt. He showed it to the officer. He asked Lou and Becky and all the servants if he hadn't been bushwhacking. They all said, 'No.' He said he wanted something to eat. They went to the well house and got him some milk.

"They camped below the house. They went to their store house and brought more rations up there in a wagon. Lou cooked and she had help. She set a big table and they had the biggest dinner. They had more hams. They had 'Lincoln Coffee' there that day. It was a jolly day. They never et up there no more or bothered round our house no more. The officer had something on his bare arm he showed. He said, when he went to leave, 'Aunt Lou, you shall not be hurt.'

"Mr. Oats had taken long before that day all his slaves to Texas. He took all but Wash Martin. They went in wagons and none of them ever come back.

"Miss Callie Edwards was older than Miss Henrietta Jackson. They kept Wash Martin going through the bottoms nearly all time from their houses at Golden Hill to Indian Bay. They kept him from one place to the other to keep him out of the war. They hired him out to school Miss Henrietta. Miss Callie Edwards died then they give him to Miss Henrietta.

"During the war Mrs. Keeps come up to our house. They heard a gun. She was jes visiting Mrs. Oats. Mrs.

Keeps went home and the bushwhackers had killed him. He was dead.

"I never seen no Ku Klux in my whole life.

"I remember the stage coach that run every two or three days from Helena to Clarendon.

"I don't remember bout freedom. Dr. Green, Hall Green's daddy, told his colored folks they was free. They told our folks. I heard em talking bout it. I was kept quiet. It was done freedom, fore I knowed it. I stayed on and done like I been doin'. I stayed on and on.

"When I was grown I come here to school and soon married. I washed and ironed and cooked all over Holly Grove. I was waiting on the table at the boarding house here at Holly Grove. Mr. Oats was talking bout naming the town. They had put the railroad through. I ask em why didn't they name the town Holly Grove. It was thick with holly trees. They named it that, and put it up on the side of the depot. That way I named the town.

"My folks give me five acres of land and Julia Woolfolk give a blind woman on the place five acres. I didn't know what to do wid it. I didn't have no husband. I was young and foolish. I let it be.

"My husband farmed. I raised my family, chopped and picked cotton and done other things along with that. I have worked all my life till way after my husband died.

"My husband could jump up, knock heels together three times before he come down. He died May 12, 1909. He was 83 years old February 16, 1909.

"I never voted. I never heard my husband say much

bout voting. I know some colored folks sold their voting rights. That was wrong.

"I lived at Baptist Bottoms two years. It lack to killed me."

Wyatt Oats and Miss Callie Edwards owned the husband of Emma Oats. She was married once and had two girls and two boys—one boy dead now. Emma lives at one of her daughters' homes.

Interviewer: Miss Irene Robertson
Person interviewed: Helen Odom and mother, Sarah Odom
Biscoe, Arkansas
Age: 30?

HELEN ODOM

"Great-grandmother was part African, Indian, and Caucasian. She had two girls before slavery ended by her own master—Master Temple. He was also Caucasian (white). She was cook and housemaid at his home. He was a bachelor. Grandmother's name was Rachael and her sister's name was Gilly. Before freedom Master Temple had another wife. By her he had one boy and two girls. He never had a Caucasian wife. In fact he was always a bachelor. Grandmother was a field hand and so was her sister, Gilly.

"But after freedom grandmother married a Union soldier. His took-on name was George Washington Tomb. He was generally called Parson Tomb (preacher). He met Grandmother Rachael in Arkansas.

"When Master Temple died his nearest relative was Jim McNeilly. He made a will leaving everything he possessed to Master McNeilly. The estate had to be settled, so he brought the two sisters to Little Rock we think to be sold. They rode horseback and walked and brought wagons with bedding and provisions to camp along the road. The blankets were frozen and stood alone. It was so cold. Grandmother was put up on the block to be auctioned off and freedom was declared! Aunt Gilly never got to the block. Grandmother married and was separated from her sister.

"Whether the other three children were brought to Arkansas then I don't know but this I know that they went by the name McNeilly. They changed their names or it was done for them. They are all dead now and my own mother is the only one now living. Their names were John, Tom, and Netline. Mother says they were sold to Johnson, and went by that name too as much as McNeilly. They remained with Johnson till freedom, in Tennessee.

"My mother's name is Sarah.

"They seem to think they were treated good till Master Temple died. They nearly froze coming to Arkansas to be sold.

"I heard this told over and over so many, many times before grandmother died. Seemed it was the greatest event of her life. She told other smaller things I can't remember to tell with sense at all. Nothing so important as her master and own father's death and being sold.

"Times are good, very good with me. Our African race is advancing with the times."

Interviewer's Comment

Teacher in Biscoe school. Father was a graduate doctor of medicine and in about 1907, '08, '09 school director at Biscoe.

Interviewer: Mrs. Bernice Bowden
Person interviewed: Jane Oliver
Route 4, near airport, Pine Bluff, Arkansas
Age: 81

JANE OLIVER

"I'm certainly one of em, cause I was in the big house. When Miss Liza married they give sister to her and I stayed with Miss Netta. Her name was Drunetta Rawls. That was in Mississippi. We come to Arkansas when I was small.

"I remember when they run us to Texas, and we stayed there till freedom come. I remember hearin' em read the free papers. Mama died in Texas and they buried her the day they read the free papers. I know. I was out playin' and Miss Lucy, that was my young mistress, come out and say, 'Jane, you go in and see your mother, she wants you.' I was busy playin' and didn't want to go in and I member Miss Lucy say, 'Poor little fool nigger don't know her mother's dyin'.' I went in then and said, 'Mama, is you dyin'?' She say, 'No, I ain't; I died when you was a baby.' You know, she meant she had died in sin. She was a christian.

"Me and Lucy played together all the time—round about the house and in the kitchen. Little Marse Henry, that was big old Marse Henry's son, he was a captain in the army. We all called him Little Marse Henry. Old mistress was good to us. Us chillun called her Miss Netta.

Best woman I ever seed. Me and Lucy growed up together. Looks like I can see just the way the house looked and how we used to go down to the big gate and play. I sits here and studies and wonders if I'd know that place today. That's what I study bout.

"I used to hear em say we only stayed in Texas nine months and the white folks brought us back.

"My uncle Simon Rawls, he took me after the war. Then I worked for Mrs. Adkins.

"I went to school a little and learned to read prints. The teacher tried to get me to write but I wouldn't do it. And since then I have wished so much I had learned to write. Oh mercy! Old folks would tell me, 'Well, when you get up the road, you'll wish you had.' I didn't know what they meant but I know now they meant when I got old.

"I was married when I was young—I don't think I was fifteen.

"Yes ma'am, I've worked hard. I've always lived in the country.

"I can remember when the white folks refugeed us to Texas. Oh we did hate the Yankees. If I ever seed a Yankee I didn't know it but I heard the white folks talkin' bout em.

"I used to hear em talk bout old Jeff Davis and Abe Lincoln.

"Bradley County was where we lived fore we went to Texas and afterward. Colonel Ed Hampton's plantation jined the Rawls plantation on the Arkansas River where it overflowed the land. I loved that better than any place I ever seed in my life.

"I couldn't say what I think of the young folks now. They is different from what we was. Yes, Lord, they is different. Sometimes I think they is better and sometimes wuss. I just thanks the Lord that I'm here—have come this far.

"When I bought this place from Mr. R.M. Knox he said, 'When I'm in my grave you'll thank me that you took my advice and put your savings in a Home.' I do thank him. I been here thirty years and I get along. God bless you."

Interviewer: Mrs. Bernice Bowden
Person interviewed: Ivory Osborne
Route 5, Box 158, Pine Bluff, Arkansas
Age: 85

IVORY OSBORNE

"Know about slavery? Sho I do—I was born in '52. Born in Arkansas? No ma'm, born in Texas.

"Oh yes, indeed, I had a good master. Good to me, indeed. I was that high when the war started. I member everything. Take me from now till dark to tell you everything I know bout slavery.

"I put in three years and five months, choppin' cotton and corn. I member the very day, on the 10th of May, old mistress blowed the conk and told us we was free.

"Oh Lord, I had a good time.

"I never was whipped.

"Ku Klux used to run me. Run me clear from the plum orchard bout a mile from the house. Run to my mistress at the big house.

"Miss Ann had eight darkies and told her stepmother, 'Don't you put your hand on em.' She didn't either.

"I went to school since 'mancipation in Nacitosh. Learned to read and write. Was in the eighth grade when

I left. Stood at the head of every class. They couldn't get me down. I done got old and forgot now.

"I didn't know the difference between slavery and free, I never was whipped.

"Did I ever vote? You know I voted, old as I am. Ain't voted in over forty years. I ain't nobody. My wife's eighty. I've had her forty years. Cose I voted the Republican ticket. You never seed a colored person a Democrat in your life.

"In slavery days we killed seventy-five or eighty hogs every year. And I don't mean shoats, I mean hogs. I ain't lost my membrance."

Interviewer: Mrs. Bernice Bowden
Person interviewed: Jane Osbrook
602 E. 21st Avenue, Pine Bluff, Arkansas
Age: 90

JANE OSBROOK

"Yes ma'm, I was livin' in slavery days. I was borned in Arkansas I reckon. I was borned within three, miles of Camden but I wasn't raised there. We moved to Saline County directly after peace was declared.

"I don't know what year I was born because you see I'm not educated but I was ninety the 27th of this last past May. Yes ma'm, I'm a old bondage woman. I can say what a heap of em can't say—I can tell the truth bout it. I believe in the truth. I was brought up to tell the truth. I'm no young girl.

"My old master was Adkison Billingsly. My old mistress treated us just like her own children. She said we had feelin's and tastes. I visited her long after the war. Went there and stayed all night.

"I member when they had the fight at Jenkins Ferry. Old Steele had 30,000 and he come down to take Little Rock, Pine Bluff and others. Captain Webb with 1,500 Rebels was followin' him and when they got to Saline River they had a battle.

"The next Sunday my father carried all us children

and some of the white folks to see the battle field. I member the dead was lyin' in graves, just one row after another and hadn't even been covered up.

"Oh yes, I can tell all bout that. Nother time there was four hundred fifty colored and five white Yankee soldiers come and ask my father if old mistress treated us right. We told em we had good owners. I never was so scared in my life. Them colored soldiers was so tall and so black and had red eyes. Oh yes ma'm, they had on the blue uniforms. Oh, we sure was fraid of em—you know them eyes.

"They said, 'Now uncle, we want you to tell the truth, does she feed you well?' My ma did all the cookin' and we had good livin'. I tole my daughter we fared ten thousand times better than now.

"I come up in the way of obedience. Any time I wanted to go, had to go to old mistress and she say, 'Don't let the sun go down on you.' And when we come home the sun was in the trees. If you seed the sun was goin' down on you, you run.

"I ain't goin' tell nothin' but the truth. Truth better to live with and better to die with.

"Some of the folks said they never seed a biscuit from Christmas to Christmas but we had em every day. Never seed no sodie till peace was declared—used saleratus.

"In my comin' up it was Whigs and Democrats. Never heard of no Republicans till after the war. I've seed a man get upon that platform and wipe the sweat from his brow. I've seed em get to fight in' too. That was done at our white folks house—arguin' politics.

"I never did go to school. I married right after the war you know. What you talkin' bout—bein' married and goin' to school? I was housekeepin': Standin' right in my own light and didn't know it."

United States. Work Projects Administration

Interviewer: Mrs. Bernice Bowden
Person interviewed: Annie Page
412-1/2 Pullen Street, Pine Bluff, Arkansas
Age: 86

ANNIE PAGE

"I was born 1852, they tell me, on the fifteenth of March. I was workin' a good while 'fore surrender.

"Bill Jimmerson was my old master. He was a captain in Marmaduke's army. Come home on thirty days furlough once and he and Daniel Carmack got into some kind of a argument 'bout some whisky and Daniel Carmack stabbed him with a penknife. Stabbed him three times. He was black as tar when they brought him home. The blood had done settled. Oh Lawd, that was a time.

"My eyes been goin' blind 'bout six years till I got so I can't excern (discern) anything.

"Old miss used to box me over the head mightily and the colored folks used to hit me over the head till seem like I could hear a bell for two or three days. Niggers ain't got no sense. Put 'em in authority and they gits so uppity.

"My brother brought me here and left me here with a colored woman named Rachael Ross. And oh Lawd, she was hard on me. Never had to do in slavery times what I had to do then.

"But the devil got her and all her chillun now I reckon. They tell me when death struck her, they asked if the

Lawd called her, and they say she just turned over and over in the bed like a worm in hot ashes."

Interviewer: Mrs. Bernice Bowden
Person interviewed: Annie Page
400 Block West Pullen, Pine Bluff, Arkansas
Age: 85

ANNIE PAGE

"Yes'm I 'member the war. I never knowed why they called it the Civil War though.

"I was born in Union County, Arkansas, 'bout a mile from Bear Creek, in 1852. That's what my old mistress tole me the morning we was sot free.

"My mistress was a Democrat. Old master was a captain in Marmaduke's army.

"I used to hope (help) spin the thread to make the soldiers' clothes. Old mistress cared for me. Lacy Jimmerson—the onliest mistress I ever had. She wanted to send us away to Texas but old master say it want no use. Cause if the Yankees won, they have to bring us back, so we didn't go.

"Did they whip us? Why I bet I can show you scars now. Old Miss whip me when she feel like fightin'. Her granddaughter, Mary Jane, tried to learn me my ABC's out of the old Blue Back Speller. We'd be out on the seesaw, but old Miss didn't know what we doin'. Law, she pull our hair. Directly she see us and say 'What you doin'? Bring that book here!'

"One day old master come home on a thirty-day furlough. He was awful hot-headed and he got into a argument with Daniel Carmack and old Daniel stobbed him right in the heart. Fore he die he say to bury him by the side of the road so he can see the niggers goin' to work.

"I never seen no Ku Klux but I heard of 'em 'rectly after the war.

"I'se blind. I jest can see enough to get around. The Welfare gives me eight dollars a month.

"My mother died soon after the war ended and after that I was jest knocked over the head. I went to Camblin and worked for Mrs. Peters. Then I runned away and married my first husband Mike Samson. I been married twice and had two children but they all dead now.

"Law, I jest scared of these young ones as I can be. I don't have no dealins with 'em."

FOLKLORE SUBJECTS
Name of interviewer: Mrs. Bernice Bowden
Subject: Apparitions
Subject: Superstitions
Subject: Birthmarks
Story:—Information

This information given by: Annie Page
Place of residence: 412-1/2 Pullen Street, Pine Bluff, Arkansas
Occupation: None Age: 86

[TR: Information moved from bottom of first page.]
[TR: Repetitive information deleted from subsequent pages.]

ANNIE PAGE

"I told 'bout old master's death. Mama had done sent me out to feed the chickens soon of a morning.

"Here was the smokehouse and there was a turkey in a coop. And when I throwed it the feed I heard somethin' sounded just like you was draggin' a brush over leaves. It come around the corner of the smokehouse and look like a tall woman. It kept on goin' toward the house till it got to the hickory nut tree and still sound like draggin' a brush. When it got to the hickory nut tree it changed and look like a man. I looked and I said, 'It's old master.' And the next day he got killed. I run to the house and told mama, 'Look at that man.' She said, 'Shut your mouth, you don't see no man.' Old miss heard and said, 'Who do you s'pose it could be?' But mama wouldn't let me talk.

"But I know it was a sign that old master was goin' to die."

Superstitions

"I was born with a caul over my face. Old miss said it hung from the top of my head half way to my waist.

"She kept it and when I got big enough she said, 'Now that's your veil, you play with it.'

"But I lost it out in the orchard one day.

"They said it would keep you from seein' ha'nts."

Birthmarks

"William Jimmerson's wife had a daughter was born blind, and she said it was her husband's fault. She was delicate, you know, and one afternoon she was layin' down and I was sittin' there fannin' her with a peafowl fan. Her husband was layin' there too and I guess I must a nodded and let the fan drop down in his face. He jumped up and pressed his thumbs on my eyes till they was all bloodshot and when he let loose I fell down on the floor. Miss Phenie said, 'Oh, William, don't do that.' I can remember it just as well.

"My eyes like to went out and do you know, when her baby was born it was blind. It's eyes just looked like two balls of blood. It died though, just lived 'bout two weeks."

Interviewer: Mrs. Bernice Bowden
Person interviewed: Fannie Parker
1908 W. Sixth Street, Pine Bluff, Arkansas
Age: 90?

FANNIE PARKER

"Yes, honey, this is old Fannie. I'se just a poor old nigger waitin' for Jesus to come and take me to Heaven.

"I was just a young strip of a girl when the war come. Dr. M.C. Comer was my owner. His wife was Elizabeth Comer. I said Marse and Mistis in them days and when old mistress called me I went runnin' like a turkey. They called her Miss Betsy. Yes Lord, I was in slavery days. Master and mistress was bossin' me then. We all come under the rules. We lived in Monticello—right in the city of Monticello.

"All I can tell you is just what I remember. I seed the Yankees. I remember a whole host of 'em come to our house and wanted something to eat. They got it too! They cooked it them selves and then they burned everything they could get their hands on. They said plenty to me. They said so much I don't know what they said. I know one thing they said I belonged to the Yankees. Yes Lord, they wanted me to tell 'em if I was free. I told 'em I was free indeed and that I belonged to Miss Betsy. I didn't know what else to say. We had plenty to eat, plenty of hog meat and buttermilk and cornbread. Yes ma'm—don't talk about that now.

"Don't tell me 'bout old Jeff Davis—he oughta been killed. Abraham Lincoln thought what was right was right and what was wrong was wrong. Abraham was a great man cause he was the President. When the rebels ceded from the Union he made 'em fight the North. Abraham Lincoln studied that and he had it all in his mind. He wasn't no fighter but he carried his own and the North give 'em the devil. Grant was a good man too. They tried to kill him but he was just wrapped up in silver and gold.

"I remember when the stars fell. Yes, honey, I know I was ironin' and it got so dark I had to light the lamp. Yes, I did!

"It's been a long time and my mind's not so good now but I remember old Comer put us through. Good-bye and God bless you!"

Interviewer: Samuel S. Taylor
Subject: Ex-slavery
Story: Birth, Parents, Master.

Person Interviewed: J.M. Parker, (dark brown)
Address: 1002 Ringo Street, Little Rock, Arkansas
Occupation: Formerly a carpenter
Age: 76

[TR: Information moved from bottom of first page.]

J.M. PARKER

"I was born in South Carolina, Waterloo, in Lawrence County, [HW: Laurens Co.] in 1861, April 5th. Waterloo is a little town in South Carolina. I believe that fellow shot the first gun of the war when I was born. I knew then I was going to be free. Of course that is just a lie. I made that up. Anyway I was born in 1861.

"Colonel Rice was our master. He was in the war too. The name Parker came in by intermarriage, you see. My mother belonged to Rice. She could have been a Simms before she married. My father's name was Edmund Parker. He belonged to the Rices also. That was his master; Colonel Rice and him were boys together. He went down there to Charleston, South Carolina to build breastworks. While down there, he slipped off and brought a hundred men away from Charleston back to Lawrence County where the men was that owned them. He was a business man, father was. Brought 'em all through the swamps. They were slaves and he brought 'em all back home. They all followed his advice.

"My mother's name was Rowena Parker after she married.

"Colonel Rice was a pretty fair man—a pretty good fellow. He was a colonel in the war and stood pretty high. Bound to be that way by him being a colonel. Seemed like him and my father had about the same number of kids. He thought there was nobody like my mother. He never whipped the slaves himself but his overseer would sometimes jump on them. The Rice family was very good to our people. The men being gone they were left in the hands of the mistress. She never touched anybody. She never had no reason to.

Pateroles

"Patterollers didn't bother us, but we were in that country. During the war, most of the men that amounted to anything were in the war and the patrolers didn't bother you much. The overseer didn't have so much power over me than. That pretty well left the colored people to come up without being abused during the war. The white folks was forced to go to the war. They drafted them just like they do now. They'd shoot a po' white man if he didn't come.

Breeding

"My master didn't force men and women to marry. He didn't put 'em together just to get more slave. Some times other people would have women and men just for that purpose. But there wasn't much of it in my country.

House, Stock, Parents' Occupations

"Our house was a frame building, boxed in with one-by-twelve like we have here in the country. That was a good house with regular flooring, tongue and groove. We was raised up in a good house. Old Colonel Rice had to protect his standing. He had good stock. My father was a carriage man. He had to keep those horses clean and they always looked good. That carriage had to shine too. Colonel Rice was a high stepper. He'd take his handkerchief and rub it over the horses hair to see if they were really clean. He would always find 'em clean though when the old man got through with them. He would drive fine stock. Had some fine horses. Couldn't trust 'em with just anybody.

"My mother was cook. She helped Mrs. Rice take care of the kids, and cooked around the house. She took care of her kids, too.

"The house we was born and bred in was built for a carriage house, but somehow or 'nother they give it to us to live in. My mother being a cook, she got what she wanted. That was a good house too. It was sealed. It had good floors. It had two rooms. It had about three windows and good doors to each room.

"We had just common furniture. Niggers didn't have much then. My father was a good mechanic though and he would make anything he wanted. We didn't have much, just common things. But all my people were mechanics, harness makers, shoemakers,—they could make anything. Young Sam Parker could make any kind of shoe. He made shoes for the white folks; Young Jacob was a blacksmith; he made horseshoes and anything else out of iron. He may still be living. In fact, he made anything he could get his hands on. My young uncles on my mother's side, I don't know much about them, because they were all mechanics. My grandfather on my mother's side could make baskets—any kind—could make baskets that would hold water.

"My father had thirteen children. Three of them are living now. My brother lives here in the city. He was born during the war and his mother was supposed to be free when he was born.

Right After the War

"That's what my mother told me. I can remember a long ways back myself. After the war, it wasn't long before they began to open up schools. They used to run school three or four months a year. Both white and colored in the country had about three or four months. That is all they had. There weren't so very many white folks that took an interest in education during slave time. Colored people got just about as much as they did right after the war. What time we went to school we went the whole day. We would come home and work in the evening like. We had pretty fair teachers. All white then at first. They didn't have no colored till afterwards. If they did, they had so few, I never heard of them.

"The first teacher I had was Katie Whitefold (white). That was in Waterloo. Miss Richardson was our next teacher. She was white too. We went to school two terms under white women. After that we began to get teachers from Columbia, South Carolina, where the normal school was.

"The white teachers who taught us were people who had been raised right around Waterloo. We never had no Northern teachers as I knows of. Our first colored teacher was Murry Evans. He a preacher. He was one of our leading preachers too. After him our colored women began to come in and stand examination wasn't so hard at that time, but they made a good showing. There were good scholars.

"I went to school too much. I went to school at Philander Smith College some, too. I went a good piece in school. Come pretty near finishing the English course (high school). I finished Good[HW: sp.?] Brown's 'Grammer of Grammers'. Professor Backensto (the spelling is the interviewer's) sent away and got it and sold it to us. We was his students. He was a white man from the North and a good scholar. We got in those grammars and got the same lessons they give him when he was in school—nine pages a lesson and we had to repeat that lesson three times. When my mother died, I was off in the normal school.

"Right after the war, my parents farmed. He followed his trade. That always gave us something to eat you know. When we farmed, we sharecropped—a third and a fourth—that is, we got a third of the cotton and a fourth of the corn. Potatoes and things like that went free. All women got an acre free. My mother always got an acre and she worked it good too. She always had her bale of cotton. And if she didn't have a bale, she laid it next to the white folks' and made it out. They knew it and they didn't care. She stood well with the white people. Helped all of 'em raise their children, and they all liked that.

"I went along with my father whenever he had a big

job and needed help. I got to be as good a carpenter as he was.

"I married out here. About eighty-five. People were emigrating to this country. There was a boom to emigrating then. Emigrating was a little dangerous when a man was trying to get hands. White folks would lay traps and kill men that were taking away their hands—they would kill white just as quick as they would black. I started out under a white man—I can't remember his name. He turned me over to Madden, a colored man who was raised in Waterloo. We came from there to Greenwood, South Carolina where everything was straight. After that we had nothing to do but get on the train and keep coming. We was with our agent then and we had no more trouble after that.

"I got off at Brinkley over at Minor Gregory's farm. He needed hands then and was glad to get us. He is dead now. I stayed in Brinkley the space of about a year. Then he gave us transportation to Little Rock. The train came from Memphis, and we struck out for Little Rock. I married after I come to Little Rock. I forget what year. But anyway my wife is dead and gone and all the children. So I'm single now.

Opinions of the Present

"I think times are about dead now. Things ought to get better. I believe things are going to get better for all of us. People have got to think more. People have got to get together more. War doesn't always make thing better. It didn't after the Civil War. And it didn't after the World

War. The young people are all right in their way. It would just take another war to learn 'em a lesson.

Support

"I can't do any work now. I get a little help from the welfare. It doesn't come regular. I need a check right now. I think it's due now. But they haven't sent it out yet. That is, I haven't got it.

"I'm a Christian. All my family were Methodists. I belong to Wesley.

Interviewer: Mary D. Hudgins
Person Interviewed: Judy Parker
Home: 618 Wade Street, Hot Springs, Ark.
Aged: 77

JUDY PARKER

For location of Wade Street, see interview with Emma Sanderson.

As the interviewer walked down Silver Street a saddle colored girl came out on a porch for a load of wood.

"I beg your pardon," she began, pausing, "can you tell me where I will find Emma Sanderson?"

"I sure can." The girl left the porch and came out to the street. "I'll walk down with you and show you. That way it'll be easier. Kind of cold, ain't it?"

"It surely is," this from the interviewer. "Isn't it too cold for you, can't you just tell me? I think I can find it." The girl had expected to be only on the porch and didn't have a coat.

"No, ma'am. It's all right. Now we're far enough for you to see. You see those two houses jam up against one and 'tother? Well Miz Parker lives in the one this way. I goes down to look after her most every day. That's where you'll find her.—No ma'am—'twaren't no bother."

The gate sagged slightly at the house "this way" of the "two jam up against one and 'tother." A large slab from an oak log in the front yard near a woodpile bore mute evidence of many an ax blow. (Stove wood is generally split in the rural South—one end of the "stick" resting against the ground, the other atop a small log.)

Up a couple of rickety steps the interviewer climbed. She knocked three times. When she was bade to enter she opened the door to find an old woman sitting near a wood stove combing her long, white hair.

Mrs. Parker was expecting the visit. A few days before the interviewer had had a visit from a couple of colored women who had "heard tell how you is investigating the old people.—been trying to get on old age pension for a long time—glad you come to get us on.——No? Oh, I see you is the Townsend woman." (An explanation of her true capacity was almost impossible for the interviewer.)

Mrs. Parker, however, seemed to comprehend the idea perfectly. She expected nothing save the chance to tell her story. Her joy at the gift of a quarter (the amount the interviewer set aside from her salary for each interviewee) was pitiful. Evidently it had been a long time since she had possessed a similar sum to spend exactly as she pleased.

"I don't rightly know how old I is. My mother used to tell me that I was a little baby, six months old when our master, Joe Potts was his name, got ready to clear out of Florida. You see he had heard tell of the war scare. So he started drifting out of the way. Bet it didn't take him long after he made up his mind. He was a right decided man. Mister Joe was.

"How did we like him? Well, he was always good to

us. He was well thought of. Seemed to be a pretty clever man, Mr. Joe did." ("Clever" in plantation language like "smart" refers more to muscular than mental activity. They might almost be used as synonyms for "hard working" on the labor level.)

"So Mr. Joe got ready to go to Texas. Law, Miss, I don't rightly know whether he had a family or not. Never heard my Mother say. Anyhow he come through Arkansas intending to drift on out into Texas. But when he got near the border 'twix't and between Arkansas and Texas he stopped. The talk about war had about settled down. So he stopped. He stopped near where the big bridge is. You know where Little River County is don't you? He stopped and he started to work. Started to make a crop. 'Course I can't remember none about that. Just what my Mother told me. But I remembers him from later.

"He went at it the good way. Settled down and tried to open up a home. They put in a crop and got along pretty good. Time passed and the war talk started floating again. That time he didn't pay much attention and it got him. It was on a Sunday morning when he went away. I never knew whether they made him go or not. But I kind of think they must of. Cause he wouldn't have moved off from Florida if he had wanted to go to war.

"He took my daddy with him! Ma'am—did he take him to fight or to wait on him—Don't know ma'am, but I sort of think he took him to wait on him. But he didn't bring him back. My daddy got killed in the war. No ma'am. I don't rightly know how he got killed. Never heard nobody say. I was just a little girl—nobody bothered to tell me much.

"Yes, that we did. We stayed on on the farm and we made a crop—the old folks did. Mr. Joe, when he went off, said "Now you stay on here, you make a crop and you use all you need. Then you put up the rest and save for me." He was a right good man, Mr. Joe was.

"No, we didn't never see no fighting. There wasn't nothing to be scared of. Didn't see no Yankees until the war was through. Then they started passing. Lawsey, I couldn't tell how many of them there was. More than you could count.

"We had all stayed on. I was the oldest of my mother's children. But she had two more after me. There was our family and my two uncles and my grandmother. Then there was some other colored folks. But we wasn't scared of the Yankees. Mr. Joe was there by that time. They camped all around in the woods near us. They got us to do their washing. Lawsey they was as filthy as hogs. I never see such folks. They asked Mr. Joe if we could do their washing. Everything on the place that come near those clothes got lousey. Those men was covered with them. I never see nothing like it. We got covered with them. No, ma'am, we got rid of 'em pretty easy. They ain't so hard to get rid of, if you keep clean.

"After it was all over Master Joe got ready to go back to Florida. He took Warley and Jenny with him. They was children he had had by a black woman—you know folks did such things in them days. He asked the rest of us if they wanted to go back too. But my folks made up their minds they didn't. You see, they didn't know how they'd get along and how long it would take them to pay for the trip back, so they stayed right where they was.

"Lots of 'em went to Rondo and some of us worked for Herb Jeans—he lived farther up Red River. After my mother died I was with my grandmother. She washed and cooked for Herb Jeans's family. I stayed on with her, helped out until I got married. I was about fifteen when that time come.

"My man owned his place. Sure he did. Owned it when I married him. He owned it himself and farmed it good. Yes ma'am we stayed with the land. He made good crops—corn and cotton, mostly. Course we raised potatoes and the truck we needed—all stuff like that. Yes, ma'am we had thirteen children. Just three of them's living. All of them is boys.

"Yes ma'am we got along good. My husband made good crops and we got along just good. But 'bout eight years ago my husband he got sick. So he sold out the farm—sold out everything. Then he come here.

"Before he died he spent every last cent—every last cent—left me to get along the very best way I kin. I stays with my son. He takes care of me. He don't make much, but he does the best he kin.

"No ma'am, I likes living down in the country. Down there near Red River it's soft and sandy. Up here in Hot Springs the rocks tear up your feet. If you's country raised—you like the country. Yes ma'am, you like the country."

As she left the interviewer handed her a quarter. At first the old woman's face was expressionless. But she moved the coin nearer to her eyes and a smile broke and widened until her whole face was a wrinkle of joy. When she turned in the doorway, the interviewer noticed that the hand jammed into an apron pocket was clutched into a possessive fist, cradling the precious twenty five cents.

Interviewer: Mrs. Bernice Bowden
Person interviewed: R.F. Parker
619 N. Hickory, Pine Bluff, Arkansas
Age: 76

R.F. PARKER

"I was born in '62. I reckon I was born in slavery times. Born in Ripley County, Missouri. Old man Billy Parker was my master, and my young master was Jim Parker.

"They bought my mother in Tennessee when she was a child. I wasn't big enough to remember much about slavery but I was big enough to know when they turned my mother loose, and we come to Lawrence County, Arkansas.

"I remember my mother sayin' she had to plow while her young master, Jim Parker, was off to war, but I don't know what side he was on.

"I remember seein' some soldiers ridin' down the road, about seventy-five of 'em. I know I run under a corn pen and hid. I thought they was after me. They stopped right there and turned their horses loose 'round that pen. I can remember that all right. They went in the white folks' house and took a shotgun. I know I remember hearin' mama talk about it. I think they had on blue clothes.

"I was goin' on seven when we come to Arkansas. I

know I'd walk a while and she'd tote me a while. But we was lucky enough to get in with some white people that was movin' to Arkansas. We was comin' to a place called 'The Promised Land.' We stayed there till '92.

"I have farmed and done public work. I worked nine years at that heading factory in the east end (of Pine Bluff).

"I used to vote. When I was in north Arkansas, I voted in all kinds of elections. But after I come down here to Jefferson County, I couldn't vote in nothin' but the presidential elections.

"I don't think the young people are goin' to amount to much. They are a heap wilder than when I was young. They got a chance to graduate now—something I didn't get to do.

"I never went to school a day in my life, but the white people where I worked learned me to read and write."

Interviewer's Comment

This man could easily pass for a white person.

Interviewer: Samuel S. Taylor
Person interviewed: Annie Parks
720 Pulaski Street, Little Rock, Arkansas
Age: About 80
Occupation: Formerly house and field work

ANNIE PARKS

"I was born and raised in Mer Rouge, Louisiana. That is between here and Monroe. I have been here in Little Rock more than twenty-five years.

"My mother's name was Sarah Mitchell. That was her married name. I don't know what her father's name was. My father's name was Willis Clapp. He was killed in the first war—the Civil War. My father went to the war from Mer Rouge, Louisiana. I don't remember him at all. But that is what my mother told me about him. My mother said he had very good people. After he married my mother, old man Offord bought him. Offord's name was Warren Offord. They buried him while I was still there in Mer Rouge. He was a old-time Mason. That was my mother's master—in olden days.

"His grandmother took my mother across the seas with her. She (his grandmother) died on shipboard, and they throwed her body into the water. There's people denies it, but my mother told me it was so. Young Davenport is still living. He is a relative of Offords. My mother never did get no pension for my father.

Slave House and Occupation

"I was born in a log house. There were two doors—a front and a back—and there were two windows. My mother had no furniture 'cept an old-time wooden bed—big bed. She was a nurse all the time in the house. I heard her say she milked and waited on them in the house. My father's occupation was farming during slavery times.

"My mother always said she didn't have no master to beat on her. I like to tell the truth. My mother's master never let no overseer beat his slaves around. She didn't say just what we had to eat. But they always give us a plenty, and there wasn't none of us mistreated.

"My father could have an extra patch and make a bale of cotton or whatever he wanted to on it. That was so that he could make a little money to buy things for hisself and his family. And if he raised a bale of cotton on his patch and wanted to sell it to the agent, that was all right.

Family

"I have a brother named Manuel Clayton. If he's living still, he is younger than I am. He is the baby boy. I doesn't remember his father at all. I had five sisters with myself and two brothers. All of them were older than me except Manuel. My mother had one brother and two sisters. Her brother's name was Lin Urbin. We always called him Big Buddy. He hasn't been so long died. My older brother is named Willis Clayton—if he's still living. Willis has a half dozen sons. He is my oldest brother. He lives way out in the country 'round Mer Rouge.

Freedom

"My mother said they promised to them money when they were freed. Some of them gave them something, and some of them didn't. My mother's folks didn't give her nothin'. The Government didn't give her nothin' either. I don't know just who told her she was free nor how. I don't remember myself.

Patrollers and Ku Klux

"I never heard much about pateroles. My mother said they used to whip you if they would catch you out without a pass. I heard her talk about the Ku Klux after freedom.

Slave Worship

"My mother could always go to church on Sunday. Her slave-time preacher was Tom Johnson. Henry Soates and Watt Taylor were slavery-time preachers too. Old man Jacob Anderson too was a great preacher in slave time. There was a big arbor where they held church. That was outdoors. There was just a wood frame and green leaves laid over it. Hundreds of people sat under there and heard the Gospel preached. The Offords didn't care how much you worshipped. If I was with them, I wouldn't have no trouble.

"In the winter time they had a small place to meet in. They built a church after the war. When I went home, eight or nine years ago, I walked all 'round and looked at all the old places.

Health

"You know my remembrance comes and goes. I ain't had no good remembrance since I been sick. I been mighty sick with high blood pressure. I can't work and I can't even go out. I'm 'fraid I'll fall down and get myself hurt or run over.

Support

"I don't get no help 'cept what my daughter gives me. I can't get no Old Age Pension. I never did get nothin' for my father. My mother didn't either. He was killed in the war, but they didn't give nobody nothin' for his death. They told me they'd give me something and then they told me they wouldn't. I'm dependent on what my daughter does for me. If I was back in Mer Rouge, I wouldn't have no trouble gettin' a pension, nor nothin' else.

Slave Marriages on the Offord Plantation

"My mother said they just read 'em together, slavery times. I think she said that the preacher married them on the Offord plantation. They didn't get no license.

Amusements

"They had quiltings and corn shuckings. I don't know what other amusements they had, but I know everything was pleasant on the Offord plantation.

"If slaves went out without a pass, my mother said her master wouldn't allow them to beat on them when they come in. They had plenty to eat, and they had substantial clothes, and they had a good fire.

Age

"I don't know how old I am. I was born before the war. My father went to the war when it begun. I had another brother that was born before the war. He don't remember nothin' about my father. I don't neither. I was too young."

Interviewer's Comment

Allowing for a year's difference between the two youngest children, and allowing that the boy was born immediately before the War, the girl could not be younger than seventy-eight. She could be older. She states all facts as through her mother, but she seems to have experienced some of the things she relates. Her memory is fading. Failure to get pension or old age assistance oppresses her mind. She comes back to it again and again. She carries her card and her commodity order with her in her pocketbook.

She had asked me to write some letters for her when her daughter interfered and said that she didn't want it done. She said that she had told the case worker that her husband worked at the Missouri Pacific Shop and that the case worker had asked her if she wouldn't provide for her mother. They live in a neat rented house. The mother weighs about a hundred and ten pounds and is tall. The daughter is about the same height but weighs about two hundred and fifty. Time and again, the old lady tried to convey to me a message that she didn't want her daughter to hear, but I could not make it out. The daughter was belligerent, as is sometimes the case, and it was only by walking in the very middle of the straight and narrow path that I managed to get my story.

Interviewer: Samuel S. Taylor
Person interviewed: Austin Pen Parnell
4314 W. Seventeenth Street, Little Rock, Arkansas
Age: 73
Occupation: Carpenter

AUSTIN PEN PARNELL

Birth and General Fact About Life

"I was born April fifteenth, 1865, the day Lincoln was assassinated, in Carroll County, Mississippi, about ten miles from Grenada. It's about half the distance between Grenada and Carrollton. Carrollton is our county seat but we went to Grenada more than we went to Carrollton.

"When I got older, I moved to Grenada and I come from there here. I was about thirty-five years old when I moved to Grenada. About 160 acres of land in Grenada was mine. I bought it, but heirs claimed the place and I had to leave. I had no land then, only a lot here and I came over here to look it over. A lady had come to Mississippi selling property and she had a plat which she said was in Little Rock not far from the capitol. Her name was Mrs. Putman. The place was on the other side of the Fourche. But I didn't know that until I came here. She misguided me. I came to Arkansas and looked at the lot and didn't want it. I made a trip over here twice before I settled on living in Little Rock. I told the others who had bought property from her the truth about its location. They asked me and I hate to lie. I didn't knock; I just answered questions and didn't volunteer nothing. They all quit making their payments, Just like I did. My land had a rock on it as big as a bale of cotton.

"Mr. Herring thought hard of me because I told the others the truth. I went into the office one day and Mr. Herring said, 'Parnell, I understand you have been knocking on me.' I said, 'Well, I'll tell you, Mr. Herring, if telling the truth about things is knocking on them, I certainly did.' He never said anything more about it, and I didn't either.

"I rented a place on Twelfth and Maple and then rented around there two or three times, and finally bought a place at 3704 West Twelfth Street. I moved to Little Rock March 18, 1911. That was twenty-seven years ago.

Parents

"My father was named Henry Parnell. He died in the year 1917 in the time of the great war. He was ninety-five years old when he died. His master had the same name. My mother's name was Priscilla Parnell. She belonged to the same family as he did. They married before freedom. My father was a farmer and my mother was a housewife and she'd work in the field too.

"My grandmother on my mother's side was named Hester Parnell. I don't know what her husband's name was. My mother, father, and grandmother were all from North Carolina. My grandmother did house and field work.

House

"My mother and father lived in a two-room house hewed out of big logs—great big logs. The logs were about four inches thick and twelve inches wide. It didn't take many of them to build a wall—about ten or twelve of them on a side. They were notched down so as to almost come together. They chinked up the cracks with mud and covered it with a board.

"I laid in bed many a night and looked up through the cracks in the roof. Snow would come through there when it snowed and cover the bed covers. We thought you couldn't build a roof so that it would keep out rain and snow, but we were mistaken. Before you would make a fire in them days, you had to sweep out the snow so that it wouldn't melt up in the house and make a mess. But we kept healthy just the same. Didn't have no pneumonia in those days.

"The house had two rooms about eight feet apart. The rooms were connected by a hall which we called a gallery in those days. The hall was covered by the same roof as the house and it had the same floor. The house sot east and west and had a chimney in each end. The chimneys were made out of sticks and mud. I can build a chimney now like that.

"It was large at the bottom and tapered at the top. It was about six or seven feet square at the bottom. It grew smaller as it went toward the top. You could get a piece of wood three and a half or four feet long in the boddom of it. Sometimes the wood would be too large to carry and you would just have to roll it in.

"The floors was boards about one by twelve. There were two doors in each room—one leading outside and the other to the hall. If there were any windows, I can't remember them. We didn't need no windows for ventilation.

"This was the house that I remember first after freedom. I remember living in it. That was about seven or eight years after freedom. My father rented it from the big man named Alf George for whom he worked. Mr. George used to come out and eat breakfast with us. We'd get that hoecake out of the ashes and wash it off until it looked like it was as clean as bread cooked in a skillet. I have seen my grandmother cook a many a one in the fire. We didn't use no skillet for corn bread. The bread would have a good firm crust on it. But it didn't get too hard to eat and enjoy.

"She'd take a poker before she put the bread in and rake the ashes off the hearth down to the solid stone or earth bottom, and the ashes would be banked in two hills to one side and the other. Then she would put the batter down on it; the batter would be about an inch thick and about nine inches across. She'd put down three cakes at a time and let 'em stay there till the cakes were firm—about five minutes on the bare hot hearth. They would almost bake before she covered them up. Sometimes she would lay down as many as four at a time. The cakes had to be dry before they were covered up, because if the ashes ever stuck to them while they were wet, there would be ashes in them when you would take them out to eat. She'd take her poker then and rake the ashes back on the top of the cakes and let 'em stay there till the cakes were done. I don't know just how long—maybe about ten or twelve minutes. She knew how long to cook them. Then she'd rake down the hearth gently, backward and forward, with the poker till she got down to them and then she'd put the poker under them and lift them out. That poker was a kind of flat iron. It wasn't a round one. Then we'd wash 'em off like I told you and they be ready to eat.

"Mr. George would eat the ash cake and drink sweet milk. 'Auntie, I want some of that ash cake and some of that good sweet milk.' We had plenty of cows.

"Two-thirds of the water used in the ash cake was hot water, and that made the batter stick together like it was biscuit dough. She could put it together and take it in her hand and pat it out flat and lay it on the hearth. It would be just as round! That was the art of it!

"When I go back to Mississippi, I'm going back to that house again. I don't remember seeing the house I was born in. But I was told it was an ordinary log house just like those all the other slaves had,—just a one-room log house.

Freedom

"My father went to the War. He was on the Confederate side. They carried him there as a worker. They cut down all the timber 'round the place where they were to keep the Yankee gunboats from shelling them and knocking the logs down on them. But them Yankees were sharp. They stayed away till everything got dry as a chip. Then they come down and set all that wood afire with their shells, and the wind seemed to be in their favor. The Rebels had to get away from there.

"He got sick before the War closed and he had to come home. His young master and the other folks stayed there four or five months longer. His young master was named Tom. When Tom came home, he waited about five or six months before he would tell them they was free. Then he said, 'You all free as I am. You can stay here if you want or you can go. You are free.' They all got together and told him that if he would treat them right he wouldn't have to do no work. They would stay and do his work and theirs too. They would work the land and he would give them their part. I don't know just what the agreement was. I think it was about a third. Anyway, they worked on shares. When the landlord furnished a team usually it was halves. But when the worker furnished his own team, it was usually two-thirds or three-fourths that the worker got. But none of them owned teams at that time. They were just turned loose. We stayed there with them people a good while. I don't know just how long, but it was several years.

Catching a Hog

"One time a slave went to steal a hog. I don't know the name of the man; I just hear my father tell what happened, and I'm repeating it. It was a great big hog and kind of wild. His plan to catch the hog was to climb a tree and carry a yeer of corn up the tree and at the same time he'd carry a long rope. He had put a running noose in the end of the rope and laid it on the ground and shelled the corn into the ring. He had the other end of the rope tied around himself; he was up the tree. About the time he got the noose pulled up around the hog so that he could tighten up on it, he dropped his hat and scared the hog. The hog didn't know he was around until the hat fell, and the falling of the hat scared it so that it made a big jump and ran a little ways off. That jerked the man out of the tree. Him falling scared the hog a second time and got him to running right. He was a big stout hog, and the man's weight didn't hold him back much. The man didn't know what to do to stop the hog. The hog was running draggin' him along, snatching him over logs. There was nothin' else he could do, so he tried prayer. But the hog didn't stop. Seemed like even the Lord couldn't stop him. Then he questioned the Lord; he said, 'Lawd, what sawt [HW: sort] of a Lawd is you? You can stop the wind; you can stop the rain; you can stop the ocean; but you can't stop this hog.'

"The hog ran till he came to a big ditch. He jumped the ditch, but the man fell in it, and that compelled the hog to stop. The man's hollering made somebody hear him and come and git him loose from the hog. He was so glad to git loose, he didn't mind losing the hog and gettin' punished. He didn't get the hog. He just got a lot of bruises. I don't remember just how they punished him.

Ku Klux Klan

"Once after the War there was a lot of colored people at a prayer meeting. It was in the winter and they had a fire. The Ku Klux come up. They just stood outside the door, but the people thought they were coming in and they got scared. They didn't know hardly how to get out. One man got a big shovelful of hot coals and ashes out of the fireplace and threw it out over them, and while they was dusting off the ashes and coals, the niggers all got away.

Patrollers

"I remember my father telling tales about the patrollers, but I can't remember them just now. There was an old song about them. Part of it went like this:

> 'Run, nigger, run
> The pateroles'll get you.
>
> That nigger run
> That nigger flew
> That nigger bust
> His Sunday shoe.
>
> Run, nigger, run
> The pateroles'll get you.'

That's all I know of that. There is more to it. I used to hear the boys sing it, and I used to hear 'em pick it out on the banjo and the guitar.

Old Massa Goes 'Way

"Old massa went off one time and left the niggers. He told 'em that he was goin' to New York. He jus' wanted to see what they would do if they thought he was away. The niggers couldn't call the name New York, and they said, 'Old massa's gone to PhilameYawk.'

"They went in the pantry and got everything they wanted to eat. And they had a big feast. While they were feasting, the old man came in disguised as a tramp—face smutty and clothes all dirty and raggedy. They couldn't tell who he was. He walked up just as though he wanted to eat and begged the boys for something to eat. The boys said to him, 'Stan' back, you shabby rascal, you; if'n they's anything left, you get some; if'n they ain't none left, you get none. This is our time. Old massa done gone to PhilameYawk and we're having a big time.'

"After they were through, they did give him a little something but they still didn't know him. I never did learn the details about what happened after they found out who the tramp was. My father told me about it.

Whipping a Slave

"I heard my father say his old master give him two licks with a whip once. Him and another man had been off and they came in. Master drove up in a double surrey. He had been to town and had bought the boys a pair of boots apiece. He told them as he got out of the surrey to take his horses out and feed them. My father's friend was there with him and he said: 'Le's get our boots before we feed the horses.' After that the master walked out on the porch and he had on crying boots. The horses heard them squeaking and they nickered.

"Master said, 'Henry, I thought I told you to feed them horses. Henry was so taken aback that he couldn't say a thing. Henry was my father, you know. Master went and got his cowhide. He said, 'Are you going to obey my orders?' About the time he said that, he hit my father twice with the cowhide, and my father said, 'Oh pray, master, oh pray,' and he let him go. He beat the other fellow pretty bad because he told him to 'Le's get the boots first.'

"Old master would get drunk sometimes and get on the niggers and beat them up. He would have them stark naked and would be beating them. Then old missis would come right out there and stop him. She would say, 'I didn't come all the way here from North Carolina to have my niggers beat up for nothin'.' She'd take hold of the cowhide, and he would have to quit. My father had both her picture and the old man's.

Prayer

"I can remember how my mother used to pray out in the field. We'd be picking cotton. She would go off out there in the ditch a little ways. It wouldn't be far, and I would listen to her. She would say to me: 'Pray, son,' and I would say, 'Mother, I don't know how to pray,' and she would say, 'Well, just say Lord have mercy.' That gave me religious inclinations. I cultivated religion from that time on. I would try to pray and finally I learned. One day I was out in the field and it was pouring down rain, and I was standing up with tears in my eyes trying to pray as she taught me to. We weren't picking cotton then. I was just walking out. My mother was dead. I would be walking out and whenever I would get the notion I would stop right there and go to praying.

"In slave times, they would have a prayer meeting out in some of the places and they would turn a pot down out in front of the door. It would be on a stick or something and raised up a short distance from the ground so that it wouldn't set flat on the ground. It seems that that would catch the sound and keep it right around there. They would sing that old song:

> 'We will camp awhile in the wilderness
> And then I'm going home.'

I don't know any more of the words of that song.

Early Schooling

"I started to school when I was about six or seven years old. I didn't get to school regular because my father had plenty of work and he had a habit of taking me out to help him when he needed me in his work.

"My first teacher was a white man named Jones. I don't remember his first name. He was a northerner and a Republican. He taught in the public school with us. His boy, John, and his girl, Louisa, went to the same school, and were in classes with us. The kids would beat them up sometimes but he didn't cut up about it. He was pretty good man.

"After him, I had a colored man named M.E. Davis as a teacher. He would say to my father, 'Henry, that is a bright boy; he will be a credit to you if you will keep him at school and give him a chance. Don't make him lose so much time.' My father would say, 'Yes, that is right.' But as soon as another job came up, he would keep me out again.

"I soon got so my learning was a help to him in his work. Whenever any figuring was to be done, I had to do it if it was done right. He never had a chance to get any schooling and he couldn't figure well. So they used to beat him out of plenty when he would work for them. One day we had picked cotton for a white man and when the time came to pay off, the man paid father, but I noticed that he didn't give him all he should have. I didn't say anything while we was standing there but after we got away I said, 'Papa, he didn't give you the right money.'

"Papa said, 'How much should he have given me?'

"I told him, and he said to me, 'Will you say that to him?'

"I said, 'Yes, papa.'

"He turned 'round and we went on back to the place and pa said, 'My boy says you didn't pay me all that was comin' to me.'

"The white man turned to me at once and said, 'How much was coming to him?'

"I told him.

"He said, 'What makes you think that?'

"I said, 'We picked so many pounds of cotton at so much per hundred pounds, and that would amount to so many dollars and so many cents.'

"When I said that, he fell over on the ground and like to killed his self laughing. He counted out the right money to my father and said, 'Henry, you better watch that little skinny-eyed nigger; he knows something.'

Present Support

"I don't got anything from the government. I live by what little I make at odd jobs."

Note: In this interview this man used correct English most of the time and the interview is given in his own words. Lapses into dialect will be noticed.

Interviewer: Miss Irene Robertson
Person interviewed: Ben Parr, Brinkley, Arkansas
Age: 85 next March (1938)

"I was born in Tennessee close to Ripley. My master was Charles Warpoo and Catherine Warpoo. They had three boys and two girls. They owned my mama and me and Gentry was the oldest child. He died last year. My mama raised twelve children. My papa belong to people over on the Mississippi River. Their name was Parr but I couldn't tell a thing about them. When I come to know about them was after freedom. There was Jim Parr, Dick Parr, Columbus Parr. We lived on their place. Both my parents was farm hands, and all twelve children wid them.

"Well, the first I recollect is that we lived on the five acre lot, the big house, and some of the slaves lived in houses around the big yard all fenced with pailings and nice pickett fence in front of Charlie Warpoo's house. We played around under the trees all day. The soldiers come nearly every day and nearly et us out of house and home. The blue coats seemed the hungriest or greediest pear lack. They both come. Master didn't go to war; his boys was too young to go, so we was all at home. My papa shunned the war. He said he didn't give a pickayune whether he be free or not, it wouldn't do no good if he be dead nohow. He didn't live with us doe (though). They kept papa pretty well hid out with stock in the Mississippi River bottoms. He wasn't scared ceptin' when he come over to see my mama and us. When we come to know anything we was free.

"I never seen nobody sold. None of my folks was sold. The folks raised my mama and they didn't want her to leave. The folks raised papa what had him at freedom. He said him and mama was married long before the war sprung up. I don't know how they married nor where. She was young when they married.

"I remember hearing mama say when you went to preaching you sit in the back of the church and sit still till the preaching was all over. They had no leaving.

"I know when I was a child people raised children, now they let them grow up. Children was sent off or out to play, not sit and listen to what grown folks had to say. Now the children is educated and too smart to listen to good advice. They are going to ruination. Mama used to have our girls knit at night and she spin, weave, sew. They would tell us how to be polite and honest and how to work. Young folks too smart to take advice now.

"Mama was cooking at the Warpoo's house; she cooked breakfast. One morning I woke up and here was a yard full of 'Feds.' I was hungry. I went through the whole regiment—a yard full—to mama hard as I could split. They didn't bother me. I was afraid they would carry me off sometimes. They was great hands to tease and worry the little Negro children.

"Over at Dyersburg, Tennessee the Ku Klux was bad. Jefferie Segress was pretty prosperous, owned his own home. John Carson whooped him, cut his ear off, treated him bad. High Sheriff they said was a 'Fed.' He put twenty-four buck shots in John Carson. That was the last of the Ku Klux at Dyersburg. The Negroes all left Dyersburg. They kept leaving. The 'Feds' was meaner to them than the owners. In 1886, three weeks before Christmas, one hundred head of Negroes got off the train here at Brinkley. The Ku Klux was the tail end of the war, whooping around. It was a fight between the 'Feds' and the old owners—both sides telling the Negroes what to do. The best way was stay at home and work to keep out of trouble.

"The bushwhackers killed Raymond Jones (black man) before the war closed. Well, I don't know what they ambushed for.

"I paid my own way to Arkansas. I brought my wife. Mama was dead.

"If the Negro is a taxpayer he ought to vote like white folks. But they can't run the government. That was tried out after that war we been talking about. Our color has faith in white folks and this is their country. I vote some. We got a good right to vote. We helped clear out the country. It is our home now.

"The present times is too fast. I can't place this young generation.

"This is my second wife I'm living wid now. She's got children. I never had a child. We gets $10 off of the Welfare and I work around at pick-up jobs. I farmed all my whole life."

Interviewer: Samuel S. Taylor
Person interviewed: Frank A. Patterson
906 Chester Street, Little Rock, Arkansas
Age: 88

FRANK A. PATTERSON

"I was born in Raleigh, North Carolina in 1850. My father was born in Baltimore, Maryland. My mother and father was sold into Bibb County, Georgia. I don't know how much they sold for. I don't know how much they paid for them. I don't know how much the speculator asked for them. Used to have them in droves and you would go in and pick 'em out and pay different amounts for them.

"I was never sold. My old boss didn't believe in selling slaves. He would buy 'em but he wouldn't sell 'em. I'll say that much for him.

Master

"I belonged to a man named Thomas Johnson Cater.

Houses

"They lived in log houses. Some of them had weatherboard houses but the majority of them was log houses. Two doors and one window. Some of them had plank floors. Some of them had floors what was hewed, you know, sills. They had stick and dirt chimneys. Some of them had brick chimneys. It depended on the master—on the situation of the master.

Furniture

"They just had bunks built up side the wall. The best experienced colored people had these teester beds. Didn't have no slats. Had ropes. They called 'em cord beds sometimes. They had tables just like we have now what they made themselves. Chairs were long benches made out of planks. Little kids had big blocks to sit on where they sawed off timber.

"They had what they called a cupboard to keep the food in. Some of them had chests made out of planks, you know. That is the way they kept it. They put a hasp and steeple on it so as to keep the children out when they was gone to the field.

Food

"They give 'em three pounds of meat a week, peck of meal, pint of molasses; some of them give 'em three to five pounds of flour on a Sunday morning according to the size of the family. The majority of them had shorts from the wheat. Some of the slaves would clean up a flat in the bottoms and plant rice in it. That was where they would allow the slaves to have truck patches.

"Some few of them had chickens that was allowed to have them. Same of them had owners that wouldn't allow their slaves to own chickens. They never allowed them to have hogs or cows. Wherever there was a family that had a whole lot of children they would allow them to have a cow to milk for to get milk for their children. They claimed the cow, but the master was the owner of it. It belonged to him. He would just let them milk it. He would just let them raise their children off of the milk it gave.

Clothes

"There was no child ever had a pair of shoes until he got old enough to go in the field. That was when he was twelve years old. That is about all I know about it.

Schooling

"I never went to school in my life. I got hold of one of them old blue back spelling books. My young boss gave it to me after I was free. He told me that I was free now and I had to think and act for myself.

Signs of War

"Before the War I saw the elements all red as blood and I saw after that a great comet; and they said there was going to be a war.

Memories of the Pre-War Campaign

"When Fillmore, Buchanan, and Lincoln ran for President one of my old bosses said, 'Hurrah for Buchanan,' and I said, 'Hurrah for Lincoln.' One of my mistresses said, 'Why do you say, 'Hurrah for Lincoln?' And I said, 'Because he's goin' to set me free.'

"During that campaign, Lincoln came to North Carolina and ate breakfast with my master. In those days, the kitchen was off from the house. They had for breakfast ham with cream gravy made out of sweet milk and they had biscuits, poached eggs on toast, coffee and tea, and grits. They had waffles and honey and maple syrup. That was what they had for breakfast.

"He told my old boss that our sons are 'ceivin' children by slaves and buyin' and sellin' our own blood and it will have to be stopped. And that is what I know about that.

Refugeeing

"At the close of the War, we had refugeed down in Houston County in Georgia.

War Memories

"Sherman's army came through there looking for Jeff Davis, and they told me that they wasn't fightin' any more,—that I was free.

"They said, 'You ain't got no master and no mistress.' They et dinner there. All the old folks went upstairs and turned the house over to me and the cook. And they et dinner. One of them said, 'My little man, bring your hat 'round now and we are going to pay you,' and they passed the hat 'round and give me a hat full of money. I thought it wasn't no good and I carried it and give it to my old mistress, but it was good.

"They asked me if I had ever seen Jeff Davis. I said 'No.' Then they said, 'That's him sittin' there.' He had on a black dress and a pair of boots and a mantilla over his shoulders and a Quaker bonnet and a black veil.

"They got up from the dining table and Sherman ordered them to 'Recover arms.' He had on a big black hat full of eagles and he had stars and stripes all over him. That was Sherman's artillery. They had mules with pots and skillets, and frying pans, and axes, and picks, grubbing hoes, and spades, and so on, all strapped on those mules. And the mules didn't have no bridles but they went on just as though they had bridles. One of the Yanks started a song when he picked up his gun.

> 'Here's my little gun
> His name is number one
> Four and five rebels
> We'll slay 'em as they come
> Join the ban'
> The rebels understan'
> Give up all the lan'
> To my brother Abraham
> Old Gen'l Lee
> Who is he?
> He's not such a man
> As our Gen'l Grant
> Snap Poo, Snap Peter
> Real rebel eater
> I left my ply stock
> Standin' in the mould
> I left my family
> And silver and gold
> Snap Poo, Snap Peter
> Real rebel eater
> Snap Poo, Snap Peter.'

"And General Sherman gave the comman', 'Silence', and 'Silence' roared one man, and it rolled all down the line, 'Silence, silence, silence, silence.' And they all got silent.

How Freedom Came

"They had a notification for a big speaking and that was in Perry, Georgia. Everybody that was able throughout the State went to that convention where that speaking was. And that is where peace was declared. Every man was his own free agent. 'No more master, no more mistress. You are your own free moral agent. Think and act for yourself.' That is how it was declared. I didn't go to the meeting. I was right there in the town. There was too many people there. You couldn't stir them with hot fire. But my mother and father went.

What the Slaves Expected

"They didn't expect anything but freedom. Some of them didn't have sense enough to secure a home for themselves. They didn't have no sense. Some of them wasn't eligible to speak for themselves. They wanted somebody to speak for them.

What They Got

"I don't know that they got anything.

Immediately After the War

"Right after the War, I stayed with the people that owned me and worked. They give me two dollars a month and my food and clothes. I stayed with them five years and then I quit. I had sense enough to quit and I went to work for wages. I got five dollars a month. And I thought that was a big salary. I didn't know no better. I learnt better by experience.

Negroes in Politics

"Just after the War, the Republicans used to have representatives at the state convention. After the Democrats got in power, they knocked all that in the head. Colored people used to be on juries. But they won't let them serve now. (Negroes served on local grand jury last year.)

"I knew one nigger politician in Georgia named I.B. Simons. He was a school-teacher. He never held any office. I knowed a nigger politician here by the name of John Bush. He had the United States Land Office. When the Democrats got in power they put him out. I knowed another fellow used to be here named Crockett Brown. He lived in Lee County, Arkansas. He was a Congressman. I don't know whether he ever got to the White House or not. I ain't never seen no account of it. I can't tell you all any more now.

Memories of Fred Douglass

"I knowed Fred Douglass. I shook hands with him and talked with him here in Little Rock. They give him the opera house. We had the first floor. The white folks had the gallery. That was when the Republicans were in power.

"He said: 'They all seem to be amazed and dumbfounded over me having a white woman for a wife.' He said, 'You all don't know that my father was my mother's master and she was as black as a crow. Don't it seem natural that history should repeat itself? have often wondered why he liked such a black woman as my mother. I was jus' a chip off the old block.'

Voting

"I voted for U.S. Grant. He was the first President we had after the Civil War. I shook hands with him twice in Little Rock. He put up at the Capitol Hotel and I was a-cooking there.

"I voted for McKinley. I saw him too. I had a walking cane with his head on it. That is about all I remember right now. He was the one that got up this gold standard. He liked to put this state under bayonet laws when he was working under that gold standard. The South was bitterly against him.

Occupation

"I followed cooking all my life. I have had the white peoples' lives in my hand all my life. I worked on the Government boat, Wichita. It went out of season and they built a boat called the Arkansas. I cooked on it. Captain Griffin was the master of it. When it went out of service, Captain Newcome from the War Department transferred me over to the Mississippi River on the Arthur Hider (?). My headquarters were in Greenville, Mississippi. It was far from home, so after nine months I quit and came home (Little Rock). Captain Van Frank give me a position on a dredge boat and the people were so bad on there I wouldn't stay. I came away. I wouldn't stay 'mongst 'em.

Religion

"I want you to know that I am a Christian and I want you to know I ain't got no compromise with nobody on God's word. I ain't got but one way and that is the way Jesus said:

Come unto me all ye that are heavy laden, and I will give you rest.
He that believeth on me shall be saved. You all fix anything anyway you want. I ain't bothered 'bout you.

"My people were good Christian people."

United States. Work Projects Administration

Interviewer: Miss Irene Robertson
Person interviewed: John Patterson, Helena, Arkansas
Age: 74

JOHN PATTERSON

"I was born near Paducah, Kentucky. Mother was never sold. She belong to Master Arthur Patterson. Mother was what folks called black folks. I never seen a father to know. I never heard mother say a thing about my father if I had one. He never was no use to me nor her neither. Mother brought me here in time of the Civil War. I was four years old. We come here to be kept from the Yankee soldiers. We was sent with some of the Pattersons. At the end of the war mother cooked for Nick Rightor (?) and his wife here in North Helena. He was a farmer but his son is a ear, eye, nose specialist.

"I farmed, cleaned house and yards for these Helena people. I was janitor at the Episcopal church in Helena sixteen years and four months. They paid me forty-five dollars a month.

"Yes ma'am, I have heard about the Ku Klux. Heard talk but never seen one.

"I never been in jail. I never been drunk. Folks in Helena will tell you John Patterson can be trusted.

"I saved up one thousand dollars, just let it slip. The present times are hard. Times are hard. I get ten dollars and comissary helps. I got one in family.

"I think mother said she was treated very good in slavery. She didn't tell me much about it.

"I own a home. It come through a will from my aunt. My uncle was a drayman here in Helena and a close liver. I want to hold to it if I can.

"If you'd ask me what all ain't took place since I been here I could come nigh telling you. We had colored officers here. Austin Barrer was sheriff. Half of the officers was colored at one time. John Jones was police. No, they wasn't friends of mine. I seen these levies built. One was here in 1897. It was rebuilt then.

"It seems to me the country is going down. When they put in the Stock Law people had to sell so much stock. Milch cows sold for six dollars a head. People that want and need stock have no place to raise it. People are not as industrious as they was and they accumolate more it seems to me. We used to make our living at home. I think that is the best way.

"I voted a Republican ticket years ago. I don't believe in women voting. The Lord don't believe in that. I belong to the Baptist church.

"Young folks don't act on education principles. Folks used to fight with fist. Now one shoots the other down. Times are not improving morally. Folks don't even think it is wrong to take things; that is stealing. They drink up all the money they can get. I don't see no colored folks ever save a dollar. They did long time ago. Thaes worse in some ways.

"I forgot our plough songs:

'I wonder where my darling is.'

'Nigger makes de cotton and de
White man gets the money.'

"Everybody used to sing. We worked from sun to sun; we courted and was happy. People not happy now. They are craving now. About four o'clock we all start up singing. Sing till dark."

United States. Work Projects Administration

Interviewer: Samuel S. Taylor
Person interviewed: Sarah Jane Patterson
2611 Orange Street, North Little Rock, Arkansas
Age: 90

SARAH JANE PATTERSON

"I was born in Bartow County, Georgia, January 17, 1848. You can go there and look in that Bible over there and you will find it all written down. My mama kept a record of all our ages. Her old mistress kept the record and gave it to my mother after freedom.

Parents

"My parents were Joe Patterson and Mary Adeline Patterson. My mother's name before she married was Mary Adeline Huff. My grandfather on my mother's side was named Huff. My mother's sisters were Mahala, and Sallie. And them's the onliest two I remember. She had two brothers but I don't remember their names.

How Freedom Came

"I was living in Bartow County in north Georgia when freedom came. I don't remember how the slaves found it out. I remember them saying, 'Well, they's all free.' And that is all I remember. And I remember some one saying—asking a question, 'You got to say master?' And somebody answered and said, 'Naw.' But they said it all the same. They said it for a long time. But they learned better though.

Family

"I have brother Willis, Lizzie, Mary, Maud, and myself. There was four sisters and one brother. I had just one child—a boy. He lived to be a grown man and raised a family. His wife had three children and all of them is gone. The father, the mother, and the children. I was a woman. I wasn't no man. I just had one child, but the Lord blessed me. I have three sisters and a brother dead.

Master

"My old master's name was John Patterson and my old mistress was named Lucy Patterson. She had a son named Bill and a son named Tommy and a son named Charles, and a boy named Bob, and a girl named Marion. We are so for apart they can't help me none. I know Bob's boys are dead because they got killed in a fight in Texas.

Crippled in Slave Time

"I been crippled all my life. We was on the lawn playing and the white boy had been to the pond to water the horses. He came back and said he was going to run over us. We all ran and climbed up on the top of a ten rail fence. The fence gave 'way and broke and fell down with us. I caught the load. They all fell on me. It knocked the knee out of place. They carried me to Stilesboro to Dr. Jeffrey, a white doctor in slavery time. I don't know what he did, but he left me with my knee out of joint after he treated it. I can't work my toes and I have to walk with that stick.

Soldiers

"I was a tot when I seen the soldiers coming dressed in blue, and I run. They was very nice to the colored people, never beat 'em or nothin'. I was in Bartow County when they come through. They took a lot of things, but I can't remember exactly what it was. I 'tended to the children then—both the white and colored children, but mostly the white.

Good Masters

"My old master, John Patterson, never beat up the women and men he bossed.

Patrollers

"I have heard people talk about the pateroles raising sand with the niggers. Some of the niggers would say they got whipped. I was small. I would hear 'em say, 'The pateroles is out tonight.'

Ku Klux Klan

"I have seed the old Ku Klux. That was after freedom. They came 'round to my old master where my mama stayed. They were just after whipping folks. Some of them they couldn't whip.

Support

"I used to get a little money from Mr. Dent long as he was living. I would go over there and he would give me a dollar or two. Since he's been dead, his wife don't have much to give me. She gives me something to eat sometimes but she doesn't have any money now that her husband is dead.

"I can't get up to the Welfare. Crippled as I am, I can't walk up and down those stairs, and I can't git there nohow. I been tryin' to git some one to take me up there.

"Mr. Pratt helps me from time to time, but he ain't sent me nothin' now in a good while. He's right smart busy, but if I go to him, I spect he'll stir up somethin' for me.

Travels

"I wouldn't never a left Bartow County, but the white people made out that this was a rich country and you could make so much out here, and we moved out here. We was young then. We came out on the train. It was a long time back but it was too far to came on a wagon. I don't remember just how long ago it was.

Occupation

"I used to quilt until my fingers got too stiff. I got some patterns in there now if you want to see them."

Interviewer's Comment

The old lady took me in the house and showed me about a dozen quilts, beautifully patterned and made. She had also some unfinished tops. She says that she does not have much of a sale for them now because the "quality of folks" who liked such things well enough to buy them "is just about gone."

She is crippled and unable to walk with facility. She has a great deal of difficulty in getting off and on her porch. Still she does not impress one as feeble so much as just disabled in one or two particulars. She has a crippled knee, and both of her hands are peculiarly stiff in the finger joints, one more so than the other. If it were not for the disabilities, as old as she is, I believe that she could give a good account of herself.

I didn't have the heart to tell the old lady that her Bible record is not what she thinks it is. It is not the old original record which her mistress possessed. Neither is it the copy of the record of her mistress which her mother kept. From questioning, I gather that the old mistress dictated the original record to some one connected with her mother, might have written it out herself on a sheet of paper. From time to time, as new deaths and births occurred, scraps of paper containing them were added to the first paper, and as the papers got worn, blurred, and dog-eared, they were copied—probably not without errors. Time came when the grandchildren up in the grades and with semi-modern[HW:?] ideas copied the scraps into the family Bible. By that time aging and blurring of the original lead pencil notes, together with recopying, had invalidated the record till it is no longer altogether reliable.

The births recorded in the Bible are as follows and in the exact order given below:

      Mary Patterson 10-11-1866
      Harris Donesson 3-13- 72
      Lilley Donesson 7-21- 85
      Pearly Donesson 3-29- 92
      Silvay Williams 8-29- 84

Beney Williams 11-24- 85
Millia A. Williams 12-30- 88
Joe Patterson 10- 3- 77
H. Patterson 7-29- 79
Maria E. Patterson 11-19- 81
Jennie Patterson 12-24- 84
Alex Patterson 7- 5- 86
James Patterson 6-20- 90
Janie Patterson 1-27- 60
Amanda Patterson 1-28- 63
James Rafield Walker 8-11- 99
Cornelius Walker 7-21-1902
Willie Walker 11-20- 03
Elias Walker 7-21- 11
Emmet Brown 1-23- 22
Leon Harris 12-13- 21

The following marriages were given:

May Lee Brown 2-26-1926
James Walker Brown 2-21- 35
Jennie Walker 6-20- 15
Lillie Jean Walker 12-6- 36

The name of Sarah Jane Patterson is not in the list. The list itself is not chronological. It is written in ink but in the stiff cramped hand to be expected of a school child not yet thoroughly familiar with the pen. The eye fixes on the name of Janie Patterson, 1-27-1860. It does not seem probable that this is correct if it is meant to be Sarah Jane. Sarah Jane could give no help except to answer questions about the manner in which the record was made.

These considerations led me to set the record aside in

my own mind so far as Sarah Jane Patterson's age is concerned and to take her word. She has a very clear conception of the change from slavery to freedom. Her memories are blurred and indistinct, but she recollects that this matter was during slavery times and that during freedom. It seems that she had the care of the smaller children during slavery time—at the time she saw the soldiers marching through. This was not during the time of freedom, because she distinguished clearly the Ku Klux time. She would have to be at least eighty to have cared for children. Her tenacious memory of ninety may have some foundation, therefore.

Moreover where writing is done in lead pencil and hurriedly, six is often made to look like four and a part of eight may become blurred till it looks like a zero. That would account for 1848 being transcribed as 1860. There would be nothing unusual, however, in a Sarah Jane and a Jane. I neglected to cover that point in a question.

Interviewer: Samuel S. Taylor
Person interviewed: Solomon P. Pattillo
1502 Martin Street, Little Rock, Arkansas
Age: 76
Occupation: Formerly farmer, teacher, and small dealer—now blind

SOLOMON P. PATTILLO

"I was born November 1862. I was three years old at the time of the surrender. I was born right here in Arkansas—right down here in Tulip, Dallas County, Arkansas. I have never been out of the state but twice.

Refugeeing

"My daddy carried me out once when they took him to Texas during the war to keep the Yanks from setting him free.

"Then I went out once long after slavery to get a load of sand. On the way back, my boat nearly sank. Those are the only two times I ever left the state.

Parents

"My father's name was Thomas Smith, but the Pattillos bought him and he took the name of Pattillo. I don't know how much he sold for. That was the only time he was ever sold. I believe that my father was born in North Carolina. It seems like to me I recollect that is where he said he was born.

"My mother was born in Virginia. I don't know how she got here unless she was sold like my father was. I don't know her name before she got married. Yes, I do; her name was Fannie Smith, I believe.

Houses

"We lived in old log cabins. We had bedsteads nailed to the wall. Then we had them old fashioned cordboard springs. They had ropes made into springs. That was a high class bed. People who had those cord springs felt themselves. They made good sleeping. My father had one. Ropes were woven back and forth across the bed frame.

"We had those old spinning wheels. Three cuts was a day's work. A cut was so many threads. It was quite a day to make them. They had hanks too. The threads were all linked together.

"My mother was a spinner. My father was a farmer. Both of them worked for their master,—old Massa, they called him, or Massa, Mass Tom, Mass John or Massta.

War Recollections

"I remember during the war when I was in Texas with a family of Moody's how old Mistiss had me packing rocks out of the yard in a basket and cleaning the yard. I didn't know it then, but my daddy told me later that that was when I was in Texas,—during the war. I remember that I used to work in my shirt tail.

"The soldiers used to come in the house somewhere and take anything they could get or wanted to take.

Pateroles

"When I was a boy they had a song, 'Run, Nigger, run; The Pateroles will get you.' They would run you in and I have been told they would whip you. If you overstayed your time when your master had let you go out, he would notify the pateroles and they would hunt you up and turn you over to him.

Church Meetings

"Way long then, my father and mother used to say that man doesn't serve the Lord—the true and living God and let it be known. A bunch of them got together and resolved to serve Him any way. First they sang in a whisper, 'Come ye that love the Lord.' Finally they got bold and began to sing in tones that could be heard everywhere, 'Oh for a thousand tongues to sing my Great Redeemer's praise.'

After the War

"After the war my father fanned—made share crops. I remember once how some one took his horse and left an old tired horse in the stable. She looked like a nag. When she got rested up she was better than the one that was took.

"His first farm was down here in Dallas County. He made a share crop with his former master, Pattillo. He never had no trouble with him.

Ku Klux

"I heard a good deal of talk about the Ku Klux Klan, but I don't know anything much about it. They never bothered my father and mother. My father was given the name of being an obedient servant—among the best help they had.

"My father farmed all his life. He died at the age of seventy-two in Tulip, near the year 1885, just before Cleveland's inauguration. He died of typhoid pneumonia. My mother was ninety-six years old when she died in 1909.

Little Rock

"I came to Little Rock in 1894. I came up here to teach in Fourche Dam. Then I moved here. I taught my first school in this county at Cato. I quit teaching because my salary was so poor and then I went into the butcher's business, and in the wood business. I farmed all the while.

"I taught school for twenty-one years. I always was a successful teacher. I did my best. If you contract to do a job for ten dollars, do as much as though you were getting a hundred. That will always help you to get a better job.

"I have farmed all my life in connection with my teaching. I went into other businesses like I said a moment ago. I was a caretaker at the Haven of Rest Cemetery for sometime.

"I was postmaster from 1904 to 1911 at Sweet Home. At one time I was employed on the United States Census.

"I get a little blind pension now. I have no other means of support.

Loss of Eyes

"The doctor says I lost my eyesight on account of cataracts. I had an operation and when I came home, I got to stirring around and it caused me to have a hemorrhage of the eye. You see I couldn't stay at the hospital because it was costing me $3 a day and I didn't have it. They had to take one eye clean out. Nothing can be done for them, but somehow I feel that the lord's going to let me see again. That's the way I feel about it.

"I have lived here in this world this long and never had a fight in my life. I have never been mistreated by a white man in my life. I always knew my place. Some fellows get mistreated because they get out of their place.

"I was told I couldn't stay in Benton because that was a white man's town. I went there and they treated me white. I tried to stay with a colored family way out. They were scared to take me. I had gone there to attend to some business. Then I went to the sheriff and he told me that if they were scared to have me stay at their home, I could stay at the hotel and put my horse in the livery stable. I stayed out in the wagon yard. But I was invited into the hotel. They took care of my horse and fed it and they brought me my meals. The next morning, they cleaned and curried and hitched my horse for me.

"I have voted all my life. I never had any trouble about it.

"The Ku Klux never bothered me. Nobody else ever

did. If we live so that everybody will respect us, the better class will always try to help us."

Interviewer: Miss Irene Robertson
Person interviewed: Carry Allen Patton
Forrest City, Arkansas
Age: 71

CARRY ALLEN PATTON

"I was born in Shelby County, Tennessee. My parents was Tillie Watts and Pierce Allen. He come from Louisiana reckly (directly) after the surrender. My mother come from Virginia. She was sold in Virginia and brought to middle Tennessee close to Murfreesboro and then brought to Memphis and sold. She was dark and my father was too. They was living close to Wilmar, Arkansas when the yellow fever was so bad. I don't remember it. Heard them talk about it.

"I heard my mother say how Mr. Jake Watts saved his money from the Yankees. They had a great big rock flat on both sides. They put on the joints of big meat to weight it down when they salted it down in a barrel. They didn't unjoint the meat and in the joint is where it started to spoil. Well, he put his silver and gold in a pot. It was a big round pot and was smaller around the top. He dug a hole after midnight. He and his two boys James and Dock put the money in this hole in the back yard. They covered the pot with the big flat rock and put dirt on that and next morning they planted a good big cedar tree over the rock, money and all.

"Old Master Jake died during the War and their house

was burned but James lived in one of the cabins in the yard. Dock went to the War. My mother said when they left, that tree was standing.

"My mother run off. She thought she would go cook for the men in the camps but before she got to the camps a wagon overtook her and they stole her. They brought her to Memphis and sold her on a block. They guarded her. She never did know who they was nor what become of them. They kept her in the wagon on the outskirts of the city nearly a month. One man always stayed to watch her. She was scared to death of both of them. One of the men kept a jug of whiskey in the wagon and drunk it but he never would get dead drunk so she could slip off.

"Mr. Johnson bought her and when the surrender come on, Master Johnson took his family and went to Texas. She begged him to take her to nurse but he said if it wasn't freedom he would send her back to Master James Watts and he would let her go back then. He give her some money but she never went back. She was afraid to start walking and before her money give clear out she met up with my father and he talked her out of going back.

"She had a baby pretty soon. It was by them men that stole her. He was light. He died when he got nearly grown. I recollect him good. I was born close to Memphis, the boy died of dysentery.

"When my mother was sold in Virginia she was carried in a wagon to the block and thought she was going to market. She never seen her folks no more. They let them go along to market sometimes and set in the wagon. She had a little pair of gloves she wore when she was sold her grandma had knit for her. They was white, had half thumb and no fingers. When she died I put them in her coffin. She had twins born dead besides me. They was born close to Wilmar, Arkansas.

"We farmed all my life in Arkansas and Mississippi. I married in Mississippi and we come back here before Joe died. I live out here and in Memphis. My son is a janitor at the Sellers Brothers Store in Memphis. My daughter cooks about here in town and I keep her children. I rather farm if I was able.

"I think young folks, both colors, shuns work. Times is running away with itself. Folks is living too fast. They ride too fast and drinks and do all kinds of meanness.

"My father was a mighty poor hand at talking. He said he was sold in a gang shipped to Memphis from New Orleans. Master Allen bought him. He was a boy. I don't know how big. He cleaned fish—scaled them. He butchered and in a few months Mr. Allen set him free. It was surrender when he was sold but Mr. Allen didn't know it or else he meant to keep him on a few years. When he got loose he started farming and farmed till he died. He farmed in Tennessee, Mississippi, and Arkansas. He owned a place but a drouth come along. He got in debt and white folks took it.

"I married in Mississippi. My husband immigrated from South Carolina. He was Joe Patton. I washed and ironed and farmed. I rather farm now if I was able.

"I never got no gov'ment help. I ain't posing it. It is a fine thing. I was in Tennessee when it come on. They said I'd have to stay here six months. I never do stay."

Interviewer: Mrs. Annie L. LaCotts
Person interviewed: Harriett McFarlin Payne
Dewitt, Arkansas
Age: 83

HARRIETT MCFARLIN PAYNE

"Aunt Harriett, were you born in slavery time?"

"Yes, mam! I was big enough to remember well, us coming back from Texas after we refugeed there when the fighting of the war was so bad at St. Charles. We stayed in Texas till the surrender, then we all come back in lots of wagons. I was sick but they put me on a little bed and me and all the little chillun rode in a 'Jersey' that one of the old Negro mammies drove, along behind the wagons, and our young master, Colonel Bob Chaney rode a great big black horse. Oh! he nice-looking on dat horse! Every once and awhile he'd ride back to the last wagon to see if everything was all right. I remember how scared us chillun was when we crossed the Red River. Aunt Mandy said, 'We crossin' you old Red River today, but we not going to cross you any more, cause we are going home now, back to Arkansas.' That day when we stopped to cook our dinner I picked up a lot little blackjack acorns and when my mammy saw them she said, 'Throw them things down, chile. They'll make you wormy.' (I cried because I thought they were chinquapins.) I begged my daddy to let's go back to Texas, but he said, 'No! No! We going with our white folks.' My mama and daddy belonged to Col. Jesse Chaney, much of a gentleman, and his wife Miss Sallie was the best mistress anybody ever had. She was a Christian. I can hear her praying yet! She wouldn't let one of her slaves hit a tap on Sunday. They must rest and go to church. They had preaching at the cabin of some one of the slaves, and in the Summertime sometimes they had it out in the shade under the trees. Yes, and the slaves on each plantation had their own church. They didn't go galavanting over the neighborhood or country like niggers do now. Col. Chaney had lots and lots of slaves and all their houses were in a row, all one-room cabins. Everything happened in that one room,—birth, sickness, death and everything, but in them days niggers kept their houses clean and their door yards too. These houses where they lived was called 'the quarters'. I used to love to walk down by that row of houses. It looked like a town and late of an evening as you'd go by the doors you could smell meat a frying, coffee making and good things cooking. We were fed good and had plenty clothes to keep us dry and warm.

"Along about time for de surrender, Col. Jesse, our master, took sick and died with some kind of head trouble. Then Col. Bob, our young master, took care of his mama and the slaves. All the grown folks went to the field to work and the little chillun would be left at a big room called the nursing home. All us little ones would be nursed and fed by an old mammy, Aunt Mandy. She was too old to go to the field, you know. We wouldn't see our mammy and daddy from early in the morning till night when their work was done, then they'd go by Aunt Mandy's and get their chillun and go home till work time in the morning.

"Some of the slaves were house negroes. They didn't

go to work in the fields, they each one had their own job around the house, barn, orchard, milk house, and things like that.

"When washday come, Lord, the pretty white clothes! It would take three or four women a washing all day.

"When two of de slaves wanted to get married, they'd dress up nice as they could and go up to the big house and the master would marry them. They'd stand up before him and he'd read out of a book called the 'discipline' and say, 'Thou shalt love the Lord thy God with all thy heart, all thy strength, with all thy might and thy neighbor as thyself.' Then he'd say they were man and wife and tell them to live right and be honest and kind to each other. All the slaves would be there too, seeing the 'wedden'.

"Our Miss Sallie was the sweetest best thing in the world! She was so good and kind to everybody and she loved her slaves, too. I can remember when Uncle Tony died how she cried! Uncle Tony Wadd was Miss Sallie's favorite servant. He stayed in a little house in the yard and made fires for her, brought in wood and water and just waited on the house. He was a little black man and white-headed as cotton, when he died. Miss Sallie told the niggers when they come to take him to the grave yard, to let her know when they got him in his coffin, and when they sent and told her she come out with all the little white chillun, her little grandchillun, to see Uncle Tony. She just cried and stood for a long time looking at him, then she said, 'Tony, you have been a good and faithful servant.' Then the Negro men walked and carried him to the graveyard out in a big grove in de field. Every plantation had its own graveyard and buried its own folks, and slaves right on the place.

United States. Work Projects Administration

"If all slaves had belonged to white folks like ours, there wouldn't been any freedom wanted."

Interviewer: Miss Irene Robertson
Person interviewed: John Payne
Brinkley, Ark.
Age: 74

JOHN PAYNE

"I was born in Georgia, close to Bowles Spring, in Franklin County. My mama's master was Reverend David Payne. He was a Baptist preacher. My mama said my father was Monroe Glassby. He was a youngster on a neighboring plantation. He was white. His father was a landowner. I think she said it was 70 miles east of Atlanta where they went to trade. They went to town two or three times a year. It took about a week to go and come.

"From what Mama said they didn't know it was freedom for a long time. They worked on I know till that crop was made and gathered. Somebody sent word to the master, Rev. David, he better turn them slaves loose. Some of the hands heard the message. That was the first they knowed it was freedom. My mama said she seen soldiers and heard fighting. She had heard that if the Yankees won the war all the slaves be free. She set to studyin' what she would do. She didn't know what to do. So when she heard it she asked If she had to be free. She told Rev. David she wanted to stay like she had been staying. After I was up a good size boy we went to Banks County. She done house work and field work too and I done farm work. All kinds and from sun-up till dark every day. Sometimes I get in so late I have to make a torch light to see how to put the feed in the troughs. We had plenty litard—pine knots—they was rich to burn.

"I used to vote but I quit since I come to Arkansas. I come in 1902. I paid my own way and wrote back for my family. I paid their way too. I got one little grandaughter, 20 years old. She is off trying to make her way through college. My wife had a stroke and she can't do much no more. I got a piece of a house. It need repairs. I can't hardly pay my taxes. I can't work much. I got two cows and six little pigs. I got eighty acres land. I worked fourteen years for John Gazolla and that is when I made enough to buy my place. I am in debt but I am still working. Seems like one old man can't make much."

Interviewer: Miss Irene Robertson
Person Interviewed: Larkin Payne
Brinkley, Ark.
Age: 85

LARKIN PAYNE

"I was born in North Carolina. I don't recall my moster's name. My parents was Sarah Hadyn and John Payne. They had seven children. None of them was sold. My pa was sold. He had three sons in the Civil War. None of em was killed. One was in the war four years, the others a good portion of two years. They was helpers.

"Grandma bought grandpa's, freedom. My great grandma was an Indian woman. My mother was dark brown. My father was tolerable light. When I was small child they come in and tell bout people being sold. I heard a whole lot about it that way. It was great grandma Hadyn that was the Indian. My folks worked in the field or anywhere as well as I recollect.

"When freedom come on my folks moved to East Tennessee. I don't know whether they got good treatment or not. They was freedom loving folks. The Ku Klux never bothered us at home. I heard a lot of em. They was pretty hot further south. I had two brothers scared pretty bad. They went wid some white men to South Carolina and drove hogs. The white men come back in buggies or on the train—left them to walk back. The Ku Klux got after them. They had a hard time getting home. I heard the Ku Klux was bad down in Alabama. They had settled down fore I went to Alabama. I owned a home in Alabama. I took stock for it. Sold the stock and come to Arkansas. I had seven children. We raised three.

"When my folks was set free they never got nothing. The mountain folks raised corn and made whiskey. They made red corn cob molasses; it was good. They put lye in the whiskey; it would kill you. They raised hogs plenty. My folks raised hogs and corn. They didn't make no whiskey. I seen em make it and sell it too.

"I heard folks say they rather be under the home men overseers than Northern overseers. They was kinder to em it seem like. I was jes beginnin' to go to the field when freedom come on. I helped pile brush to be burned before freedom. I farmed when I was a boy; pulled fodder and bundled it. I shucked corn, slopped pigs, milked, plowed a mule over them rocks, thinned out corn. I worked twenty days in East Tennessee on the section. I cut and haul wood all winter.

"My parents both died in Arkansas. We come here to get to a fine farmin' country. We did like it fine. I'm still here.

"I have voted. I vote if I'm needed. The white folks country and they been runnin' it. I don't want no enemies. They been good to me. I got no egercation much. I sorter follows bout votin'. We look to the white folks to look after our welfare.

"I get $8.00 and commodities. I work all I can git to do."

Interviewer: Miss Irene Robertson
Person interviewed: Cella Perkins
Marvell and Palestine, Arkansas
Age: 67

CELLA PERKINS

"I was born close to Macon, Georgia. Mama's old mistress, Miss Mari (Maree) Beth Woods, brung her there from fifteen miles outer Atlanta.

"After emancipation Miss Mari Beth's husband got killed. A horse kicked him to death. It shyed at something and it run in front of the horse. He held the horse so it couldn't run. It kicked the foot board clean off, kicked him in the stomach. His boy crawled out of the buggy. That's the way we knowed how it happened. She didn't hurt the boy. His name was Benjamin Woods.

"Pa went to war with his master and he never come back to mama. She never heard from him after freedom. He got captured and got to be a soldier and went 'way off. She didn't never know if he got killed or lost his way back home.

"Mama cooked and kept up the house. Miss Mari Beth kept a boarding house in Macon till way after I was a big girl. I stood on a box and washed dishes and dried them for mama.

"Mr. Ben was grown when we come to Arkansas. He got his ma to go to Kentucky with him and I heard about

Arkansas. Me and mama come to Palestine. We come in a crowd. A man give us tickets and we come by our lone selves till we got to Tennessee. A big crowd come from Dyersburg, Tennessee. Ma got to talking and found out we was headed fo' the same place in Arkansas.

"Ma talked a whole heap at tines more 'an others (times) about slavery times. Her master didn't take on over her much when he found out she was a barren woman. The old man Crumpton give her to his youngest daughter, Miss Mari Beth. She always had to do all kinds of work and house turns.

"After mama's slavery husband didn't come back and she was living in Macon, she fell in love with another man and I was a picked-up baby. Mama said Miss Mari Beth lost faith in her when I was born but she needed her and kept her on. Said seem like she thought she was too old to start up when she never had children when her papa owned her. They didn't like me. She said she could trust mama but she didn't know my stock. He was a black man. Mama was black as I is.

"Miss Mari Beth had a round double table. The top table turned with the victuals on it. I knocked flies three times a day over that table.

"I never had a store-bought dress in my life till mama bought me one at Madison, Arkansas. I wanted a pure white dress. She said if we made a good crop she was going to give me a dress. All the dresses I ever had was made out of Miss Mari Beth's dresses but I never had a pure white one. I never had one bought for me till I was nearly grown. I was so proud of it. When I would go and come back, I would pull it off and put it away. I wore it one summer white and the next summer I blued it and had a new dress. I had a white dress nearly every year till I got too old to dress up gay now. I got a white bonnet and apron I wears right now.

"Mama said Master Crumpton bought up babies to raise. She was taken away from her folks so soon she never heard of them. Aunt Mat raised her up in Atlanta and out on his place. He had a place in town but kept them on a place in the country. He had a drove of them. He hired them out. He hired mama once to a doctor, Dr. Willbanks. Mama said old master thought she would learn how to have children from him the reason he sent her there so much. When they had big to-dos old master sent mama over there. She never seen no money till about freedom. She loved to get hired out to be off from him. They all had young babies about but her. He was cross and her husband was cross. She had pleasure hired out. She said he didn't whoop much. He stamped his foot. They left right now.

"I hab three girls living; one here (Palestine), one at Marvell, and one in St. Louis. My youngest girl teaches music at a big colored school. She sends me my money and I lives with these girls. I been up there and I sure don't aim to live in no city old as I is. It's too dangerous slow as I got to be and so much racket I never slept a night I was there. I was there a month. She brung me home and I didn't go back.

"I cooked and washed and ironed and worked in the field. I do some work yet. I helps out where I am.

"The times is better I think from accounts I hear. This

generation all living too fast er lives. They don't never be still a minute."

Pine Bluff District
FOLKLORE SUBJECTS
Name of Interviewer: Martin & Barker
Subject: Ex-Slaves—Slavery Times

This Information given by: Maggie Perkins
Place of Residence: W. 6th. St.

[TR: Information moved from bottom of first page.]

MAGGIE PERKINS

My folks lived in S. Carolina and belonged to Col. Bob Baty and his family.

If I should lay down tonight I could tell when my folks were going to die, because the Lawd would tell me in a vision.

Just before my grandmother died, I got up one morning and told my aunt that granma was dead. Aunt said she did not want me telling lies.

Then I saw another aunt laying on the bed, and she had her hand under her jaw. She was smiling. The house was full of people. After awhile they heard that her aunt was dead too, and after that they paid attention to me when I told them somebody was going to die.

I'se a member of the Holiness Church. I believes step up right and keep the faith.

I seen my aunt walking up and down on a glass. The Lawd tells me in a vision to step right up and see the faith.

I am living in Jesus. He is coming to Pine Bluff soon. He is going to separate the lions from the sheep.

I was born in slavery times. I member folks riding around on horses.

Them days I used to wash my mistis feet and legs, and sometimes I would fall asleep against my mistis knees. I tells the young fry to give honor to the white folks, and my preacher tell 'em to obey the white folks, dat dey are our best friends, dey is our dependence and it would be hard getting on if we didn't have em to help us.

Spirits—Me and my husband moved into a house that a man, "uncle Bill" Hearn died in, and we wanted dat house so bad we moved right in as soon as he was taken out, we ate supper and went to bed.

By the time we got to sleep we heard sounds like someone was emptying shelled corn, and I hunched up under my husband scared to death and then moved out the next day. The dead haven't gone to Heaven. When death comes, he comes to your heart. He has your number and knows where to find you. He won't let you off, he has the key.

Death comes and unlocks the heart and twists the breath out of that heart and carries it back to God.

Nobody has gone to Heaven, no one can get pass Jesus until the day of his redemption, which is judgement day.

We can't pass the door without being judged. On the day of ressurection the trumpet will sound and us will wake up out of he graveyard, and come forth to be judged. The sea shall give up its dead. Every nation will have to appear before God and be judged in a twinklin of an eye. If you aren't prepared before Jesus comes, it will be too late. God is everywhere, he is the almight. God is a nice God, he is a clean God, he is a good God. I would be afraid to tell you a lie for God would strike me down.

Eight years ago I couldn't see, I wore specs 3 years. I forgot my specs one morning, I prayed for my eyesight and it was restored that morning.

Our marster was a good man. De overseers sometimes wuz bad, but dey did not let marsters know how dey treated their girl slaves. My grandmother was whipped by de overseers one time, it made welts on her back. My sister Mary had a child by a white man.

To get joy in de morning, get up and pray and ask Him to bless you. God will feed all alike, he is no respector of persons. He shows no extra favors twixt de rich and de poor.

United States. Work Projects Administration

Interviewer: Bernice Bowden
Person interviewed: Marguerite Perkins
West Sixth and Catalpa Streets, Pine Bluff, Arkansas
Age: 81

MARGUERITE PERKINS

"I was born in slavery times, Miss. I was born in South Carolina, Union County. I was born in May.

"I know I 'member old Missy. I just been washin' her feet and legs when they said the Yankees was comin. Old Miss' name was Miss Sally. Her husband was a colonel. What is a colonel?

"I got some white cousins. They tell me they was the boss man's chillun.

"Yes'm, I reckon Miss Sally was good to me. I'm a old nigger. All us niggers belonged to Colonel Beatty. I went to school a little while but I didn't learn nothin'.

"I use to be a nurse girl and sleep right upstairs.

"Missus, you know people just walkin along the street droppin dead with heart trouble and white women killin men. I tell you lady it's awful.

"I been married just once. The Lord took him out o' my house one Sunday morning 'fore day.

"The thing about it is I got that high blood pressure. Well, Missus, I had it five years ago and I went to Memphis and the Lord healed me. All we got to do is believe in the Lord and He will put you on your feet.

"I had four sisters and three brothers and all of 'em dead but me, darlin.

"Now let me tell you somethin'. Old as I is, I ain't never been to but one picture show in my life. Old as I is, I never was on a base ball ground in my life. The onliest place I go now is to church."

Interviewer: Miss Irene Robertson
Person interviewed: Rachel Perkins, Goodwin, Arkansas
Age: ? Baby during the Civil War

RACHEL PERKINS

"I was born in Greensboro, Alabama. Sallie Houston and Peter Houston was my parents. They had two girls and a boy. They died when they was small, but me. They always told me mother died when I was three days old in the cradle. I don't fur a fact know much about my own people. Miss Agnes took me to raise me fur a house girl. She nursed me wid her Mary. My mother's and father's owners was Alonso Brown and Miss Agnes Brown. Their two girls was Mary and Lucy and their three boys was Bobby, Jesse, and Frank. Miss Agnes rocked the babies to sleep in a big chair out on the gallery. We slept there all night. Company come and say, 'Where the babies?' Miss Agnes take them back and show us off. They say, 'Where the little black chile?' They'd try to get me to come go live wid them. They say they be good to me. I'd tell 'em, 'No, I stay here.' It was good a home as I wanted. We slept on the front gallery till Lucy come on, then we had sheep skin pallets. She got the big chair. She put us out there because it was cool.

"I left Miss Agnes when I got to be my own woman. Didn't nobody toll me off. I knowed I ought to go to my own race of people. They come after me once. Then they sent the baby boy after me what I had nursed. I wanted to go but I never went. Miss Lucy and Miss Mary both in college. It was lonesome for me. I wanted to go to my color. I jus' picked up and walked on off.

"My girl is half Indian. I'm fifteen years older than my girl. Then I married Wesley Perkins, my husband. He is black fur a fact. He died last fall. I married at my husband's brother's by a colored preacher. Tom Screws was his name. He was a Baptist preacher.

"I never went to school a day in my life. I can't read. I can count money. Seem lack it jus' come natural. I never learned it at no one time. It jus' come to me.

"In warm weather I slept on the gallery and in cold weather I slept by the fire. I made down my own bed. I cleaned the house. I took the cows off to the pasture. I nursed the babies, washed and dried the dishes. I made up the beds and cleaned the yards.

"Master Brown owned two farms. He had plenty hands on his farms. I did never go down to the farms much but I knowed the hands. On Saturday little later than other days they brought the stock to the house and fed. Then they went to the smokehouse for their rations. He had a great big garden, strawberries, and grape arbors.

"One thing I had to do was worm the plants. I put the worms in a bottle and leave it in the row where the sun would dry the worms up. When a light frost come I would water the plants that would wilt before the sun riz and ag'in at night. Then the plants never felt the frost. Certainly it didn't kill 'em. It didn't hurt 'em.

"Julane was the regular milk woman. She milked and strained the milk. I churned and 'tended to the chickens. Miss Agnes sot the hens her own self. She marked the eggs with a piece of charcoal to see if other hens laid by the setting hen. If they did she'd take the new egg out of the nest.

"We had flower gardens. We had mint, rosemary, tansy, sage, mullen, catnip, horseradish, artichokes, hoarhound—all good home remedies.

"I never knowed when we moved to that farm. I was so small. I heard Miss Agnes Brown say I was a baby when they moved to Boldan depot, not fur from Clinton, Mississippi.

"When I left Miss Agnes I went to some folks my own color on another farm 'joining to their farm. Of course I took my baby. I took Anna and I been living with Anna ever since. What I'd do now without her. (Anna is an Indian and very proud of being half Indian.) My husband done dead.

"I get eight dollars welfare help. And I do get some commodities. Anna does all right but she got hit on the shoulder and about lost use of her arm. One of the railroad hands up here got mad and hit her. I had doctors. They done it a little good. It's been hurt three years or more now.

"I wisht I knowd where to find a bed of mullen. Boil it down to a syrup and add some molasses, boil that down. It makes a good syrup for coughs and colds.

"I never went to white folks' church none hardly. Miss Agnes sent me along with her cook to my own color's church.

"My husband sure was good to me. We never had but one fight. Neither one whooped.

"This young generation is going backward. They tired of training. They don't want no advice. They don't want to work out no more. They don't know what they want. I think folks is trifling than they was when I come on. The times is all right and some of the people. I'm talking about mine and yo' color both."

Interviewer: Mrs. Bernice Bowden
Person interviewed: Dinah Perry
1800 Ohio Street, Pine Bluff, Arkansas
Age: 78

DINAH PERRY

"Yes ma'am, I lived in slavery times. They brought me from Alabama, a baby, right here to this place where I am at, Mr. Sterling Cockril.

"I don't know zackly when I was born but I member bout the slave times. Yes ma'am, I do. After I growed up some, I member the overseer—I do. I can remember Mr. Burns. I member when he took the hands to Texas. Left the chillun and the old folks here.

"Oh Lord, this was a big plantation. Had bout four or five hundred head of niggers.

"My mother done the milkin' and the weavin'. After free times, I wove me a dross. My mother fixed it for me and I wove it. They'd knit stockin's too. But now they wear silk. Don't keep my legs warm.

"I member when they fit here in Pine Bluff. I member when 'Marmajuke' sent word he was gain' to take breakfast with Clayton that mornin' and they just fit. I can remember that was 'Marmajuke.' It certainly was 'Marmajuke.' The Rebels tried to carry me away but the wagon was so full I didn't get in and I was glad they didn't. My mother was runnin' from the Rebels and she hid under the cotehouse. After the battle was over she come back hero to the plantation.

"I had three brothers and three sisters went to Texas and I know I didn't know em when they come back.

"I member when they fit here a bum shell fell right in the yard. It was big around as this stovepipe and was all full of chains and things.

"After free time my folks stayed right here and worked on the shares. I was the baby chile and never done no work till I married when I was fifteen.

"After the War I went to school to white teachers from the North. I never went to nothin' but them. I went till I was in the fifth grade.

"My daddy learned me to spell 'lady' and 'baker' and 'shady' fore I went to school. I learned all my ABC's too. I got out of the first reader the second day. I could just read it right on through. I could spell and just stand at the head of the class till the teacher sent me to the foot all the time.

"My daddy was his old mistress' pet. He used to carry her to school all the time and I guess that's where he got his learnin'.

"After I was married I worked in the field. Rolled logs, cut brush, chopped and picked cotton.

"I member when they had that 'Bachelor' (Brooks-Baxter) War up here at Little Rock.

"After my chillun died, I never went to the field no

more. I just stayed round mongst the white folks nussin'. All the chillun I nussed is married and grown now.

"All this younger generation—white and colored—I don't know what's gwine come of em. The poet says:
'Each gwine a different way
And all the downward road.'"

United States. Work Projects Administration

Interviewer: Mrs. Bernice Bowden
Person interviewed: Dinah Perry
1002 Indiana, Pine Bluff, Arkansas
Age: 78

[TR: Appears to be same as last informant despite different address.]

DINAH PERRY

"I'se bawn in Alabama and brought here to Arkansas a baby. I couldn't tell what year I was bawn 'cause I was a baby. A chile can't tell what year he was bawn 'less they tells him and they sure didn't tell me.

"When I'd wake up in the mawnin' my mother would be gone to the field.

"Some things I can remember good but you know old folks didn't 'low chillun to stand around when they was talkin' in dem days. They had to go play. They had to be mighty particular or they'd get a whippin'.

"Chillun was better in them days 'cause the old folks was strict on 'em. Chillun is raisin' theirselves today.

"I 'member one song they used to sing

>'We'll land over shore
>We'll land over shore;
>And we'll live forever more.'

"They called it a hymn. They'd sing it in church, then they'd all get to shoutin'.

"Superstitions? Well, I seen a engineer goin' to work the other day and a black cat run in front of him, and he went back 'cause he said he would have a wreck with his train if he didn't. So you see, the white folks believes in things like that too.

"I never was any hand to play any games 'cept 'Chick. Chick.' You'd ketch 'hold a hands and ring up. Had one outside was the hawk and some inside was the hen and chickens. The old mother hen would say

> 'Chick-a-ma, chick-a-ma, craney crow,
> Went to the well to wash my toe;
> When I come back my chicken was gone,
> What time is it, old witch?'

One chicken was s'posed to get out and then the hawk would try to ketch him.

"We was more 'ligious than the chillun nowadays. We used to play preachin' and baptisin'. We'd put 'em down in the water and souse 'em and we'd shout just like the old folk. Yes ma'am."

Interviewer: Mrs. Bernice Bowden
Person interviewed: Alfred Peters, 1518 Bell Street,
Pine Bluff, Arkansas
Age: 78

ALFRED PETERS

"I was born seven miles from Camden.

"I was 'leven months old when they carried us to Texas. First thing I remember I was in Texas.

"Lucius Grimm was old master. He's been dead a long time. His wife died 'bout two years after the Civil War and he died twenty-five years after.

"I 'member durin' of the war he buried his stuff---silverware and stuff—and he never took it up. And after he died his brother's son lived in California, and he come back and dug it up.

"The Yankees burned up four hundred bales of cotton and taken the meat and two cribs of corn.

"I heard 'em talk 'bout the Ku Klux but I never did see 'em.

"My mother said old Mars Lucius was good to his folks. She said he first bought her and then she worried so 'bout my father, he paid twenty-five hundred dollars for him.

"Biggest part of my life I farmed, and then I done carpenter work.

"I been blind four years. The doctor says it's cataracts.

"I think the younger generation goin' to cause another war. They ain't studyin' nothin' but pleasure."

Interviewer: S.S. Taylor
Person interviewed: Mary Estes Peters,
3115 W. 17th Street, Little Rock, Arkansas
Age: 78

MARY ESTES PETERS

Biographical

Mary Estes Peters was born a slave January 30, 1860 in Missouri somewhere. Her mother was colored and her father white, the white parentage being very evident in her color and features and hair. She is very reticent about the facts of her birth. The subject had to be approached from many angles and in many ways and by two different persons before that part of the story could be gotten.

Although she was born in Missouri, she was "refugeed" first to Mississippi and then here, Arkansas. She is convinced that her mother was sold at least twice after freedom,—once into Mississippi, one into Helena, and probably once more after reaching Arkansas, Mary herself being still a very small child.

I think she is mistaken on this point. I did not debate with her but I cross-examined her carefully and it appears to me that there was probably in her mother's mind a confused knowledge of the issuance of the Emancipation Proclamation in 1862. Lincoln's Compensation Emancipation plan advocated in March 1863, the Abolition in the District of Columbia in 1862 in April, the announcement of Lincoln's Emancipation intention in July 1862, the prohibition of slavery in present and future territories, June 19, 1862, together with the actual issuance of the Emancipation in September 1862, and the effectiveness of the proclamation in January 1, 1863, would well give rise to an impression among many slaves that emancipation had been completed.

As a matter of fact, Missouri did not secede; the Civil War which nevertheless ensued would find some slaveholders exposed to the full force of the 1862 proclamation in 1863 at the time of its first effectiveness. Naturally it did not become effective in many other places till 1865. It would very naturally happen then that a sale in Missouri in the latter part of 1862 or any time thereafter might be well construed by ex-slaves as a sale after emancipation, especially since they do not as a rule pay as much attention to the dates of occurrences as to their sequence. This interpretation accords with the story. Only such an explanation could make probable a narrative which places the subject as a newborn babe in 1860 and sold after slavery had ceased while still too young to remember. Her earliest recollections are recollections of Arkansas.

She has lived in Arkansas ever since the Civil War and in Little Rock ever since 1879. She made a living as a seamstress for awhile but is now unable to sew because of fading eyesight. She married in 1879 and led a long and contented married life until the recent death of her husband. She lives with her husband's nephew and ekes out a living by fragmentary jobs. She has a good memory and a clear mind for her age.

Slave After Freedom

"My mother was sold after freedom. It was the young folks did all that devilment. They found they could get some money out of her and they did it. She was put on the block in St. Louis and sold down into Vicksburg, Mississippi. Then they sold her into Helena, Arkansas. After that they carried her down into Trenton (?), Arkansas. I don't know whether they sold her that time or not, but I reckon they did. Leastways, they carried her down there. All this was done after freedom. My mother was only fifteen years old when she was sold the first time, and I was a baby in her arms. I don't know nothing about it myself, but I have heard her tell about it many and many a time. It was after freedom. Of course, she didn't know she was free.

"It was a good while before my mother realized she was free. She noticed the other colored people going to and fro and she wondered about it. They didn't allow you to go round in slave times. She asked them about it and they told her, 'Don't you know you are free?' Some of the white people too told her that she was free. After that, from the way she talked, I guess she stayed around there until she could go some place and get wages for her work. She was a good cook.

Mean Mistress

"I have seen many a scar on my mother. She had mean white folks. She had one big scar on the side of her head. The hair never did grow back on that place. She used to comb her hair over it so that it wouldn't show. The way she got it was this:

"One day her mistress went to high mass and left a lot of work for my mother to do. She was only a girl and it was too much. There was more work than she could get done. She had too big a task for a child to get done. When her old mistress came back and her work was not all done, she beat my mother down to the ground, and then she took one of the skillets and bust her over the head with it—trying to kill her, I reckon. I have seen the scar with my own eyes. It was an awful thing.

"My mother was a house servant in Missouri and Mississippi. Never done no hard work till she came here (Arkansas). When they brought her here they tried to make a field hand out of her. She hadn't been used to chopping cotton. When she didn't chop it fast as the others did, they would beat her. She didn't know nothing about no farmwork. She had all kinds of trouble. They just didn't treat her good. She used to have good times in Missouri and Mississippi but not in Arkansas. They just didn't treat her good. In them days, they'd whip anybody. They'd tie you to the bed or have somebody hold you down on the floor and whip you till the blood ran.

"But, Lawd, my mother never had no use for Catholics because it was a Catholic that hit her over the head with that skillet—right after she come from mass.

Food

"My mother said that they used to pour the food into troughs and give it to the slaves. They'd give them an old, wooden spoon or something and they all eat out of the same dish or trough. They wouldn't let the slaves eat out of the things they et out of. Fed them just like they would hogs.

"When I was little, she used to come to feed me about twelve o'clock every day. She hurry in, give me a little bowl of something, and then hurry right on out because she had to go right back to her work. She didn't have time to stay and see how I et. If I had enough, it was all right. If I didn't have enough, it was all right. It might be pot liquor or it might be just anything.

"One day she left me alone and I was lying on the floor in front of the fireplace asleep. I didn't have no bed nor nothing then. The fire must have popped out and set me on fire. You see they done a whole lot of weaving in them days. And they put some sort of lint on the children.

"I don't reckon children them days knowed what a biscuit was. They just raked up whatever was left off the table and brung it to you. Children have a good time nowadays.

"People goin' to work heard me hollering and came in and put out the fire. I got scars all round my waist today I could show you.

"Another time my mother had to go off and leave me. I was older then. I guess I must have gotten hungry and wanted to get somethin' to eat. So I got up and wandered off into the woods. There weren't many people living round there then. (This was in Trenton (?), Arkansas, a small place not far from Helena.) And the place was [HW: not] built up much then and they had lots of wolves. Wolves make a lot of noise when they get to trailin' anything. I got about a half mile from the road and the wolves got after me. I guess they would have eat me up but a man heard them howling, and he knew there wasn't no house around there but ours, and he came to see what was up, and he beat off the wolves and carried me back home. There wasn't nare another house round there but ours and he knew I must have come from there.

"Mother was working then. It was night though. They brung the news to her and they wouldn't let her come to me. Mother said she felt like getting a gun and killin' them. Her child out like that and they wouldn't let her go home.

"That must have happened after freedom, because it was the last mistress she had. Almost all her beatings and trouble came from her last mistress. That woman sure gave her a lot of trouble.

Age, Good Masters

"All I know about my age is what my mother told me.

"The first people that raised my mother had her age in the Bible. She said she was about fifteen years old when I was born. From what she told me, I must be about seventy-eight years old. She taught me that I was born on Sunday, on the thirtieth of January, in the year before the War.

"My mother's name was Myles. I don't know what her first master's name was. She told me I was born in Phelps County, Missouri; I guess you'd call it St. Louis now. I am giving you the straight truth just as she gave it to me.

"From the way she talked, the people what raised her from a child were good to her. They raised her with their children. Them people fed her just like they fed their own children.

Color and Birth

"There was a light brownskin boy around there and they give him anything that he wanted. But they didn't like my mother and me—on account of my color. They would talk about it. They tell their children that when I got big enough, I would think I was good as they was. I couldn't help my color. My mother couldn't either.

"My mother's mistress had three boys, one twenty-one, one nineteen, and one seventeen. Old mistress had gone away to spend the day one day. Mother always worked in the house. She didn't work on the farm in Missouri. While she was alone, the boys came in and threw her down on the floor and tied her down so she couldn't struggle, and one after the other used her as long as they wanted for the whole afternoon. Mother was sick when her mistress came home. When old mistress wanted to know what was the matter with her, she told her what the boys had done. She whipped them and that's the way I came to be here.

Sales and Separations

"My mother was separated from her mother when she was three years old. They sold my mother away from my grandmother. She don't know nothing about her people. She never did see her mother's folks. She heard from them. It must have been after freedom. But she never did get no full understanding about them. Some of them was in Kansas City, Kansas. My grandmother, I don't know what became of her.

"When my mother was sold into St. Louis, they would have sold me away from her but she cried and went on so that they bought me too. I don't know nothing about it myself, but my mother told me. I was just nine months old then. They would call it refugeeing. These people that had raised her wanted to get something out of her because they found out that the colored people was going to be free. Those white people in Missouri didn't have many slaves. They just had four slaves—my mother, myself, another woman and an old colored man called Uncle Joe. They didn't get to sell him because he bought hisself. He made a little money working on people with rheumatism. They would ran the niggers from state to state about that time to keep them from getting free and to get something out of them. My mother was sold into Mississippi after freedom. Then she was refugeed from one place to another through Helena to Trenton (?), Arkansas.

Marriages

"My mother used to laugh at that. The master would do all the marryin'. I have heard her say that many a time. They would call themselves jumpin' the broom. I don't know what they did. Whatever the master said put them together. I don't know just how it was fixed up, but they helt the broom and master would say, 'I pronounce you man and wife' or something like that.

Ku Klux

"My mother talked about the Ku Klux but I don't know much about them. She talked about how they would ride and how they would go in and destroy different people's things. Go in the smoke house and eat the people's stuff. She said that they didn't give the colored people much trouble. Sometimes they would give them something to eat.

"When they went to a place where they didn't give the colored people much to eat, what they didn't destroy they would say, 'Go get it.' I don't know how it was but the Ku Klux didn't have much use for certain white people and they would destroy everything they had.

"I have lived in Arkansas about all my life. I have been in Little Rock ever since January 30, 1879. I don't know how I happened to move on my birthday. My husband brought me here for my rheumatism.

"I married in 1879 and moved here from Marianna. I had lived in Helena before Marianna.

Voting

"The niggers voted in Marianna and in Helena. They voted in Little Rock too. I didn't know any of them. It seems like some of the people didn't make so much talk about it. They did, I guess, though. Many of the farmers would tell their hands who they wanted them to vote for, and they would do it.

"Them was critical times. A man would kill you if he got beat. They would say, 'So and so lost the lection,' and then somebody would go to Judgment. I remember once they had a big barbecue in Helena just after the 'lection. They had it for the white and for the colored alike. We didn't know there was any trouble. The shooting started on a hill where everybody could see. First thing you know, one man fell dead. Another dropped down on all fours bleeding, but he retch in under him and dragged out a pistol and shot down the man that shot him. That was a sad time. Niggers and white folks were all mixed up together and shooting. It was the first time I had ever been out. My mother never would let me go out before that.

Seamstress

"I ain't able to do much of anything now. I used to make a good living as a dressmaker. I can't sew now because of my eyes. I used to make many a dollar before my eyes got to failing me. Make pants, dresses, anything. When you get old, you fail in what you been doing. I don't get anything from the government. They don't give me any kind of help."

Interviewer: Mrs. Bernice Bowden
Person interviewed: John Peterson, 1810 Eureka Street,
Pine Bluff, Arkansas
Age: 80

JOHN PETERSON

"I was small but I can remember some 'bout slavery days. I was born down here in Louisiana.

"I seed dem Yankees come through. Dey stopped dere and broke up all de bee gums. Just tore 'em up. And took what dey could eat and went on. Dey was doin' all dey could do. No tellin' what dey didn't do. People what owned de place just run off and left. Yankees come dere in de night. I 'member dat. Had ever'thing excited, so my white folks just skipped out. Oh, yes, dey come back after the Yankees had gwine on.

"You could hear dem guns shootin' around. I heered my mother and father say de Yankees was fightin' to free slavery.

"Run off? Oh Lawd, yes ma'am, I heered 'em say dey was plenty of 'em run off.

"George Swapsy was our owner. I know one thing, dey beat me enough. Had me watchin' de garden to keep de chickens out. And sometimes I'd git to playin' and fergit and de chickens would git in de garden, and I'd pay for it too. I can 'member dat. Yes'm, dat was before freedom. Dey was whippin' all de colored people—and me too.

"Yes'm, dey give us plenty to eat, but dey didn't give us no clothes. I was naked half my time. Dat was when I was a little fellow.

"We all belonged to de same man. Dey never did 'part us. But my mother was sold away from her people—and my father, too. He come from Virginia.

"No ma'am, dey didn't have a big plantation—just a little place cleared up in the woods.

"He didn't have no wife—just two grown sons and dey bof went to the war.

"Mars George died 'fore peace declared. He was a old fellow—and mean as he could be.

"I never went to school till I was sixteen or seventeen years old. Dere was a colored fellow had a little learnin' and we hired him two nights in de week for three dollars a month. Did it for three years. I can read a little and write my own name and sort of 'tend to my own business.

"Yes'm, I used to vote after I got grown. Yes'm, I did vote Republican. But de white people stopped us from votin'. Dat was when Seymour and Blair was runnin', and I ain't voted none since—I just quit. I've known white people to go to the polls wif der guns and keep de colored folks from votin'.

"Oh, dey was plenty of Ku Klux. I've known 'em to ketch people and whip 'em and kill 'em. Dey didn't bother me—I didn't give 'em a chance. Ku Klux—I sure 'member dem.

"Younger generation? Well, Miss, you're a little too hard for me. Hard to tell what'll become of 'em. I know one thing—dey is wiser. Oh, my Lawd! A chile a year old know more'n I did when I was ten. We didn't have no chance. Didn't have nobody to learn us nothin'. People is just gittin' wuss ever' day. Killin' 'em up ever' day. Wuss now than dey was ten years ago."

United States. Work Projects Administration

Interviewer: Miss Irene Robertson
Person interviewed: Louise Pettis, Brinkley, Arkansas
Age: 59

LOUISE PETTIS

"My mama was born at Aiken, South Carolina. She was Frances Rotan. I was born at Elba, South Carolina, forty miles below Augusta, Georgia. My papa was born at Macon, Georgia. Both my parents was slaves. He farmed and was a Baptist preacher. Mama was a cook.

"Mama was owned by some of the Willis. There was three; Mike, Bill, and Logie Willis, all brothers, and she lived with them all but who owned her I don't know. She never was sold. Papa wasn't either. Mama lived at Aiken till papa married her. She belong to some of the Willis. They married after freedom. She had three husbands and fifteen children.

"Mama had a soldier husband. He took her to James Island. She runned off from him. Got back across the sea to Charleston to Aunt Anette's. She was mama's sister. Mama sent back to Aiken and they got her back to her folks. Aunt Anette had been sold to folks at Charleston.

"Grandma was Rachel Willis. She suckled some of the Willis children. Mama suckled me and Mike Willis together. His mama got sick and my mama took him and raised him. She got well but their names have left me. When we got sick the Willis women would send a hamper basket full of provisions, some cooked and some to be cooked. I used to sweep their yards. They was white sand and not a sprig of grass nor a weed in there.

"Mama and papa was both slavery niggers and they spoke mighty well of their owners.

"Papa said in slavery times about two nights in a week they would have a dance. He would slip off and go. Sometimes he would get a pass. He was a figger caller till he 'fessed religion. One time the pattyrollers come in. They said, 'All got passes tonight.' When they had about danced down my daddy got a shovelful of live coals and run about scattering it on the floor. All the niggers run out and he was gone too. It was a dark night. A crowd went up the road and here come the pattyrollers. One run into grapevines across the road and tumbled off his horse. The niggers took to the woods then. Pa tole us about how he studied up a way to get himself and several others outer showing their passes that night. Master never found that out on him.

"During the War they sent a lot of the meat to feed the soldiers on and kept the skins and sides. They tole them if the Yankees ask them if they had enough to eat say, 'See how greasy and slick I is.' They greased their legs and arms to make them shine and look fat. The dust made the chaps look rusty.

"Papa saved his young mistress' life. His master was gone to war. He had promised with others to take care of her. The Yankees come and didn't find meat. It was buried. They couldn't find much. They got mad and burned the house. Pa was a boy. He run up there and begged folks not to burn the house; they promised to take care of everything. Papa begged to let him get his mistress and three-day-old baby. They cursed him but he run in and got her and the baby. The house fell in before they got out of the yard. He took her to the quarters. Papa was overstrained carrying a log and limped as long as he lived.

"Pa was hired out and they was goner whoop him and he run off and got back to the master. Ma nor pa was never sold.

"We had a reason to come out here to Arkansas. A woman had a white husband and a black one too. The black husband told the white husband not come about there no more. He come on. The black man killed the white man at his door. They lynched six or seven niggers. They sure did kill him. That dissatisfied all the niggers. That took place in Barnwell County, South Carolina. Three train loads of us left. There was fifteen in our family. We was doing well. My pa had cattle and money. They stopped the train befo' and behind us—the train we was on. Put the Arkansas white man in Augusta jail. They stopped us all there. We got to come on. We was headed for Pine Bluff. We got down there 'bout Altheimer and they was living in tents. Pa said he wasn't goiner tent, he didn't run away from South Carolina and he'd go straight back. Mr. Aydelott got eight families on track at Rob Roy to come to Biscoe. We got a house here. Pa was old and they would listen at what he said. He made a speech at Rob Roy and told them let's come to Biscoe. Eleven families come. He had two hundred or three hundred dollars then in his pocket to rattle. He could get more. He grieved for South Carolina, so he went back and took us but ma wanted to coma back. They stayed back there a year or two. We made a crop. Pa was the oldest boss in his crowd. We all come back. There was more room out here and so many of us.

"The schools was better out there. I went to Miss Scofield's College. All the teachers but three was colored. There was eight or ten colored teachers. It was at Aiken, South Carolina. Miss Criley was our sewing mistress. Miss Criley was white and Miss Scofield was too. I didn't have to pay. Rich folks in the North run the school. No white children went there. I think the teachers was sent there.

"I taught school out here at Blackton and Moro and in Prairie County about. I got tired of it. I married and settled down.

"We owns my home here. My husband was a railroad man. We lives by the hardest.

"I don't know what becoming of the young generation. They shuns the field work. Times is faster than I ever seen them. I liked the way times was before that last war (World War). Reckon when will they get back like that?"

Interviewer: Miss Irene Robertson
Person interviewed: Henry C. Pettus, Marianna, Arkansas
Age: 80

HENRY C. PETTUS

"I was born in Wilkes County, near Washington, Georgia. My mother's owners was Dr. Palmer and Sarah Palmer. They had three boys; Steve, George, and Johnie. They lived in Washington and the farm I lived on was five miles southeast of town. It was fifty miles from Augusta, Georgia. He had another farm on the Augusta Road. He had a white man overseer. His name was Tom Newsom and his nephew, Jimmie Newsom, helped. He was pretty smooth most of the time. He got rough sometimes. Tom's wife was named Susie Newsom.

"Dick Gilbert had a place over back of ours. They sent things to the still at Dick Gilbert's. Sent peaches and apples and surplus corn. The still was across the hill from Dr. Palmer's farm. He didn't seem to drink much but the boys did. All three did. Dr. Palmer died in 1861. People kept brandy and whiskey in a closet and some had fancy bottles they kept, one brandy, one whiskey, on their mantel. Some owners passed drinks around like on Sunday morning. Dr. Palmer didn't do that but it was done on some places before the Civil War. It wasn't against the law to make spirits for their own use. That is the way it was made. Meal and flour was made the same way then.

"Mother lived in Dr. Palmer's office in Warren County. It was a very nice log house and had a fence to make the front on the road and the back enclosed like. Inside the fence was a tanyard and house at some distance and a very nice log house where Mr. Hudson lived. Dr. Palmer and Mr. Hudson had that place together. The shoemaker lived in Washington in Dr. Palmer's back yard. He had his office and home all in the same. Mr. Anthony made all the shoes for Dr. Palmer's slaves and for white folks in town. He made fine nice shoes. He was considered a high class shoemaker.

"Mother was a field hand. She wasn't real black. My father never did do much. He was a sort of a foreman. He rode around. He was lighter than I am. He was old man Pettus' son. Old man Pettus had a great big farm—land! land! land! Wiley and Milton Roberts had farms between Dr. Palmer and old man Pettus' farm. Mother originally belong to old man Pettus. He give Miss Sarah Palmer her place on the Augusta Road and his son the place on which his own home was. They was his white children. He had two. Mother was hired by her young mistress, Dr. Palmer's wife, Miss Sarah. Father rode around, upheld by the old man Pettus. He never worked hard. I don't know if old man Pettus raised grandma or not; he never grandpa. He was a Terral. He died when I was small. Grandpa was a field hand. He was the only colored man on the place allowed to have a dog. He was Dr. Palmer's stock man. They raised their own stock; sheep, goats, cows, hogs, mules, and horses.

"None of us was ever sold that I know of. Mother had three boys and three girls. One sister died in infancy. One sister was married and remained in Georgia. Two of my brothers and one sister come to Arkansas. Mother brought us boys to a new country. Father got shot and died from the womb. He was a captain in the war. He was shot accidentally. Some of them was drinking and pranking with the guns. We lived on at Dr. Palmer's place till 1866. That was our first year in Arkansas. That was nearly two years. We never was abused. My early life was very favorable.

"The quarters was houses built on each side of the road. Some set off in the field. They must have had stock law. We had pastures. The houses was joining the pasture. Mr. Pope had a sawmill on his place. The saw run perpendicularly up and down. He had a grist mill there too. I like to go to mill. It was dangerous for young boys. Mr. Pope's farm joined us on one side. Oxen was used as team for heavy loads. Such a contrast in less than a century as trucks are in use now. I learned about oxen. They didn't go fast 'ceptin' when they ran away. They would run at the sight of water in hot weather. They was dangerous if they saw the river and had to go down a steep bank, load or no load the way they went. If it was shallow they would wade but if it was deep they would swim unless the load was heavy enough to pull them down. Oxen was interesting to me always.

"Children didn't stay in town like they do now. They was left to think more for themselves. They hardly ever got to go to town.

"We raised a pet pig. Nearly every year we raised a pet pig. When mother would be out that pig would get my supper in spite of all I could do. The pig was nearly as large as I was. I couldn't do anything. We had a watermelon patch and sometimes sold Dr. Palmer melons.

He let us have a melon patch and a cotton patch our own to work. Mother worked in moonlight and at odd times. They give that to her extra. We helped her work it. They give old people potato patches and let the children have goober rows. Land was plentiful. Dr. Palmer wasn't stingy with his slaves—very liberal. He was a man willing to live and let live so far as I can know of him.

"During the Civil War things was quiet like where I was. The soldiers didn't come through till after the war was over. Then the Union soldiers took Washington. They come there after the surrender.

Freedom

"The Union soldiers came in a gang out from Washington all over the surrounding country, scouting about, and notified all the black folks of freedom. My folks made arrangements to stay on. Two colored men went through the country getting folks to move to southwest Georgia but before mother decided to move anywhere along come two men and they had a helper, Mr. Allen. It was Mr. William H. Wood and Mr. Peters over here on Cat Island. They worked from Washington, Georgia. We consented to leave and come to Arkansas. We started and went to Barnetts station to Augusta, to Atlanta. There was so many tracks out of order, bridges been burnt. We crossed the river at Chattanooga, then to Nashville, then to Johnsonville. We took a boat to Cairo, then to Memphis, then on to some landing out here. Well, I never heard. We went to the Woods' place and made a crop here in Arkansas in 1866. I worked with John I. Foreman till 1870 and went back to the Woods' farm till 1880. Then I went to the Bush place (now McCullough farm). I farmed all along through life till the last twelve years. I started preaching in 1875. I preach yet occasionally. I preached here thirty-six years in the Marianna Baptist church. I quit last year. My health broke down.

"Chills was my worst worry in these swamps. We made fine crops. In 1875 yellow fever come on. Black folks didn't have yellow fever at first but they later come to have it. Some died of it. White folks had died in piles. It was hard times for some reason then. It was hard to get something to eat. We couldn't get nothing from Memphis. Arrangements was made to get supplies from St. Louis to Little Rock and we could go get them and send boats out here.

"In 1875 was the tightest, hardest time in all my life, A chew of tobacco cost ten cents. In 1894-'95 hard times struck me again. Cotton was four and five cents a pound, flour three dollars a barrel, and meat four and five cents a pound. We raised so much of our meat that didn't make much difference. Money was so scarce.

"Ku Klux—I never was in the midst of them. They was pretty bad in Georgia and in northeast part of this county. They was bad so I heard. They sent for troops at Helena to settle things up at about Marion, Arkansas now. I heard more of the Ku Klux in Georgia than I heard after we come here. And as time went on and law was organized the Ku Klux disbanded everywhere.

"Traveling conditions was bad when we came to Arkansas. We rode in box cars, shabby passenger coaches. The boats was the best riding. As I told you we went way around on account of burnt out and torn up bridges. The South looked shabby.

"I haven't voted since 1927 except I voted in favor of the Cotton Control Saturday before last.

"Times has come up to a most deplorable condition. Craving exists. Ungratefulness. People want more than they can make. Some don't work hard and some won't work at all. I don't know how to improve conditions except by work except economical living. Some would work if they could. Some can work but won't. Some do work hard. I believe in bread by the sweat of the brow, and all work.

"The slaves didn't expect anything. They didn't expect war. It was going on a while before my parents heard of it. I was a little boy. They didn't know what it was for except their freedom. They didn't know what freedom was. They couldn't read. They never seen a newspaper like I take the Commercial Appeal now. I went to school a little in Arkansas. My father being old man Pettus' son as he was may have been given something by Miss Sarah or Dr. Palmer or by his white son, but the old man was dead and I doubt that. Father was killed and mother left. Mother knew she had a home on Dr. Palmer's land as long as she needed one but she left to do better. In some ways we have done better but it was hard to live in these bottoms. It is a fine country now.

"I own eighty acres of land and this house. (Good house and furnished well.) We made six bales of cotton last year. My son lives here and his wife—a Chicago reared mulatto, a cook. He runs my farm. I live very well."

Interviewer: Miss Irene Robertson
Person interviewed: Dolly Phillips, Clarendon, Arkansas
Age: 67

DOLLY PHILLIPS

"I ain't no ex-slave. I am 67 years old. I was born out here on the Mullins place. My mother's master was Mr. Ricks and Miss Emma Ricks.

"My mother named Diana and my father Henry Mullins. I never saw my grand fathers and I seen one grandma I remembers. My mother had ten children. My father said he never owned nuthin' in his life but six horses. When they was freed they got off to their selves and started farming. See they belong to different folks. My father's master was a captain of a mixed regiment. They was in the war four years. I heard 'em say they went to Galveston, Texas. The Yankees was after 'em. But I don't know how it was.

"I heard 'em say they put their heads under big black pot to pray. They say sing easy, pray easy. I forgot whut all she say.

"I lives wid my daughter. I gets commodities from the Welfare some. The young folks drinks a heap now. It look lack a waste of money to me."

Interviewer: Miss Irene Robertson
Person Interviewed: Tony Piggy
Brinkley, Ark.
Age: 75

TONY PIGGY

"I was born near Selma, Alabama, but I was raised in Mississippi. My grandpa was sold from South Carolina to Moster Alexander Piggy. He didn't talk plain but my papa didn't nother. Moster Piggy bought a gang of black folks in South Carolina and brought em into the state of Alabama. My papa was mighty near full-blood African, I'll tell you. Now ma was mixed.

"I'm most too young to recollect the war. Right after the war we had small pox. My uncle died and there was seven children had em at one time. The bushwhackers come in and kicked us around—kicked my uncle around. We lived at Union Town, Alabama then.

"Aunt Connie used to whip us. Mama had no time; she was a chambermaid (housewoman). The only thing I recollect bout slavery time to tell is Old Mistress pour out a bushell of penders (peanuts) on the grass to see us pick em up and set out eating em. When they went to town they would bring back things like cheese good to eat. We got some of what they had most generally. She wasn't so good; she whoop me with a cow whip. She'd make pull candy for us too. I got a right smart of raisin' in a way but I growed up to be a wild young man. I been converted since then.

"Well, one day pa come to our house and told mama, 'We free, don't have to go to the house no more, git ready, we all goin' to Mississippi. Moster Piggy goiner go. He goner rent us twenty acres and we goner take two cows and a mule.' We was all happy to be free and goin' off somewhere. Moster Piggy bought land in Mississippi and put families renters on it. Moster Piggy was rough on the grown folks but good to the children. The work didn't let up. We railly had more clearin' and fences to make. His place in Alabama was pore and that was new ground.

"There was all toll nine children in my family. Ma was named Matty Piggy. Papa was named Ezra Piggy. Moster Alexander Piggy's wife named Harriett. I knowed Ed, Charley, Bowls, Ells, and Liza. That's all I ever knowd.

"I have done so many things. I run on a steamboat from Cairo to New Orleans—Kate Adams and May F. Carter. They called me a Rouster—that means a working man. I run on a boat from Newport to Memphis. Then I farmed, done track work on the railroad, and farmed some more.

"The young generation ain't got respect for old people and they tryin' to live without work. I ain't got no fault to find with the times if I was bout forty years younger than I is now I could work right ahead."

Interviewer: Bernice Bowden
Person interviewed: Ella Pittman
2409 West Eleventh Street, Pine Bluff, Arkansas
Age: 84

ELLA PITTMAN

"Yes ma'm, I was born in slavery days. I tell you I never had no name. My old master named me—Just called me 'Puss.' and said I could name myself when I got big enough.

"My old master was named Mac Williams. But where I got free at was at Stricklands. Mac Williams' daughter married a Strickland and she drawed me. She was tollable good to me but her husband wa'nt.

"In slavery times I cleaned up the house and worked in the house. I worked in the field a little but she kept me busy in the house. I was busy night and day.

"No ma'm, I never did go to school—never did go to school.

"After I got grown I worked in the farm. When I wasn't farmin' I was doin' other kinds of work. I used to cut and sew and knit and crochet. I stayed around the white folks so much they learned me to do all kinds of work. I never did buy my children any stockins—I knit 'em myself.

"After old Master died old Miss hired us out to Ben Deans, but he was so cruel mama run away and went back to old Miss. I know we stayed at Ben Deans till they was layin the crop by and I think he whipped mama that morning so she run away.

"Yes ma'm, I sho do member bout the Klu Klux—sho do. They looked dreadful—nearly scare you to death. The Klu Klux was bad, and the paddyrollers too.

"I can't think of nothin' much to tell you now but I know all about slavery. They used to build 'little hell', made something like a barbecue pit and when the niggers didn't do like they wanted they'd lay him over that 'little hell'.

"I've done ever kind of work—maulin rails, clearin up new ground. They was just one kind of work I didn't do and that was workin' with a grubbin' hoe. I tell you I just worked myself to death till now I ain't able to do nothin'."

Interviewer's Comment

Ella Pittman's son, Almira Pittman was present when I interviewed his mother. He was born in 1884. He added this information to what Ella told me:

"She is the mother of nine children—three living. I use to hear mama tell about how they did in slavery times. If she could hear good now she could map it out to you."

I asked him why he didn't teach his mother to read and write and he said, "Well, I tell you, mama is high strung. She didn't have no real name till she went to Louisiana."

These people live in a well-furnished home. The living room had a rug, overstuffed furniture and an organ. Ella was clean.

Interviewer: Mrs. Bernice Bowden
Person interviewed: Ella Pittman
2417 W. Eleventh Street, Pine Bluff, Arkansas
Age: 84

[TR: Appears to be same as last informant despite different address.]

ELLA PITTMAN

"Here's one that lived then. I can remember fore the Civil War started. That was in the State of North Carolina where I was bred and born in March 1853. Mac Williams, he was my first owner and John Strickland was my last owner. That was durin' of the war. My white folks told me I was thirteen when peace was declared. They told me in April if I make no mistake. That was in North Carolina. I grewed up there and found my childun there. That is—seven of them. And then I found two since I been down in here. I been in Arkansas about forty years.

"When the war come I heard em say they was after freein' the people.

"My mother worked in the field and old mistress kep' me in the house. She married a widow-man and he had four childun and then she had one so there was plenty for me to do. Yes ma'm!

"I ain't never been to school a day in my life. They didn't try to send me after freedom. I had a very, very bad, cruel stepfather and he sent all his childun to school but wouldn't send me. I stayed there till I was grown. I sho did. Then I married. Been married just once. Never had but that one man in my life. He was a very good man, too. Cose he was a poor man but he was good to me.

"Yes ma'm, I sho did see the Ku Klux and the paddy-rollers, too. They done em bad I tell you.

"I know they was a white man they called Old Man Ford. He dug a pit just like a barbecue pit, and he would burn coals just like you was goin' to barbecue. Then he put sticks across the top and when any of his niggers didn't do right, he laid em across that pit. I member they called it Old Ford's Hell.

"I had a bad time fore freedom and a bad time after freedom till after I married. I'm doin' tollably well now. I lives with my son and his wife and she treats me very well. I can't live alone cause I'se subject to inagestin' and I takes sick right sudden.

"I'm just as thankful as I can be that I'm gettin' along as well as I is.

"I stayed in the North in Detroit one year. I liked it very well. I liked the white people very well. They was so sociable. My son lives there and works for Henry Ford. My oldest son stays in Indiana.

"It was so cold I come back down here. I'se gettin' old and I needs to be warm. Good-bye."

Interviewer: Samuel S. Taylor
Person interviewed: Sarah Pittman
1320 W. Twentieth Street, Little Rock, Arkansas
Age: About 82

SARAH PITTMAN

"I never saw nothing between white folks and colored folks. My white folks were good to us. My daddy's white folks were named Jordan—Jim Jordan—and my mama's folks were Jim Underwood. And they were good. My mama's and father's folks both were good to the colored folks. As the song goes, 'I can tell it everywhere I go.' And thank the Lord, I'm here to tell it too. I raised children, grandchildren, and great-grandchildren you see there. That is my great-grandson playing there. He is having the time of his life. I raised him right too. You see how good he minds me. He better not do nothin' different. He's about two years old.

"I was born in Union Parish, Louisiana way up yonder in them hills, me and my folks, and they come down here.

"Jim Jordan married one of the Taylor girls—Jim Taylor's daughter. The old folks gave mama to them to do their housework. My father and mama didn't belong to the same masters. He died the first year of the surrender. He was a wonderful man. He was a Jackson. On Saturday night he would stay with us till Sunday. On Sunday night he would go home. He would play with us. Now he and mama both are dead. They are gone home and I am waiting to go. They're waiting for me in the kingdom there. As the song says, 'I am waiting on the promises of God.'

"My mama did housework in slave time. I don't know what my father did. In them days you done some working from plantation to plantation. Them folks is all gone in now near about. Guess mine will be the next time.

Early Childhood

"First thing I remember is staying at the house. We et at the white folks' house. We would go there in the evening before sundown and git our supper. One time Jim Underwood made me mad. Mama said something he didn't like. And he tied her thumbs together and tied them to a limb. Her feet could touch the ground—they weren't off the ground. He said she could stay there till she thought better of it.

"Before the surrender I didn't do nothing in the line of work 'cept 'tend to my mother's children. I didn't do no work at all 'cept that. My white folks were good to me. All my folks 'cept me are gone. My grandmas and uncles and things all settin' up yonder. All my children what is dead, they're up yonder. I ain't got but three living, and they're on their way. Minnie and Mamie and Annie, that is all I got. Mamie's the youngest and she's got grandchildren.

How Freedom Came

"The way we learned that freedom had come, my uncle come to the fence and told my mama we were free and I went with her. Sure he'd been to the War. He come back with his budget. Don't you know what a budget is?

You ain't never been to war, have you? Well, you oughter know what a budget is. That's a knapsack. It had a pocket on each side and a water can on each shoulder. He come home with his budget on his back, and he come to the fence and told mama we was free and I heered him.

Right After Freedom

"Right after freedom my mama and them stayed with the same people they had been with. The rest of the people scattered wherever they wanted to But my uncle come there and got mama. They moved back to the Taylors then where my grandma was. Wouldn't care if I had some of that good old spring water now where my grandma lived!

"None of my people were ever bothered by the pateroles or the Ku Klux.

"We come to Arkansas because we had kinfolks down here. Just picked up and come on. I been here a long time. I don't know how long, I don't keep up with nothing like that. When my husband was living I just followed him. He said that this was a good place and we could make a good living. So I just come on. When he died, those gravediggers dug his grave deep enough to put another man on top of him. But that don't hurt him none. He's settin' in the kingdom. He was a deacon in the church and his word went. The whole plantation would listen to him and do what he said. Everybody respected him because he was right. I was just married once and no man can take his place. He was the first one and the best one and the last one. He was heaven bound and he went on there. I don't know just how long I was married. It is in the Bible. It is in there in big letters. I can't get that right now. It's so big and heavy. But it's in there. I think we left it in Detroit when I was there, and it ain't come back here yet. But I know we lived together a long time.

"I remember the old slave-time songs but I can't think of them just now. 'Come to Jesus' is one of them. 'Where shall I be when the first trumpet sounds?', that's another one. Another one is: 'If I could, I surely would; Set on the rock where Moses stood—first verse or stanza. All of my sins been taken away, taken away—chorus. Mary wept and Martha moaned, Mary's gone to a world unknown—second verse or stanza. All of my sins are taken away, taken away—chorus."

"I don't think nothing 'bout these young folks. When they was turned loose a lot of them went wild and the young folks followed their leaders. But mine followed me and my daddy.

"My grandmother had a big old bay horse and she was midwife for the white and the colored folks. She would put her side saddle on the old horse and get up and go, bless her heart; and me and my cousin had to stay there and take care of things. She's gone now. The Lord left me here for some reason. And I'm enjoyin' it too. I have got my first cussin' to do. I don't like to hear nobody cuss. I belong to the church. I belong to the Baptist church and I go to the Arch Street Church."

Interviewer: Miss Irene Robertson
Person interviewed: Mary Poe, Forrest City, Arkansas
Age: 60

MARY POE

"My papa used to tell about two men he knowd stealing a hog. He was Wyatt Alexander. He was feeding one evening and the master was out there too that evening. They overheard two colored men inside the crib lot house. They was looking at the hogs. They planned to come back after dark and get a hog. The way it turned out master dressed up ragged and got inside that night. The first man come. They got a shoat and killed it, knocked it in the head. The master took it on his back to the log cabin. When he knocked, his wife opened the door. She seen who it was. She nearly fell out and when he seen who it was he run off. The master throwed the hog down. They all got the hot water and went to work. He left a third there and took part to the other man. He done gone to bed and he took a third on home. He said he wanted to see if they needed meat or wanted to keep in stealing practice. He didn't want them to waste his big hog meat neither. Said that man never come home for two weeks, 'fraid he'd get a whooping. No, they said he never got a whooping but the meat was near by gone.

"Seem lack hog stealing was common in North Carolina in them days from the way he talked.

"Papa said he went down in the pasture one night to get a shoat. He said they had a fine big drove. He got one knocked over an' was carrying it out across the fence to the field. He seen another man. He couldn't see. It was dark. He throwed the hog over on him. The man took the shoat on to his house and papa was afraid to say much about it. He said way 'long towards day this man come bringing about half of that hog cleaned and ready to salt away. They got up and packed it away out of sight.

"My mother was named Lucy Alexander, too."

Interviewer: Miss Irene Robertson
Person interviewed: W.L. Pollacks
Brinkley, Arkansas
Age: 68

W.L. POLLACKS

"I was born in Shelby County Tennessee. My folks all come from Richmond, Virginia. They come to Kentucky and then on to Tennessee. I am 68 years old. My father's master was Joe Rollacks and Mrs. Chicky they called his wife. My mother's master was Joe Ricks and they all called his wife Miss Fee. I guess it was Pheobe or Josephine but they never called her by them names. Seemed like they was all kin folks. I heard my mother say she dress up in some of the white folks dresses and hitch up the buggy, take dinner and carry two girls nearly grown out to church and to big picnics. She liked that. The servants would set the table and help the white folks plates at the table. Said they had a heap good eating. She had a plenty work to do but she got to take the girls places where the parents didn't want to go. She said they didn't know what to do wid freedom. She said it was like weening a child what never learned to eat yet. I forgot what they did do. She said work was hard to find and money scarce. They find some white folks feed em to do a little work. She said a nickle looked big as a dollar now. They couldn't buy a little bit. They like never get nough money to buy a barrel of flour. It was so high. Seem like she say I was walking when they got a barrel of flour. So many colored folks died right after freedom.

They caught consumption. My mother said they was exposed mo than they been used to and mixing up in living quarters too much what caused it. My father voted a Republican ticket. I ain't voted much since I come to Arkansas. I been here 32 years. My farm failed over in Tennessee. I was out lookin' round for farmin' land, lookin' round for good work. I farmed then I worked seven or eight years on the section, then I helped do brick work till now I can't do but a mighty little. I had three children but they all dead. I got sugar dibeates.

"The present times are tough on sick people. It is hard for me to get a living. I find the young folks all for their own selves. If I was well I could get by easy. If a man is strong he can get a little work along.

"The times and young generation both bout to run away wid themselves, and the rest of the folks can't stop em 'pears to me like."

Interviewer: Miss Irene Robertson
Person interviewed: "Doc" John Pope, Biscoe, Arkansas
Age: 87

"DOC" JOHN POPE

I am 87 years old for a fact. I was born in De Soto County, Mississippi, eight miles south of Memphis, Tennessee. No I didn't serve in de War but my father Gus Pope did. He served in de War three years and never came home. He served in 63rd Regiment Infantry of de Yankee army. He died right at the surrender. I stayed on de farm till the surrender. We scattered around den. My father was promised $300.00 bounty and 160 acres of land. Dey was promised dat by the Constitution of the United States. Every soldier was promised dat. No he never got nary penny nor nary acre of land. We ain't got nuthin. De masters down in Mississippi did help 'em where they stayed on. I never stayed on. I left soon as de fightin was gone. I was roamin round in Memphis and man asked me if I wanted to go to college. He sent a train load to Fitz (Fisk) University. I stayed there till I graduated. I studied medicine generally. Sandy Odom, the preacher at Brinkley, was there same time as I was. He show is old. He's up in ninety now. He had a brother here till he died. He was a fine doctor. He got more practice around here than any white doctor in this portion of de county. Fitz University was a fine college. It was run by rich folks up north. I don't know how long I stayed there. It was a good while. I went to Isaac Pope, my uncle. He was farming.

Briscoe owned the Pope niggers at my first recollection. He brought my uncle and a lot more over here where he owned a heap of dis land. It was all woods. Dats how I come here.

After de Civil War? Dey had to "Root hog or die". From 1860-1870 the times was mighty hard. People rode through the county and killed both white and black. De carpet bagger was bout as bad as de Ku Kluck.

I came here I said wid John Briscoe. They all called him Jack Briscoe, in 1881. I been here ever since cept W.T. Edmonds and P.H. Conn sent me back home to get hands. I wrote 'em how many I had. They wired tickets to Memphis. I fetched 52 families back. I been farmin and practicin all my life put near.

I show do vote. I voted the last time for President Hoover. The first time I voted was at the General Grant election. I am a Republican, because it is handed down to me. That's the party of my race. I ain't going to change. That's my party till I dies. We has our leader what instructs us how to vote.

Dey say dey goiner pay 60 cents a hundred but I ain't able to pick no cotton. No I don't get no help from de relief. I think the pore class of folks in a mighty bad fix. Is what I think. The nigger is hard hit and the pore trash dey call 'em is too. I don't know what de cause is. It's been jess this way ever since I can recollect. No times show ain't one bit better. I owns dis house and dats all. I got one daughter.

I went to Fitz (Fisk) University in 1872. The folks I told you about was there then too. Their names was Dr. E.B.

Odom of Biscoe and his brother Sandy Odom. He preaches at Brinkley now. Doc Odom is dead. He served on the Biscoe School Board a long time wid two white men.

I don't know much about the young generation. They done got too smart for me to advise. The young ones is gettin fine educations but it ain't doin 'em no good. Some go north and cook. It don't do the balance of 'em no good. If they got education they don't lack de farm. De sun too hot. No times ain't no better an de nigger ain't no better off en he used to be. A little salary dun run 'em wild.

United States. Work Projects Administration

Interviewer: Mrs. Bernice Bowden
Person interviewed: William Porter
1818 Louisiana Street, Pine Bluff, Arkansas
Age: 81
Occupation: Janitor of church

WILLIAM PORTER

"Yes'm I lived in slavery times. I was born in 1856. I was borned in Tennessee but the most of my life has been in Arkansas.

"I remember when Hood's raid was. That was the last fight of the war. I recollect seein' the soldiers marchin' night and day for two days. I saw the cavalry men and the infant men walking. I heard em say the North was fightin' the South. They called the North Yankees and the South Rebels.

"Some of the Tennessee niggers was called free niggers. There was a colored man in Pulaski, Tennessee who owned slaves.

"My father was workin' to buy his freedom and had just one more year to work when peace come. His master gave him a chance to buy his freedom. He worked for old master in the daytime and at night he worked for himself. He split rails and raised watermelons.

"My father's master was named Tom Gray at that time. Considering the times he was a very fair man.

"When the war broke up I was workin' around a barber shop in Nashville, Tennessee.

"The Queen of England offered to buy the slaves and raise them till they were grown, then give them a horse, a plow and so many acres of ground but the South wouldn't accept this offer.

"It was the rule of the South to keep the people as ignorant as possible, but my mother had a little advantage over some. The white children learned her to read and write, and when freedom came she could write her name and even scribble out a letter. She gave me my first lesson, and I started to school in '67. The North sent teachers down here after the war. They were government schools.

"I was pretty apt in figgers—studied Bay's Arithmetic through the third book. I was getting along in school, but I slipped away from my people and was goin' to get a pocket full of money and then go back. First man I worked for was a colored man and I kept his books for him and was to get one-fourth of the crop. The first year he settled with me I had $165 clear after I paid all my debts. I done very well. I farmed one more year, then I come to Pine Bluff and did government work along the Arkansas River.

"I've done carpenter work and concrete work. I learned it by doing it. I followed concrete work for a long time. I've hoped to build several houses here in Pine Bluff and a lot of these streets.

"I have a brother and sister who graduated from Fisk University.

"I think one thing about the younger generation is they need to be more educated in the way of manners and to have race pride and to be subject to the laws."

United States. Work Projects Administration

Interviewer: Thomas Elmore Lacy
Person interviewed: Bob Potter, Russellville, Arkansas
Age: 65

BOB POTTER

"Sure, you oughter remember me—Bob Potter. Used to know you when you was a boy passin' de house every day go in' down to de old Democrat printin' office. Knowed yo' brother and all yo' folks. Knowed yo' pappy mighty well. Is yo' ma and pa livin' now? No suh, I reckin not.

"I was born de seventeenth of September, 1873 right here in Russellville. Daddy's name was Dick, and mudder's was Ann Potter. Daddy died before I was born, and I never seed him. Mudder's been dead about eighteen years. Dey master was named Hale, and he lived up around Dover somewheres on his farm, but I dunno how dey come by de name Potter. Well, now, lemme see—oh, yes, dey was freed at Dover after dey come dere from North Ca'liny. I think my ma was born in West Virginia, and den dey went to North Ca'liny and den to South Ca'liny, and den come to Arkansas.

"I raised seven boys and lost five chillen. Dere was three girls and nine boys. All dat's livin' is here except one in Fresno, California. My old woman here, she tells fortunes for de white folks and belongs to de Holiness church but I don't belong to none; I let her look after de religion for de fambly." (Interjection from Mrs. Potter:

"Yes suh, you bet I belongs to de Holiness chu'ch. You got to walk in de light to be saved, and if you do walk in de light you can't sin. I been saved for a good many yeahs and am goin' on in de faith. Praise de Lawd!")

"My mudder was sold once for a hundud dollahs and once ag'in for thirty-eight hundud dollahs. Perhaps dis was jist before dey left West Virginia and was shipped to North Ca'liny. De master put her upon a box, she said, made her jump up and pop her heels together three times and den turn around and pop her heels again to show how strong she was. She sure was strong and a hard worker. She could cut wood, tote logs, plow, hoe cotton, and do ever'thing on de place, and lived to be about ninety-five yeahs old. Yas suh, she was as old or older dan Aunt Joan is when she died.

"No suh, I used to vote but I quit votin', for votin' never did git me nothin'; I quit two yeahs ago. You see, my politics didn't suit em. Maybe I shouldn't be tellin' you but I was a Socialist, and I was runnin' a mine and wo'kin' fifteen men, and dey was all Socialists, and de Republicans and Democrats sure put me out of business—dey put me to de bad.

"Dat was about twelve yeahs ago when I run de mine. I been tryin' to git me a pension but maybe dat's one reason I can't git it. Oh yes, I owns my home—dat is, I did own it, but——

"Oh Lawd, yes, I knows a lot of dem old songs like 'Let Our Light Shine,' and 'De Good Old Gospel Way,' and 'Hark From de Tomb.' Listen, you oughter hear Elder Beam sing dat one. He's de pastor of de Baptis' Chu'ch at Fort Smith. He can sure make it ring!

"De young folks of today compa'ed to dem when we was boys? Huh! You jist can't compaih em—can't be done. Why, a fo'-yeah-old young'un knows mo' today dan our grandmammies knowed. And in dem days de boys and gals could go out and play and swing togedder and behave deyselves. We went in our shu'ttails and hit was all right; we had two shu'ts to weah—one for every day and one for Sunday—and went in our shu'ttails both every day and Sunday and was respected. And if you didn't behave you sure got whupped. Dey didn't put dey arms around you and hug you and den put you off to sleep. Dey whupped you, and it was real whuppin'.

"Used to hear my mudder talk about de Ku Klux Klan puttin' cotton between her toes and whuppin' her, and dat's de way dey done us young'uns when we didn't behave. And we used to have manners den, both whites and blacks. I wish times was like dem days, but dey's gone.

"Yes, we used to have our tasks to do befo' goin' to bed. We'd have a little basket of cotton and had to pick de seeds all out of dat cotton befo' we went to bed. And we could all ca'd and spin—yes suh—make dat old spinnin' wheel go Z-z-z-z as you walked back and fo'f a-drawin' out de spool of ya'n. And you could weave cloth and make all yo' own britches, too. (Here his wife interpolated a homely illustration of the movement of "de shettle" in the loom weaving—ed.)

"Yes, I mind my mudder tellin' many a time about dem Klan-men, and how dey whupped white women to make em give up de money dey had hid, and how dey used to burn dey feet. Yes suh, ain't no times like dem old days, and I wish we had times like em now. Yes suh,

I'll sure come to see you in town one of dese days. Good mornin'."

NOTE: Bob Potter is a most interesting Negro character—one of the most genial personalities of the Old South that the interviewer has met anywhere. His humor is infectious, his voice boisterous, but delightful, and his uproarious laugh just such as one delights to listen to. And his narrations seem to ring with veracity.

Interviewer: Mrs. Bernice Bowden
Person interviewed: Louise Prayer
3401 Short West Third, Pine Bluff, Arkansas
Age: 80

LOUISE PRAYER

"I can member seein' the Yankees. My mother died when I was a baby and my grandmother raised me. I'se goin' on eighty.

"When the Yankees come we piled boxes and trunks in front of the doors and windows. She'd say, 'You chillun get in the house; the Yankees are comin'.' I didn't know what 'twas about—I sure didn't.

"I'm honest in mind. You know the Yankees used to come in and whip the folks. I know they come in and whipped my grandma and when they come in we chillun went under the bed. Didn't know no better. Why did they whip her? Oh my God, I don't know bout dat. You know when we chillun saw em ridin' in a hurry we went in the house and under the bed. I specks they'd a killed me if they come up to me cause they'd a scared me to death.

"We lived on the Williams' place. All belonged to the same people. They give us plenty to eat such as 'twas. But in them days they fed the chillun mostly on bread and syrup. Sometimes we had greens and dumplin's. Jus' scald some meal and roll up in a ball and drop in with the greens. Just a very few chickens we had. I don't love chicken though. If I can jus' get the liver I'm through with the chicken.

"When I got big enough my grandmother had me in the field. I went to school a little bit but I didn't learn nothin'. Didn't go long enough. That I didn't cause the old man had us in the field.

"If we chillun in them days had had the sense these got now, I could remember more bout things.

"I was a young missy when I married.

"I told you the best I could—that's all I know. I been treated pretty good."

Slave Narratives